Praise for *The Sor*

"In 1889, S. L. Mathers published a ᵙ ᵙ. ᵙᵙ. ᵙᵤ.ᵦ magic text, *The Key of Solomon*, based on seven manuscripts. It has been hugely influential. The manuscripts and his edition are not always easy to understand. In *The Sorcery of Solomon*, Sara Mastros has provided a deep dive into the forty-four pentacles as codified by Mathers. Drawing on a wide variety of sources, including biblical exegesis, Babylonian Talmud, Aramaic incantation bowls, Greek Magical Papyri (PGM), mathematical speculations, and her own experiences, she includes many easy-to-follow exercises for exploring them."

—Joseph Peterson, author of *The Secrets of Solomon: A Witch's Handbook from the Trial Records of the Venetian Inquisition*

"*The Sorcery of Solomon: A Guide to the 44 Planetary Pentacles of the Magician King* is much more than the subtitle might imply. It is a comprehensive work which deep-dives into the pentacles given in the Mathers's edition of the classic grimoire The Key of Solomon. Before this journey, the author deftly guides the reader through all the necessary historical and philosophical context of Solomon and Jewish magic necessary to work the pentacles, and then provides a concise and coherent system of practice which frames the use of the pentacles. As Sara Mastros states, the magic of the pentacles synergizes many roots in addition to the Jewish ones, and as such, the practices she details set the use of the pentacles in modern magic without forgetting their roots. From honoring the dead to calling on the Most High, this work is an excellent body of practice for those wishing to explore the vast depths of the magic of the Solomonic pentacles."

—David Rankine, author of *The Grimoire Encyclopaedia*

"My high school girlfriend bought me a copy of Mathers's *The Greater Key of Solomon* for my seventeenth birthday. I have used the pentacles of Solomon on and off over the decades since. I only wish I had a book like *The Sorcery of Solomon* by Sara Mastros back then! Sara manages to illuminate the past history of the pentacles while shining a light forward into the future with clear and thoughtful instruction. Not only does she fully explain the design of each pentacle, correcting many errors along the way, but she shares advice and insight gained from her own work. *The Sorcery of Solomon* delivers what it promises: a fully workable system of magic."

—Jason Miller, author of *Consorting with Spirits, Protection and Reversal Magic,* and other books and courses

"*The Sorcery of Solomon* is the book on Solomonic magic I wished I had before attempting Solomonic magic! As informative and engaging in print as she is in her classes on King Solomon, Sara L. Mastros gives you history and practice not just of *The Key of Solomon* but also the context and meaning of the tradition that is not apparent when working with a grimoire alone, making it accessible to magicians and witches of many levels of experience. I not only wish I had this book before attempting any of the grimoire tradition, but it would have been quite handy before embarking on ceremonial studies in general for the explanations of Hebrew and the pentagram alone."

—Christopher Penczak, author of the Temple of Witchcraft series

"If we are going to use the Jewish language in our magic, then we better treasure and respect those whose language it is. For centuries, Hebrew has been distorted and manipulated by occultists who adapted and appropriated the alphabet for their own gain, without understanding the depth and complexity, the multiple levels and meanings of each letter and word. In *The Sorcery of Solomon*, Sara L. Mastros sets the records straight. Her knowledge and understanding are second to none. Her wisdom and insight shine through. With clear instructions, she guides the reader through the practical use and application of the forty-four Pentacles of Solomon."

—Diti J. Morgan, author of *Aromagick*

"What stands out about *The Sorcery of Solomon* for me is the exposition of how to ask for the help of the spirit of Solomon, the master magician of Jewish lore. Also, I really like the information about working with the pentacles. The author fleshes out these magical tools and provides the reader with a very do-able and empowering way of using them."

—Harold Roth, author of *The Witching Herbs* and
The Magic of the Sword of Moses

"Sara Mastros is the real deal! To anyone well-versed in magical practice, it is clear that *The Sorcery of Solomon* is deeply rooted in genuine sorcerous work, and her writing possesses the unique power to offer great value to the most seasoned magus and the curious dabbler alike."

—Carl Nordblom, author and manager at Watkins Books, London UK

"If you want to learn about the *Key of Solomon,* there's nothing that offers the rigorous practitioner a text that is as scholarly and academic—paying detailed attention to history, folklore and linguistics—and is also as practical and personal as Sara Mastros's *The Sorcery of Solomon*. Mastros offers a point of view that is both open-minded and open-hearted to give her readers essential tools to deepen their own practice. With respect for both tradition and creativity, Mastros's *The Sorcery of Solomon* is an important addition to the library of any seriously practicing occultist."

—Mark Horn, author of *Tarot and the Gates of Light: A Kabbalistic Path to Liberation*

"In *The Sorcery of Solomon*, Sara Mastros brushes off the dust of centuries of staid armchair magic and makes it really come to life. Her excellent scholarship and the compelling brilliance of her work shines through with the clarity that only those with a deep, abiding passion for the subject can achieve. An accurate analysis of the sigils is framed by a rich historical and cultural context that allows the reader to understand their structure at a deeper level and by practical instructions that inspire practitioners into experiencing their magic and exploring new ways to work with them. The presence of Solomon resonates throughout the book, guiding the reader towards that wisdom that cannot be put into words. Those who wish to hear the voice of the Magician King can follow the steps of the courting dance delineated in section two or simply let the enchanted knowledge that flows through the pages work its magic on them."

—Giulia Turolla, scholar of witchcraft and high priestess in the Tempio di Ara tradition

"I love Sara Mastros's *The Sorcery of Solomon*. I was surprised to discover how many layers there are to the talismans I've been using for years. Sara's research, wisdom, and experience with magic makes *The Sorcery of Solomon* one of the most useful guides to the Pentacles of Solomon. I wish I'd read this years ago. She explains so much that I didn't know in an unpretentious, pragmatic way. I love the practical advice for working with the talismans; it's brilliant, and she understands and explains the way they manifest so well. Follow her instructions in the book and you'll have a method to implement a *very* powerful practice."

—Rufus Opus, author of *Seven Spheres* and *Goetic Grimoire*

"In *The Sorcery of Solomon*, Sara Mastros has written a comprehensive and unique system suitable for beginners that blends mathematics, operative sorcery, and Jewish magic with the clarity of a professional teacher and the insight of a professional practitioner."

—Alison Chicosky, author of *The Secrets of Helios* and proprietor of Practical Occult

"Sara Mastros's *The Sorcery of Solomon* stands out as a must-have resource for anyone interested in *The Clavicula Salomonis* and its pentacles. Far more than just a showcase of the forty-four planetary pentacles found in *The Key of Solomon* and what they can do—this brilliantly written user-friendly guide shows how to actually *use* them to their full potential, while allowing the reader to both utilize and appreciate the pentacles with sensitivity, awareness, and respect for the historical and cultural significance surrounding them. Mastros taps into her equally impressive academic knowledge of history and her extensive experience as a magical practitioner to enrich your understanding and application of these magical seals. I was astounded by the depth of knowledge and practical wisdom I gained from this book. Suitable for the dedicated beginner and invaluable for the experienced magician, this book provides real-world, actionable insights. It's definitely a game-changer in magical studies and Solomonic magic. Whether your goals are spiritual or practical, *The Sorcery of Solomon* will be an indispensable reference you'll continually revisit."

—Mat Auryn, author of *Psychic Witch* and *Mastering Magick*

THE

SORCERY *of* SOLOMON

THE

SORCERY *of* SOLOMON

A Guide to the
44 PLANETARY PENTACLES
of the MAGICIAN KING

SARA L. MASTROS

WEISER
BOOKS

This edition first published in 2024 by Weiser Books, an imprint of
Red Wheel/Weiser, LLC
With offices at:
65 Parker Street, Suite 7
Newburyport, MA 01950
www.redwheelweiser.com

ISBN: 978-1-57863-786-7
Library of Congress Cataloging-in-Publication Data available upon request.

Cover: King Solomon. Illustration for *Old Testament Portraits* by Cunningham Geikie (Strahan,
1878). Portraits drawn by A Rowan and engraved by G Pearson. Credit: Look and Learn
Frontispiece: King Solomon, Russian ikon from first quarter of 18th century. Kizhi monastery, Russia.
Public domain, via Wikimedia Commons
Image on page Page 107: Early Hebrew conception of the Universe, by Tom-L,
CC BY 4.0 creativecommons.org/licenses/by/4.0, via Wikimedia Commons.
Pages 143, 180, 183: Heinrich Cornelius Agrippa's Malachim Script,
from Charles Walker Collection / Alamy Stock Photo

Cover and interior by Sky Peck Design
Typeset in Times New Roman

Printed in the United States of America
IBI
10 9 8 7 6 5 4 3 2 1

"Teacher sought to find delightful words,
to write correctly matters of Truth."

—Kohelet 12:10

*For my mother, of blessed memory, for my Nan Sarah,
of blessed memory, for Solomon, Magician King,
and for all my other ancestors in k'lal Israel.*

A Note Regarding the Organization of Contents

Those who are familiar with *The Key of Solomon the King* by S. L. Mathers will know that the pentacles are ordered by planet and by number. Because my book is primarily intended as a teaching text, I have reordered the planetary progression of the pentacles. As you can see in Table of Contents that follows, in this book we start with the pentacles of the Moon and end with the pentacles of Saturn. This is largely because the pentacles of the Moon and Mercury are the most applicable to studying magic, so I chose to teach those first, so you could use them to "level up" your learning of the rest of the book. In addition, within each planetary section, I have sometimes rearranged the order of resentation of pentacles to put first the ones that are easier to understand so that they can be used, both magically and as learning examples, to help unlock later pentacles. The pentacles themselves are numbered to match Mathers's order, for ease of comparison, but they are not presented in Mather's numerical order. Additionally, for ease of reference, I have given each pentacle a name. These names are not traditional.

Contents

"And furthermore, my son, be admonished: of making many books
there is no end; and much study is a weariness of the flesh."[2]

—*Kohelet* 12:12

Acknowledgments

Thank you to all the authors, named and unnamed, who first introduced me to Solomonic magic, including Andrew Lang, James Blish, Eliza Marian Butler, Sirdar Ikbal Ali Shah, S. L. Mathers, Benjamin Rowe, Poke Runyon, Stephen Skinner, and Joseph H. Peterson. Thank you to the many friends, colleagues, and co-magicians, named and unnamed, with whom I've learned and practiced Solomon magic, including Simon Zealot, Alison Chicosky, Jason Miller, Jake Stratton-Kent, all my coven-siblings, and my brilliant, inspiring, exciting students.

Special thanks to Judika Illes (my fabulous editor), Kathryn Sky-Peck (who made all the excellent illustrations), Jane Hagaman (the diligent managing editor, who kept the whole process running smoothly), and all the other people at Weiser Books who helped make this book happen. Thank you to all my beta readers, but especially Kate, Zach, and Joseph, whose comments were especially helpful. Personal thanks to Simon, Chase, and my other Witch House family; your support was invaluable. Thank you!

Introduction

A Note from the Author

S ince childhood, I have had a series of related dreams. I am in a labyrinthine library, musty, dusty, and full of joy. It is not any library I know in waking life, but a combination of many libraries, real and fictional, plausible and impossible. I hunt the stacks for a book, a magic book, which I can sense but not find. It shimmers and glimmers and tinkles just outside of my grasp. In some dreams, I do eventually find it. Most often it is a very old, very large, leatherbound book, but it appears differently in each dream. I always wake up as soon as I lay my hand on it. I have dreamed this dream, on and off, for more than forty years, ever since I learned to read.

I suspect I am not the only magician who harbors a yearning to discover a long-lost magical tome, not just *about* magic, but alight and alive with a palpable *spirit* of magic. I imagined such books were not just tools but allies and teachers and companions. When I was young, I thought the famed grimoires were the magic books after which I sought. Sadly, when I finally laid hands on them, it was not so. The word "grimoire" shares a root with "grammar"; grimoires are the textbooks of magic. They were not the magic books I craved, but they were excellent teachers.

The night I decided to write this book for you, I dreamt the dream once again. That time, I found it! The book was huge—three feet tall, two feet wide, and at least six inches thick. It was too big for me to move. I called a strong friend/co-magician to help, and he moved it onto a large library table for me. Then, wonder of wonders, I managed to open it before awakening. On the page to which I opened, with which I was permitted to commune for only a moment, was a secret you will learn by the end of this book.

Only a handful of times in my decades of searching have I met such books "in the wild." However, with long effort and much study, I have learned to make my own awake, alive magic books, and one of my many goals in this book is to teach you how to make them, too. Later in this book, you'll learn to make a book of Solomonic pentacles, but the principles you'll learn easily translate to other types of magic books.

Another objective of this book is to give you all the context—magical, cultural, and linguistic—to fully understand the forty-four planetary pentacles

Samuel Liddell (MacGregor) Mathers presents in his edition of the *Key of Solomon*. I adore the pentacles, and I am doing my best to convey both my love and my decades of experience with them to you. However, my hope is that you will use this book as a springboard to learn how to delve into all sorts of cryptic texts and be able to understand them using a combination of necromantic, linguistic, and sorcerous techniques.

I have done my best to provide clear, cogent translations and commentary, but I am neither a linguist nor a historian, and I am certainly not a rabbi. I am a student, lover, and descendant of Solomon, and it is my most sincere goal to serve as his scribe and *hermeneutes*.[3] This book is not a work of scholarship. It is a *game* of scholarship, and I encourage you to play.

Who Is This Book For?

The only prerequisites to learn from this book are a strong command of written English and the desire to learn new things. As Solomon would say, you need only the inclination of your heart to understanding.[4]

If this book is your first experience with magic, you have made a brave, but possibly daunting, choice. If you are a nerd (like me), I think you will find the work that this book might require from you both fun and rewarding. If you would prefer a gentler introduction before beginning, I recommend my course "Introduction to Witchcraft: Thirteen Lessons in Practical Spellcraft." You can learn more about that course, as well as the companion course to this book, at *WitchLessons.com*. If you have decided to start with this book, I recommend you read the entire book, in order, before attempting any of the exercises, rituals, or magic. However, when I was a beginner, I would have ignored that advice and started enchanting immediately. Fortune favors the bold.

If you are an experienced magician who has *not* worked much Solomonic magic, I recommend you skim parts one and two, and then dive right into part three. If, after finishing part three, you're still enjoying yourself, go back to the beginning, and follow the instructions to make a magic book of your own.

If you are an experienced Solomonic magician, read the rest of this paragraph, and then close your eyes, ask Solomon to guide your hand, and open to a random page. Read that and think about why it was chosen for you. Next, read the chapter titled "Magic: Sorcery & Seals." After that, once again ask Solomon to send you to the right page for you. Having done that, if you're still enjoying this book, read it in whatever order catches your fancy, making a magic book as instructed, or using it as inspiration to inform your own methods.

If you are extra-nerdy (again, like me!), I encourage you to go read the section called "The True Tree of Knowledge Is the Fruit of PRDS" in the "Solomon Extras" section at *MastrosZealot.com* before you move on to the main text, but if you're not into the crunchy details of textual exegesis, skip it.

No matter your background, I would very much like to hear your questions, complaints, and musings on this book. I believe magic is best when it is collaborative, communal, and constantly evolving. I encourage you to consult the list of online resources at the end of this book to find us.

Some Questions and Answers about Cultural Appropriation

Q: Do I have to be Christian to do Solomonic magic?
A: No, absolutely not. Solomon wasn't Christian, and neither is his magic.

Q: Do I have to be Jewish to use this book?
A: No, but you do have to be comfortable working with the G-d[5] of Israel.[6]

Q: Do I have to be a monotheist?
A: No. Solomon wasn't a monotheist, much to the chagrin of the Talmudic[7] sages.

Q: What about cultural appropriation?
A: Cultural appropriation of Judaism involves removing Jewish cultural treasures from their Jewish context, and then using them to oppress and marginalize Jews. For example, Christian churches hosting Passover seders for Easter is cultural appropriation of Judaism, partly because the seder is, in its essence, about the special relationship between the people Israel and our god, but primarily because of the millennia-long tradition of Christian churches and communities "celebrating" Passover with blood libel, pogroms, and other campaigns of terror and genocide against their Jewish neighbors. The Key of Solomon, in the form we know it today, draws on a long tradition of Jewish magic, but was almost certainly written by non-Jews, for non-Jews. The edition on which we focus in this book is by S. L. Mathers, who was assuredly not Jewish,

although his wife Moina—herself an artist, mystic, magician, and scholar of great skill—was the scion of a prominent Jewish family.[8] It is unclear how much Moina contributed to her husband's edition of the text. The book you are currently reading was written by a Greek/Jewish witch and is intended for both Jewish and non-Jewish witches and other magicians.

Q: So, can Christians and Pagans do Jewish magic?

A: Yes. Most Jewish magic does not require the practitioner to be Jewish, so long as they practice respectfully. It becomes appropriative when non-Jews attempt to lay claim to the special relationship between Israel and our G-d (as, for example, most Christian theology does). None of the magic in this book does that, although there are a few passages which some may consider problematic. In those cases, I have provided alternatives.

As in any magic, I encourage you to rewrite, carefully and respectfully, anything that doesn't feel right to you. We discuss some specifics to keep in mind in Chapter 3.ב.

Q: Wait! But isn't the Key of Solomon actually Christian? Aren't you (a Jew) just appropriating Christianity?

A: As I mentioned, cultural appropriation occurs when the appropriated treasures are used in a way which oppresses and marginalizes the people from whom they were taken. So, no.

Q: Is it "kosher" for Jews to do Christian magic?

A: Many rabbis are of the opinion that it's not "kosher" for Jews to do any magic, even Jewish magic. Some rabbis are of the opinion that magic doesn't exist. If you actually want an official *halachic* (Jewish legal) opinion, you should consult your own rabbi. However, there is very little Christian magic in this book, save for a small amount in the Mars chapter.

Q: How should Jews approach Christian magic?

A: What follows is a joke, but also an important fact about sorcery: The best way for Jews to do Christian magic is to put on your best Mel Brooks voice, strike your best Groucho Marx pose, and preface any Christian oration with (something like) "G-d of Abraham, G-d of Isaac, G-d of Jakob, hear me now, as you did for my ancestors of old. As our cousin Jesus would have said. . . ." This sort of ritualistic name-dropping, where one speaks in the name of another magician, is a very common sorcerous technique in all

Levantine magic, and most magics which inherit from those traditions. Later in this book, you'll learn to speak with the authority of Solomon.

To Use This Book for Trance

Although this book is primarily designed as a textbook, it can also be used as an object of ecstatic magical contemplation. This book was written from a specific trance state, which has both a sound and a smell, and replicating that smell and sound can help you enter the book more deeply. The smell of this book is the Solomon offering incense whose recipe appears in the *The Big Book of Magical Incense.* Plain frankincense is also a nice choice.

The "soundtrack" which this book is designed to accompany is a free online noise machine[9] by Dr. Ir. Stéphane Pigeon, featuring Dave Tawfik on duduk and Ido Romano on oud, and which was inspired by the Semitic root word SLM, the mother of the Arabic *salaam* and Hebrew *shalom,* both of which mean "peace." As we discuss in great detail later, this is also the root of Solomon's name.

If you wish to engage with this book as a magical artifact, here is one method. You will develop your own as you get to know the book better.

- Clean and prepare yourself. Ideally, wear festive white garments.

- Arrange a comfortable position to read, with adequate lighting, paper and pen for taking notes, and a glass of water. You may also want some bookmarks or sticky notes.

- Set the noise machine to any starting mode that seems right to you, and then set it to animate, providing a continuously evolving background in which the voice of Solomon, and the voice of the book herself, can manifest.

- Light incense for Solomon.

- Enter into magical space/time/consciousness by the method of your choice.

- Invite Solomon and the spirit of the book to join you in conversation . . .

- Settle in to read. You can choose to read in order or flip around as the spirits move you.

PART ONE

Historic & Cultural Context

When I study any text, I try to ground my study in a basic understanding: who wrote the book, for whom they wrote it, and why they chose to do so. First, we take a very brief tour of Solomonic magic, beginning with the biblical books attributed to Solomon, and moving our way up in history until we reach the early Renaissance, when the oldest known copies of the pentacles were written. Next, we zoom in to specifically look at what was going on in Jewish, crypto-Jewish, and pseudo-Jewish magic and mysticism around the time the Key was developing. In the next section, we briefly look into the textual history of the pentacles themselves. Finally, we look specifically at S. L. Mathers (and his wife Moina) and his (their?) edition of the Key of Solomon, on which we will focus in part three of this book.

1.1

What Is Solomonic Magic?

Although usage of the word "Solomonic" varies greatly among speakers, to me, what makes a text Solomonic is that it claims to speak with the voice of Solomon. What makes a magician Solomonic is that they can actually do so.

While originally rooted in the sorcerous styles and traditions of Jewish antiquity, Solomonic magic is a living cross-cultural tradition. There is no time over the last several thousand years during which it was not being practiced, debated, and constantly reinvented. Right now, moment by moment, as you read this book, you and I are participating in the Solomonic tradition.

Growing, changing, and adapting *generation with generation*,[1] the Solomonic current is braided through the so-called "Western mystery tradition," both influencing and being influenced by the many magical paradigms, cultures, and styles encountered along the way. Those cultures and practices include Babylonian astrotheology, Egyptian priestcraft, Jewish amulet writing, Greek *goetia,* Roman witchcraft, Arabic astrological magic, both Ashkenaz and Sefardic folk magic, Catholic, Orthodox Christian, and Muslim ceremonial magic, Afro-Caribbean sorcery, and a variety of contemporary Anglophone magics. What connects these many Solomonic styles is their claim of Solomon as a teacher of specialized technical knowledge that grants "power and dominion over a supernatural reality, which by means of universal sympathy (the relationship between each and every element of the cosmos), is connected with this mundane reality."[2]

1.2

Biblical Texts Attributed to Solomon

There is a vast and fascinating history of magical, mystical, and religious texts which ascribe themselves to Solomon, primarily in Greek, Hebrew, Latin, and Arabic, all of which are rooted in a larger Pan-Levantine tradition broadly called "Wisdom Literature."[1] In this chapter, we briefly review several such texts. I encourage you to note both their variety and their similarity; keep in mind how manifold ancient roots spread into the many-branched tree that is Solomonic magic.

The oldest surviving examples of Solomonic texts are contained in the Tanakh,[2] the Hebrew bible. Much wickedness has been worked to and by and in the name of these texts, and it can be difficult to set aside that baggage and read them with clear eyes and an open mind. At Gibeon, Solomon asked for "a heart that listens," and I encourage you to do the same.

In addition to the several books, which we discuss below, two of the canonical Psalms[3] are sometimes understood by Christians to have been written by Solomon. The first, Psalm 72, is ascribed to him on account of its title "Of Solomon." However, Jews traditionally understand it to be the magical words sung over the infant Solomon by his father David. Whether or not it is intended for that purpose, it is excellent as a blessing over babes, particularly those born into privilege and power.

The other is Psalm 127, midway through the "Songs of Ascent" (Tehillim 120–134). They are so called because they were traditionally sung by pilgrims as they made their way to the acropolis of Jerusalem on Mount Moriah. Others suggest they model the ascent of the stairs to Solomon's Temple. I imagine Solomon singing 127 as he made his way up to the high place at Gibeon, a biblical story[4] which I will recount in Part Two. Like 72, Rashi, the great medieval French rabbi, and I believe this to be a psalm (mythically) composed by David about Solomon.

The oldest surviving full text attributed to Solomon is usually called "Proverbs," a translation of its Hebrew name משלי (*Mishle*), itself a plural of משל (*mashal*),[5] which means "teaching example" or "allegory." As with all books of the Torah, it is named after its first word. It is generally understood to be a collection of short wisdom lessons, intended to be taught within the home (rather than in an academic or temple setting). These written teachings were almost certainly built on a very ancient, primarily oral, Pan-Levantine Wisdom tradition. In places, the text closely parallels other written sources from the region, including both Egyptian[6] and cuneiform[7] texts. There are six identifiable books within that which we call Proverbs. The oldest (Proverbs 25–29) appears to have been written in its current form in the 7th century BCE. The introduction (Proverbs 1–9) is likely the newest section, written in its current form in the 4th century BCE.

The next oldest surviving Solomonic text we discuss is my favorite: Kohelet, which Christians call Ecclesiastes. The word "Kohelet" is usually translated as either "teacher" or "preacher," but it literally means "woman who can hold the attention of an assembly." The book called Kohelet describes itself as "The words of Kohelet, son of David, king in Jerusalem," and is thus traditionally credited to Solomon, despite the title being female. Opinions vary on why the female form is used. Most traditional Jewish interpretations (by men) suggest that it is because the inspiring voice of the text, Wisdom, is female, and so Solomon took a female title for himself in her honor.

In the form we know it today, it was probably written between 450 and 200 BCE. Unlike Proverbs, the language of Kohelet implies it was composed by a single author, surely a powerful magician-bard, rather than being a compilation of many texts. A notable exception is the epilogue (12:9–14), which is almost universally understood as an addition by a later scribe. Even a cursory reading of the text makes clear why it was added; without it, Kohelet is shockingly heterodox.

The narrator of Kohelet, traditionally understood to be Solomon in exile, is deeply jaded. He is deeply skeptical about the value of organized religion and rejects the notion that eschatology is useful in the quest to lead a good life. He recounts his many struggles to know true Wisdom, to reconcile the cruel and seemingly capricious nature of human existence with the notion of an all-powerful, all-good G-d. Nearly all scholars agree: based only on its content, it is surprising that this book "made the cut" into biblical canon. In my opinion, it is due to the undeniable magical power and poetry of the book, which even the epilogue cannot undercut. More than any other, this book seems to me to genuinely capture the voice of Solomon which I personally experience. If you have never read it, you should.

Finally, we come to the great Song of Songs, sometimes called the Song of Solomon. Most likely written in the 3rd century BCE, the Song of Songs is the Torah's great hymn of love, and the newest piece of the canonical Hebrew bible traditionally attributed to Solomon. The book begins: "This is the song of songs, which is Solomon's." Its blatantly erotic character led to some disagreement about its inclusion in the official canon, but its beautiful poetry and irrefutable magic carried the day. The great Rabbi Akiva said of it: "The world was never as worthy as on the day that the Song of Songs was given to Israel, for all the Writings are holy, but the Song of Songs is the holiest of the holies."[8] The Song of Songs is at once a hymn to erotic love, a script for ritual theater,[9] a description of the love between Israel and our G-d, and a metaphor for the divine intercourse of *kabbalat shabbat*.[10] As magicians, I encourage you to read it as a script for *hieros gamos*.[11] As initiates of Solomon, I encourage you to read it as his love letter to Wisdom.

Written in the final century BCE, "The Wisdom of Solomon" is the newest biblical[12] text we discuss. In its currently known form, the text is in Greek, and I believe it was composed in that language. Of particular interest to magicians is chapter 7, Solomon's ode to Wisdom in which he relates how: ". . . Prudence[13] was given to me . . . the spirit Sophia[14] came into me."[15]

He then proceeds to tell how G-d ". . . gave me unerring knowledge of what is, knowledge of the structure of the world and the doings of the elements; the beginning and end and middle of times, the alternation of the solstices and the changes of the seasons, the cycles of the year and the constellations of stars, the natures of animals and the temperament of wild beasts, the powers of spirits and the reasonings of men, the varieties of plants and the virtues of roots; I learned both what is occult and what is overt, for Wisdom, the maker of all things, taught me." Surely familiar to any magician, this is a catalog of (some of the) technical knowledge that undergirds all sorcery.

1.3

Amulets & Exorcisms

Over the next several centuries, Solomon acquired a very strong reputation as an exorcist. He came to be seen as a great sorcerer, able to command demons by reason of his specialist knowledge. The famed Jewish historian Josephus, writing in the 1st century CE, reports such with little fanfare; implying it was a common understanding. "God also enabled him to learn that skill which expels demons: which is a science useful, and sanative [healing] to men. He composed such incantations also by which distempers are alleviated. And he left behind him the manner of using exorcisms; by which they drive away demons; so that they never return: and this method of cure is of great force unto this day."[1] Josephus continues, describing a specific exorcism at which he was present. ". . . The manner of the cure was this: he put a ring that had a root of one of those sorts mentioned by Solomon to the nostrils of the demoniac, after which he drew out the demon through his nostrils:[2] and when the man fell down immediately, he abjured him to return into him no more: making mention of Solomon, and reciting the incantations which he composed."[3]

Among the so-called Dead Sea Scrolls are fragments of an exorcism psalm which begins: ". . . in the name of HaShem . . . Solomon and he will invoke . . . in order to be delivered of any plague of the spirits and the demons and the Liliths,[4] the owls and the jackals; these are the demons and the prince of animosity is Belial, who rules over an abyss of darkness."[5] This surviving scroll was probably written in the 1st century CE, but it is unclear when its text was first composed.

Both Jewish and non-Jewish sorcerers of late antiquity were unquestionably seeking the aid of Solomon explicitly to work magic. For example, in one selection from the Greek Magical Papyri[6] we read the following incantation, titled The Great Name for Favor: ". . . Everyone fears your great power. Give to me all good things: the strength of Akryskylos, the speech of Euonos, the eyes of Solomon, the voice of Abrasax, the grace of Adōnios the god. Come to me Kypris every day. The hidden name bestowed on you is this: THOATHOĒTHEATHOOYTHAETHŌUSTHOAITHITHĒTHOINTHŌ: grant me victory, repute, beauty toward all men and all women." As another example, in one Jewish incantation bowl, we read: ". . . I will bind you with the bond with which the seven stars . . . the devils are bound . . . with the bond of El Shaddai and with the sealing of King Solomon . . ."[7] We discuss yet another type of amulet featuring Solomon, a precursor to the modern Saint George's medal, in the chapter on Mars pentacles.

1.4

Grimoires

Although often spoken of as a single text, *The Testament of Solomon* is, in fact, an entire family of related Grecophone Jewish (or pseudo-Jewish) texts. The oldest surviving fragments are from the 5th century CE.[1] Complete texts survive from the 1400s. *The Testament of Solomon* presents us with a "'pre-Talmudic demonology,' and one might add, Palestinian demonology. . . . the Text comes to be of real assistance in reconstructing the thought world of the Palestinian Jew in the 1st century . . ."[2] However, the Testament is not an exclusively Jewish text: "despite many features in the body of the work that are unmistakably Jewish . . . , there are many more that are attributable to pagan, and particularly Gnostic, influence. . . . And there are, too, a number of distinctively Christian features."[3]

A demon catalog wrapped in a folkloric frame story, the Testament begins by explaining how Solomon got his magic ring from Archangel Michael and used it to build the Temple. This is followed by an extensive demon catalog. Of each demon, Solomon inquires: "τις ει σύ, τίς κλήσις σου." The first part is easy to translate: "Who are you?" The next is commonly understood as "What is your name?" but it more literally means "How are you called?" For each demon, the book teaches a name, a physical description, and a list of their powers and astrological offices. Solomon then compels them to say in which angel's name they can be subdued, and they each answer. Finally, he seals each demon to his service and compels them to work building the Temple. Here again, it is Solomon's technical knowledge, particularly his knowledge of names, which allows him to work magic.

By the late Byzantine era, the wizardly Solomon of the medieval grimoire tradition was beginning to arise. *The Magical Treatise of Solomon*, also known as the *Hygromanteia*,[4] describes itself as Solomon's instructions to his son, Rehoboam. Solomon explains of his magic that it rests on a foundation of specialized technical knowledge: "The entire art, grace and force of what is sought dwells in plants, words and stones. First of all, know the positions of the seven planets . . . " and then details a system of planetary hours along with the activities most auspicious in each. For example, on Saturdays, the seventh hour belongs to the Moon, and is recommended for speaking with demons. The hours are also assigned to angels and demons. For interested readers, I strongly recommend the study of the *Hygromanteia*, but it is not a prerequisite to the material in this book.

The *Oathbound Book of Honorius* is a high medieval grimoire, the oldest surviving manuscripts of which date to the 14th century. The book begins with a brief prologue, explaining that it was written by Honorius of Thebes, and contains the collected wisdom of more than 800 master magicians. After the prologue, the book lays out technical knowledge for magic, which it describes as "works of Solomon."

Sometime in the 13th or 14th century, a new text called the Key of Solomon began to appear in Italy. It is with this text that the pentacles in this book are traditionally connected, and so I'll discuss its history and content extensively in chapter 1.6.

1.5

A Survey of Medieval European Jewish Magic and Mysticism

Although most readers will be at least passingly familiar with the history of Christian Europe in the late Middle Ages and early Renaissance, the history of Jews during that time is less well known, but it provides a vital context for the study of the Hebrew pentacles. In this section, I hope to give you just a taste of that rich and fascinating history. If you wish to learn more, I recommend the work of Dr. Henry Abramson.

Ashkenazi (European) Jewry was experiencing a mystic revival in the late 12th and early 13th centuries. At that time, particularly in Christian-controlled[1] Western Europe, living as a Jew was dangerous. Never fully accepted by their Christian neighbors, beginning in the 11th century, Jewish populations were under assault by wave after wave of Catholic Crusaders bent on ethnic cleansing. En route to kill Muslim "infidels" in Israel, these Catholic Crusaders were happy to stomp out local Jewish "infidels" as well.

At the end of the 12th century, the pope established the Inquisition, which quickly spread to all of Central and Western Europe. Although originally intended to put an end to the Cathars and other Christian "heretics," much of the wrath of the Catholic Inquisition fell on Jews. Unsurprisingly, this time of extreme hardship inspired many Jews to turn inward, becoming mystics, searching to understand *why*.

Against the backdrop of these difficult times, let us turn our eyes to one particular example. Rabbi Eleazer ben Jakob of Worms (c. 1176–1238), also called Eleazer the Potion-Maker,[2] was the most prominent author of the Hasidei[3] Ashkenaz (European Jewish Pietist) movement. At the age of twenty, Reb Eleazer was already a prominent rabbi, scholar, and scientist, who was married to a prominent scroll merchant. Following the brutal murder of his beloved wife and young children by Christian Crusaders in the autumn of 1196, he turned inward and became a mystic. Seeing so many of his family and community wiped out, Eleazer worried that Jewish communal knowledge would be lost, and so he set out to collect and preserve that wisdom in writing. Over the next forty-two years, Rabbi Eleazer produced dozens of important works,[4] covering the wisdom and teachings of his ancestors and teachers, as well as his own discoveries and creations. His preservationist instincts were well founded; by the end of the 13th century, the Hasidei Ashkenaz were almost gone, but their sacred wisdom lives on. Among his many teachings, he is said to have introduced (or, at least, popularized) Kabbalah in Seferad,[5] where it flowered extravagantly.

Centered in Castille, the 13th century Golden Age of Kabbalah produced many well-known authors, including Abraham Abulafia and Moshe (Moses) de Leon. Along with many anonymous authors, they produced many of the foundational works of modern Kabbalah, including the Zohar. It is unclear to what extent these works were 1) copied from sources of great antiquity and authenticity, 2) composed ex nihilo from the minds of their 13th century authors, and/or 3) written with the aid of spirits conjured during automatic writing. In support of option three, for example, Rabbi David of Pancorbo said about Moshe de Leon's composition of the Zohar, "R. Moses was a conjurer of the Writing Name, and through its power did he write everything connected with this book."[6]

Among the many anonymous authors of this period was a collective of mystics whom we now call the "Circle of Contemplation." Around 1230 CE, the Circle produced a huge library of texts, including a text[7] called *The Book of Contemplation,* which claims as its author Rabbi Hammai, a title which means "Teacher Seer." Although the text is less well known today than some other Kabbalistic works of the period, its influence on Kabbalah, and thence on ceremonial magic, was profound. It presents a complex cosmology, focusing on ten (categories of) angelic powers which will seem familiar to modern students of grimoire magic. For Kabbalah nerds who want to learn more, I strongly recommend *The Books of Contemplation: Medieval Jewish Mystical Sources* by Mark Verman.

It is against this background of revolutionary Jewish mysticism that the pentacles of Solomon appear to have emerged, as we will discuss in the next section.

1.6

The Key of Solomon & The Book of Seals

Like many Solomonic texts (including this one), most versions of the Key of Solomon open with a claim to speak with the authority of Solomon. In particular, the text is framed as the teaching of Solomon to his son, Rehoboam. The frame story continues, saying that, upon the death of Rehoboam, the text was hidden in his sepulcher and later rediscovered by Babylonian magicians, who could not understand it. Eventually, it came into the possession of one Toz the Greek,[1] who, with Divine aid, unlocked the secrets of the book.

The text is traditionally broken into (at least) two parts. In Book I, we are taught several experiments (exercises) in practical magic, and instructions for the conjuration and compulsion of demons and spirits of the dead. In part two, detailed instructions are given for the preparation of both the magician(s) and their tools for those operations. In some, but not most, manuscripts of the Key of Solomon, there is another short section between the two books, which presents the so-called planetary pentacles, a collection of Hebrew magical seals. It is these on which this book focuses.

The origins of the Key of Solomon are, like those of most magical texts, cloaked in mystery. Although we talk about it as a single book, it is really a family of closely related books, in multiple languages. The exact relationship between these texts is unclear. There are some ways in which the youngest versions of the Key of Solomon are also the oldest versions of the *Testament of Solomon*. Different parts of a single manuscript may have multiple "origin stories," and, like almost all magical works, the texts themselves are not reliable narrators as to their origins.

Most scholars believe that, in the form in which we know it today, the Key probably dates to the 14th or 15th century and was most likely originally composed in Latin. However, because the overwhelming majority of researchers on this topic do not read Hebrew, European language versions of the text are much more widely and deeply studied than Hebrew manuscripts, which makes it hard to get a complete picture.

In this book, we will be primarily focusing on a relatively recent English edition of the Key, by S. L. Mathers. Working as a magical rhapsode (or "stitcher of stories"), Mathers wove together many older editions of the Key of Solomon to produce his own version. Because this is the version which most modern Anglophone magicians, including myself, first encounter, I will take only a moment to discuss some of the manuscripts Mathers consulted before moving on to speak about his edition.

Abraham Colorno was an Italian-Jewish engineer of the mid-1500s. In addition to being a brilliant engineer, he was an accomplished mathematician, translator, and archaeologist. He authored a number of mathematical texts, both practical and theoretical, and was an expert performer of card tricks. It is said that, in or around 1580, at the request of Federico II of Gonzaga, the Duke of Mantua, he translated a Hebrew manuscript of *Mafteah Shlomo* (Key of Solomon) into Italian. From that Italian translation sprung a family of mostly French translations. It is from these sources that Mathers appears to have drawn most of his material.

Because in this book we are particularly interested in the pentacles, another important manuscript for our purposes is a 1729 Hebrew manuscript currently in the Rosenthaliana Collections at the University of Amsterdam.[2] That text explains that it was transcribed by Isaac Zekel ben Yidel Kohen Worms from a London copy written by Judah Perez.[3] At first, this appears to be a standard copy of the Key, but after the main text is appended another, ספר האותות (*Sefer H'Otot*, The Book of Seals), of unknown origin. This short text presents pentacles which look similar to those given by Mathers, but which contain far more, and different, text. Although a complete translation and analysis of that text is outside the scope of this book,[4] I have occasionally referenced it in relation to corrupt or difficult to interpret pentacles. The first page of *Sefer H'Otot* reads:

The Book of Seals

They are the Pentaculae or Pentaganot also, those which came from the father of all sages Solomon the King, peace be upon him, and how many impressive and wonderful things [are] in them, and whoever is like the sage, who will come after the king [who] has not yet been created, for all wisdom is revealed [to him] and all hidden things they are all revealed [to him], as it says in the scripture: Happy is He that created for Himself in His world and that gave a king like this to His nation Israel. May He see their poverty and hardship and take them out of the iron furnace from between the legs of a pig, take them out, guide them, carry them on the wings of eagles like the day of their exodus from the land of Egypt, and eye to eye they will witness the return of The Lord to Zion, may The Lord do so soon and in our days.

8 ♄ Saturn

7 ♃ Jupiter

6 ♂ Mars

7 ☉ Sun

6 ♀ Venus

3 ☿ Mercury

6 ☽ Moon

And another 14 attributed to the Psalm

"For the conductor, on neginot" [Psalm 67]
and each one to one,
the stars [planets] and one
that was copied from the book of the wizards[5]
Between them all they are 58.

1.7

The Mathers Edition of the Key of Solomon

In 1889, George Redway, of London, published a new English edition of the Key of Solomon, interpreted and edited by Samuel Liddell (MacGregor) Mathers, one of the founders of the (then very new) Hermetic Order of the Golden Dawn. According to Mathers, after examining many of the manuscripts we discussed in the previous chapter, his goal was to stitch them together to form a single, coherent magic book. In order to understand his text, it's important to learn a little bit about his life.

Samuel Liddell Mathers was born in January of 1854, the long wished-for miracle baby of an older couple, long childless. His father, William M. Mathers, died when Samuel was still very young, so, growing up, it was just him and his mother, with whom he had a close bond. Although he was poor, he attended the prestigious Bedford School, no doubt owing to his excellence in both academics and athletics.

The young Mathers had two interests, which were to remain his focus throughout his life: war and magic. He studied both the history and strategy of European warfare, as well as what we would now call "martial arts," particularly fencing and boxing. While we would today categorize his magical interests as Hermetic, I think it is more accurate to say that he was deeply interested in all the magics to which he had access, primarily those of Greek, Egyptian, and Hebrew antiquity. Partly due to his own work, those magics coalesced over the course of the late 19th and early 20th centuries into a new kind of Anglophone magic that we today call "Hermetic."

In late 1877, at the age of twenty-three, Samuel Mathers was initiated into Freemasonry, and just a few months later, he was raised to the level of Master Mason. In 1882, he became a Rosicrucian. In 1885, his mother died, and, shortly thereafter, Mathers moved to London. He became a regular at the British Museum, often spending long days in the Egyptian galleries and the Reading Room, poring over magical manuscripts, including those that would inform his edition of the Key of Solomon.

Samuel Mathers was a tall, muscular, good-looking man. The poet William Butler Yeats, Mathers's initiated brother in the Golden Dawn, would later describe him as having a "gaunt resolute face and an athletic body . . ." and said that he was "a figure of romance." I like to imagine that it was that aura of butch romance that first attracted the attention, in 1887, of an art student drawing in the Egyptian galleries. Her name was Mina Bergson. She would soon become his wife, co-magician and priestess, and take the name by which we know her today—Moina Mathers.

Very little is known about the mysterious Moina; she was a deeply private person. In fact, her magical motto, when she joined the Golden Dawn, was *Vestigia Nulla Retrorsum* ("No Backwards Steps"), which is often understood in the sense of "Leave No Trace." Below, I will tell you what I know of her, almost all of which I learned in Mary K. Greer's excellent book, *Women of the Golden Dawn*, but some of which I learned directly from Moina's spirit.

Mina was born in 1865 in Switzerland, but her family moved to Paris, where she grew up, when she was two. Her father, Michael, was a talented musician and professor of music. However, rising antisemitism, combined with his violent mood swings (perhaps due to bipolar disorder), made it difficult for him to keep a job, and the family moved often.

Michael was the scion of a prominent Polish Jewish family. His grandmother, Mina's great grandmother, was Temerl (Tamar) Bergson, an extremely wealthy woman who founded a bank, ran a salt company, built many synagogues and study houses, and almost single-handedly funded the most prominent scholars of the emerging Hasidic movement in Poland. However, Temerl was not only a financial backer of the movement, but also an important scholar and teacher in her own right. She was so important to the movement that she was addressed by the honorific title of Reb (teacher), an honor almost unheard of for women of her day.

Mina's older brother was the philosopher Henri Bergson. However, he left for boarding school in 1868, when he was nine, and Mina was only three, and so it is unclear how much contact the two had. When Mina was fifteen, she won a scholarship to study painting at the prestigious Slade School of Art in London. In 1887, when she was twenty-three and he was thirty-three, Mina first met Samuel. Very shortly thereafter, Samuel helped to found the Golden Dawn, along with William Robert Woodman and William Wynn Wescott. Owing to her private nature, and the patriarchy of their day,[1] it's not clear how involved Mina was in that endeavor. Personally, I suspect she was more deeply involved than is commonly given credit.

Similarly, it is unclear how involved Mina was in the study, compilation, and translation of the Key of Solomon. While Samuel Mathers brought far more Hebrew and Jewish knowledge to Solomonic magic than most gentiles, Mina had a good Jewish education, likely much better even than most Jews, owing to her familial relationship to Reb Temerl and the scholarly elite of Hasidism. This education would likely have included both a grounding in Kabbalah and access to important texts largely unknown, at that time, to gentiles. Additionally, Mina was a natural clairvoyant and an excellent magician. William Ayton, a later initiate of the Golden Dawn, described her as "the most advanced [magician] of all."

In 1888, Mina officially became the first initiate of the Golden Dawn and a year later, she and Samuel married.[2] Their marriage was strongly opposed by the Bergsons, not only because Samuel was not Jewish, but also because they considered him a feckless dilettante with no hopes of earning enough to support a family.[3] It is also possible that Mina's parents also saw something in the much older Samuel that the young Mina didn't yet see. Over the next decades, Samuel Mathers would transform himself from a promising scholar of the occult into a dictatorial cult leader. One imagines that the same need for control probably played out in his marriage as well, and that was certainly not what the cosmopolitan Bergsons wanted for their brilliant and beautiful daughter. After her marriage, Mina Bergson changed her name to Moina Mathers and was thereafter largely estranged from her family of birth.

The Mathers edition of the Key of Solomon was first published shortly after their marriage. This edition is particularly notable for the brief section (Chapter 18) between Parts One and Two, in which the forty-four planetary pentacles are introduced. It is unclear whence Mathers learned these pentacles. Personally, I believe that he had access to a copy of *Sefer H'Otot,* which contains very similar pentacles, and that he and Moina engaged in a series of adorcistic invocations of Solomon to channel their own versions of the pentacles. Wherever they came from, it is the Mathers pentacles that are most commonly used today, and to which we now turn our attention.

PART TWO

The SLM Method

The approach I recommend for beginners in Solomonic magic is a three-pillared one I called the SLM method. In the SLM acronym, S stands for **Solomon.** Often, in discussions by beginner (and sometimes non-beginner) magicians online, I see questions like "What is the best spirit I can summon to help me learn Solomonic magic?" The answer to that question is surely Solomon, the great Magician King, whose magic this is! In the SLM method we work with Solomon as a beloved teacher, guide, ally, and initiator.

The L in SLM stands for **Logos** and primarily relies on informed and inspired deployment of Names of Power. While it is debatable whether or not Solomonic magic is Jewish, the planetary pentacles discussed in this book are undeniably Hebrew. Like almost all Hebrew magic, they rely on the knowledgeable and skillful application of Hebrew magical words and Names of Power. In order to better understand these names, we learn a little bit of Hebrew and then discuss several important Names of Power.

Finally, the third pillar of the SLM method is **Magic.** In this book, we proceed with the assumption that magic is real. Like, really, really *real*.

2.1

Solomon: Life & Lore

Solomon, the son of David, is one of the greatest figures in Jewish mytho-history. He was perhaps the most powerful king of ancient Israel, as well as one of the most fabled magicians of all time. He built the Holy Temple and made pacts with the angels, demons, and djinn. While the core of Solomon's legend is Jewish, he is also an important figure in Persian, Arabic, Ethiopian, and Christian mythology and folklore. Solomon's story is generally understood to be set in the late 10th century BCE. However, Solomon's oldest surviving hagiography is spread across the second Book of Samuel and the first book of Kings, both written in the mid-6th century BCE, and is retold with additional details in the Book of Chronicles, which dates to the mid-4th century BCE. Historians believe that, if a figure like the biblical Solomon ever existed, it was probably not in the 10th century, but more likely in the 8th.

Before I say anything else about him, let me say this: Solomon is not a shining exemplar of a human being. He was a womanizer and a slaver, a tyrant and a conqueror. Yet, like all human beings, Solomon is not wholly defined by his failures, and there is much about him to celebrate as well. His most essential quality as a mythic figure, the greatness that has sustained him in human minds and hearts for millennia, is, of course, his wisdom. Mythically, Solomon is the wisest man who ever lived.

Additionally, he is widely regarded (not just by Jews, but by Muslims, Christians, and Pagans as well) as an avatar of magic. He built the great Temple in Jerusalem and made treaties with angels, djinn, and demons. He spoke the languages of all the plants and animals and wrote the grimoires. In both Jewish and Muslim folklore, he is the foremost archetype of the wizard, and it is in this vein that we magicians work with and learn from him. The hagiography that follows is stitched together primarily from biblical texts, but also includes material from a variety of other historical, religious, folkloric, and mythopoetic sources. It should not be mistaken for a scholarly account of historical events. As with any myth, there are many ways to tell this tale. This one is mine.

A Hagiography of Solomon, Magician King

Torah tells us that Solomon's mother, Batsheva (Bathsheba), was the daughter of Eliam, an Israeli warrior and counselor to King David. Because "bat" means "daughter" in Hebrew, I believe Batsheva's name means "daughter of Sheba." Thus, I imagine her mother was from Sheba,[1] a powerful and wealthy African civilization far to the south.[2] While still very young, Batsheva was married to Uriah the Hittite, a close friend and counselor of King David, and an elite commander in his army. While Uriah was at war, David and Batsheva had an affair, and Batsheva became pregnant. In order to keep their adultery from being discovered, and to protect his own reputation, David sent Uriah on a suicide mission and then married the newly widowed Batsheva.

Adultery is a grievous matter in Judaism; to defile the sacred covenant between man and wife is understood to also defile the sacred marriage of G-d and Israel. How much more so to *shtup* the wife of a friend, and then send him to his death to cover it up?! Nathan the Prophet came to David and remonstrated with him, urging him to repent his traitorous wrongdoing. Eventually, David came to regret his behavior and repented, but it was too late. Batsheva's child died before they were old enough to be given a name. Time passed, and Batsheva once again became pregnant. This child survived and was named Solomon or in Hebrew שלמה (*Shlomo*). This name, which is closely related to "shalom" (which means "peace"), was chosen to indicate that G-d and David had made their peace.

Solomon was not the natural heir; he had several older half-brothers. However, even as a child, Solomon was undeniably brilliant and charismatic. He was tutored in wisdom by Nathan the Prophet, who gave him his sacred name of Jedidiah, the Beloved of Jah. It is said that as a teenager, Solomon could already speak dozens of languages and knew the ancient stories and wisdom teachings not only of the Israelites, but of their neighbors as well. He had a gift for logic and strategy, and was a charismatic leader, an ebullient public speaker, and a bit of a playboy.

David grew old, and Queen Batsheva and Nathan the Prophet allied to become the powers behind the throne. When political struggles erupted over who would succeed David, they steered the conversation to young Solomon.[3] Exerting their influence, they extracted a decree from David that Solomon would succeed him. This decision was not popular, particularly with the more conservative elements of the court. Many, including military command, favored David's oldest surviving son, Adonijah. In a quick and strategic coup, Solomon, Nathan,

---

25

and Batsheva outfoxed the military, and Solomon ascended to his father's throne in 970 BCE. He then immediately purged those who had supported Adonijah and installed a new, younger, and more progressive government

As the new king of Israel, Solomon was sworn to three oaths, which are detailed in *Devarim* (Deuteronomy) 17. Essentially, he promised to rule wisely and justly, and not to:

1. Proliferate weapons.
2. Hoard wealth.
3. Exploit lovers.[4]

As you will see, in his time on the throne, Solomon broke all three oaths, and both he and his people suffered because of his failure.

Shortly after he became king, Solomon married the daughter of the Pharaoh of Egypt, a political alliance that brought him great wealth and prestige personally, as well as cementing Israel's role as a major regional power. Soon, Solomon began construction of a great palace and temple, projects long dreamed of by his father.

Legendarily, he was aided in that process by a workforce of djinn and other spirits, led by Ashmodai, the demon king. (Christians call this figure Asmodeus.) Some say these djinn were enslaved to Solomon, others that they were enslaved to Ashmodai, with whom Solomon made compact. Still others say that the djinn served Solomon of their own will, for their own djinnish reasons.

The early years of Solomon's reign were devoted to building and infrastructure projects. Yet, when the building was done, he wasn't sure what to do. In search of answers, Solomon went north, into the wild places. Taking a secret path, he began to climb, singing the song his father had taught him: "I will lift my eyes to the mountains; whence does my help come."[5]

He came at last to the altar at the high place of Gibeon, and there he made abundant sacrifice. He burned large quantities of incense and set his heart on his goal. He sought a dream[6] from the Lord of Dreams, to help and guide him as king over Israel. And thus, it came to pass. In his dream, the sky split open, and a sound like thunder rolled across the heavens. In the thunder was a Voice, and this is what the voice said to the king: **"Request what you would have me give to you."**

Solomon, most clever, had prepared for just this moment. He knew just what he would ask: "You have made me king in place of my Beloved father;[7] but I am a little child. I do not know how to lead. . . . Grant your servant a listening mind, [and] a teachable heart . . ."[8]

26

This pleased G-d enormously, and the mountaintops rang with Their thunderous laughter. **"Because you asked for this—because you did not ask for long life, and you did not ask for riches, and you did not ask for the deaths of your enemies, but instead you asked for discernment in dispensing justice—I now do as you have spoken. I grant you a wise and discerning mind; never before has there been anyone like you, nor will your like arise again. But I also grant you what you did not ask for—both riches and glory all your life—the likes of which no king has ever had."**[9]

As it is said: "God endowed Solomon with wisdom and discernment in great measure, with understanding as vast as the sands on the seashore . . . He spoke with[10] trees, from the cedar in Lebanon to the hyssop that grows out of the wall; and he spoke with beasts, birds, creeping things, and fishes."[11]

Thus, Solomon became a magician. He came to know the secrets of the natural world; he could speak the languages of the plants and animals, and even of the stars and winds. He learned the secret names of the angels, djinn, demons, and other spirits. He entered into partnership with some and brokered treaties with others. He continued to build up the city of Jerusalem, providing it with a modern infrastructure that was the envy of the region. Solomon ruled wisely and well, and Israel flourished.

His wisdom grew into fame, and rumors of him came to the attention of the Queen of Sheba, herself a brilliant, wise, and much-blessed ruler. Her people were a nation of star worshippers, and she was not just their queen, but also their priestess, magician, and chief astronomer. Like Solomon, she could speak the languages of nature and was in alliance with the old powers of Earth and Sky. With her retainers and counselors, and bringing rare and precious gifts, she traveled north to see the hotshot magician-king with her own eyes.

Some say it was love at first sight. Others tell of a slow courtship. Some say that they were merely friends, and not lovers at all. However, what all know is that the two great minds sang in each other's presence. Each tested the other with riddles and puzzles, and they taught each other all they knew. It was a productive and joyful collaboration of equals. Alas, there could be no future in it. They both had responsibilities to their people, and he could no more leave Israel for Sheba than she could remain in Israel with him. Regretfully, they said their goodbyes, and the queen, with her courtiers and counselors, made her way back home, having traded her gifts for many mundane, magical, and mystical treasures, the most precious of which was in her womb. Menelik, the

Queen of Sheba's son by Solomon, went on to establish the imperial line of Ethiopia, but that is a tale for another day.[12]

Time passed, and eventually so did Nathan. Without Nathan or the Queen of Sheba, without a wise equal to give him counsel, Solomon lost perspective, and became corrupt. He married thousands of women, hoarded vast stockpiles of wealth, and waged unjust wars of conquest on his neighbors. As the people always do, Israel paid a steep price for their wicked king. Hard times were on the land.

Having lost his partners, Solomon lost his wisdom, and so lost his way as well as his holy protection. He was tricked by the demon king Ashmodai, his long-time frenemy, into giving up his magic ring and with it, his power to command. Solomon was exiled into the desert, and Ashmodai, wearing both the guise of Solomon and his magic ring, ruled over Jerusalem. His reign was much as you might expect a demon's would be. While injustice, poverty, famine, and war plagued his people, Solomon wandered as a beggar in foreign lands. Many say that it was during this time that he wrote the book of Kohelet.

Solomon eventually came to the court of the King of Ammon (modern day Jordan), where he talked his way into a job in the kitchens. Using his knowledge as an herbalist, he cooked delicious and healing food and thus quickly rose to the role of head chef. His skilled use of spices and herbs also piqued the attention of the king's young daughter, the lovely Na'amah,[13] herself a budding sorceress. Over time, love blossomed between them. Eventually, Solomon told his story to her, confessed his wrongdoing, and accepted chastisement and advice from Na'amah. Having made his peace with G-d, he and Na'amah eloped, intending to win back his crown. They made their marriage vows on the banks of the sea, where they caught a large golden fish for their wedding feast. When they cut open the fish, they were greatly astonished to find Solomon's magic ring in its belly!

Thus blessed, the pair made their way back to Jerusalem, where Solomon defeated the demon king Ashmodai and liberated his people. He ruled once more in justice and wisdom, with the wise Na'amah at his side,[14] for all the remaining years of his life, until death them did part.

• • •

There are many lessons to be learned from Solomon's story, but I believe the most important is this: **Without wise peers empowered to call him on his**

bullshit, even the wisest person in the world was corrupted by power. It is for this reason, as well as many others, that I strongly encourage all magicians to find partners and colleagues with whom to study and work.

2.2

Courting Solomon among the Mighty Dead

There are, of course, almost as many methods for courting spirits as there are magicians, perhaps more! I, myself, employ dozens of methods. The method introduced in this chapter is very loosely modeled on Greek Orthodox Christian ikon techniques and can easily be adapted for working with anyone among the Mighty Dead. Ikons (also spelled "icons") are two-dimensional idols, usually of Jesus, Mary, or a saint. They are used in some, but not all, forms of Christian worship. They are most often painted on wood, although they also exist in other forms. Like idols in other traditions, they have a variety of uses, but are most often used as a "portal" for accessing the spirit in question.

Who Are the Mighty Dead?

The Mighty Dead are simply those dead humans who retain a high level of personal coherence long after their death. As I understand it, a dead person's ability to interact with the living world is partly a matter of skill, and partly a matter of "linkage." When mediums (living people who possess the ability to talk to the dead) die, they often retain the ability to speak with the living. More powerfully determinative, however, is the linkage of the spirit back to the world of the living; what is remembered lives.

And so, at its most basic, that is what we have to offer to the Dead. Our memories and interactions with them give them a foothold of manifestation in the world, which offers them a leg up on their climb to deification. What they have to offer us varies based on who they are. However, the Mighty Dead all have something in common: whatever they offer is potent enough that millions of people have kept their names known, and their stories told, for a very long time. That's nearly always worth investigating! Mighty Dead are folk heroes and saints, semi-deified tribal ancestors, and local legends. They vary substantially among each other, as much as any group of humans. However, one thing they all have in common is that they are the sort of people who are eager to speak with others; there are no introverts among the Mighty Dead.

How to Work with the Mighty Dead

For most people, building a relationship with the Mighty Dead rests on three foundations: 1) learning about their life and hagiography, 2) making devotional offerings, and 3) seeking contact and visitation. If you're reading this book in order, you've already learned quite a bit about Solomon and will learn much more as you continue to read. However, I encourage you to seek out even more learning about Solomon and his times. Although I will not discuss them in detail in this book, I particularly recommend you read folktales featuring Solomon to expand and deepen your understanding of him.

Honoring the Dead with Devotional Offerings

This is not the only way to honor the Dead. Every culture, and every practitioner, has their own methods. You'll develop your own praxis, which works for you, over time. This is just one example to get you started. Depending on your mediumship skills, this ritual can help establish contact. For most people, the easiest way to seek contact with the dead is to invite them, by name, to visit you in your dreams at the end of the ritual, which we discuss further later. This ritual can be used at any time, but it is most effective at liminal times that are traditionally associated with the dead, such as Halloween, New Years, the night of a New Moon,[1] sunrise, or sunset. It is also excellent on the birthday, feast day, or death day of the person you are honoring. For Solomon, the first night of Hanukkah is an especially propitious night, as is his Greek festival, the Sunday of the Holy Forefathers.[2]

In my preferred method of offering, you'll need an image of Solomon, to "hold space" for him. You should choose one that speaks to you. My favorite is the frontispiece of this book. It is an 18th century Russian Orthodox ikon from the Kizhi Pogost, a historic church in Russia noted for its extraordinary architecture and art. I like this particular image for many reasons. I like that he is young. I like that he is pointing at the Temple. I especially adore his kind, wise eyes, which are so easy to fall into. Additionally, I appreciate that the ikon clearly depicts him as biracial; many images seem to erase his mother's inheritance entirely. I cannot read what is written on the scroll, which I believe to be in Old Church Slavonic, but similar Greek ikons have scrolls with the beginning of Proverbs 9, legendarily written by Solomon: "Wisdom has built her house; She has hewn out her seven pillars."

To begin the ritual, set a fancy table for Solomon and yourself, with candles and flowers, and lay out something for the two of you two eat. I like to serve honey cake and rose-flavored kefir or lassi. I do not drink alcohol, but if I did, I would offer date liquor. Set the ikon up at Solomon's place, so that you are facing each other. Turn off all electric lights, light the candles, and invite Solomon by name. Speak from your heart, telling him why you want to meet him. Tell him what you've learned about him. Remember his names aloud. Explain to him that you have made this meal for him and wish to share it with him. Ask him to join you. Bless the meal, and then eat in silence, listening for the voice of Solomon in your head. Unless you are already an experienced medium, you might need to repeat this ritual, and the one which follows, several times before getting clear contact.

After about half an hour, when you are done with your cake, thank Solomon for joining you, and tell him when you will come again. Say goodbye, and then clear the table. If possible, go immediately to bed, and try to dream of a conversation with Solomon.

I strongly encourage you to court dream visitations from Solomon. Dreams of Solomon and his writings are traditionally considered among the most significant teaching dreams: "There are three kings whose appearance in a dream is significant . . . one who [dreams of] Solomon should expect wisdom. . . . Similarly, there are . . . books of . . . Writings. . . . One who sees the book of Psalms should anticipate piety; . . . one who sees the book of Proverbs should anticipate wisdom; . . . one who [sees the] Song of Songs in a dream should anticipate piety; . . . of Ecclesiastes should anticipate wisdom."[3]

If you are not a strong dreamer, you should try some magic to aid with dream incubation—a magical practice of choosing in advance what to dream about. Dreaming is among the most powerful of magical acts, but one which is under assault in our society. A culture that glorifies ubiquitous intoxication and pervasive sleep deprivation has stolen your dreams from you. Take them back.

2.3

Take Back Your Dreams

Evidence of human fascination with dreaming goes back as far as evidence can go. Dreaming is among the most natural of human activities, but it is not exclusive to humans. There is good reason to believe that all amniotes—mammals, birds, and reptiles—dream. The first step in any kind of oneiromancy, or dream magic, is learning to remember your dreams.

Every night, before falling asleep, speak aloud (something like) "I will sleep well, dream powerfully, and awaken refreshed, remembering my dreams," and then drink a sip of water. When you awaken, immediately write down anything you can remember of your dream. Some advice on this topic: who wants their dreams to come true will write them in a notebook and the day and the time and the place.[1]

After that, before getting out of bed, the first thing you should do is take a sip of the same glass of water, and then try to write more. I have been told by many people that your mind doesn't like two such similar events as the sips of water before and after sleeping being separated by blankness, and so it will try to fill in the gap by remembering more of your dreams. Honestly, I'm a little skeptical about that reasoning, but it does seem to work!

On days when you can manage to sleep a little later than normal, set an alarm for about two hours before you have to be up. Wake up, write down any dreams you can remember, and move around for a little bit to make sure you're really awake; this is a good time for a bathroom break. Then go back to sleep. The dreams in that second sleep are likely to be much easier to remember. Talmud relates that "Rab Hisda said: [There is no reality in] any dream without a fast. Rab Hisda also said: An uninterpreted dream is like an unread letter. Rab Hisda also said: Neither a good nor a bad dream is fulfilled in every detail."[2] Spend some time thinking about what your dream means, but not too much time. Practice this technique until you can reliably remember dreams several times each week. Once you can, it's time to learn to incubate.

Dream Incubation

Dream incubation is an important initial step to many other kinds of dream magic and has been considered a fundamental magical art in a wide variety of cultures. In Judaism, this practice is called She'elat Halom or Asking a Dream. It can be thought of as a kind of divination. In the dream world, you seek out information and solutions to problems; it really is as simple as that.

The first step in dream incubation is to choose a topic about which you'd like to dream. The easiest kinds of dreams for beginners to incubate are erotic dreams and the finding of solutions to problems about which you are anxious. It is this second type in which I will instruct you.

1. First, write a clear statement of the dream you'd like to incubate. For beginners, it is usually easiest to write this in the form of a question to which you seek an answer, but you can also script a scenario you'd like to play out.

2. Find or make a single simple symbol to represent the desired dream. It could be a picture of a person you're feuding with, or an open book you're having trouble understanding. You can also make a sigil. If you're not very good at visualizing (I'm not!), then you can use a keyword or short phrase instead, but most people do better with pictures.

3. If possible, sleep in a special place (caves and riverbanks are very traditional). However, if you are a strong dreamer and have been practicing remembering your dreams, you should have no trouble incubating dreams in your regular bed.

4. If you wish, make a short recording of yourself speaking your dream intention and keyword, and play it on repeat at a low volume while you sleep. If you have trouble falling asleep because of the sound, try mixing it with some rain, river, or ocean noises.

5. Before falling asleep, turn the problem over and over in your head, trying to hold the symbol in your mind for as long as you can while you fall asleep. In several clinical studies, it's been found that just this is enough to incubate a dream for well more than half of subjects. (However, I suspect most of those subjects, like the subjects of many psychological experiments, were in college kids. As a general rule, teens dream more strongly than adults.)

6. If this doesn't work for you, you can try adding some magic to the mix, such as the short dream incubation spell which follows, or the Dreamer's Servant pentacle which we learn in part three.

7. Once you've gotten good at incubating problem-solving dreams, try incubating other kinds. When combined with conjuration, dream visitations from spirits can be incubated for many purposes. I encourage you to invite Solomon into your dreams.[3]

A Dream Incubation Charm[4]

Before going to sleep, use a fine-tip permanent marker to write the magic formula יא יא א כן א יהוה on one side of a whole bay leaf, and a sigil of your dream intent on the other. Place it inside your pillowcase. As you lie in bed drifting off to sleep, say: "I call upon you, Tzevaot, Michael, Raphael, and you, powerful archangel Gavriel. Do not simply pass me by on your nightly journey, but let one of you enter here, and reveal to me concerning (insert your problem)." If possible, cry yourself to sleep, thinking about your problem. Crying is an extremely common dream induction technique in Levantine magic, both ancient and modern. (To incubate an erotic dream, masturbate instead of crying, but don't climax.) When you wake, think hard about what you have dreamt, but not too hard.

Dream Visitations

In my experience, once you have experienced both, it is pretty easy to tell the difference between a genuine prophetic or spirit-visitation dream and a "normal" dream. There is a texture and quality to visitations that is quite distinct from most dreams. Commenting on Joseph's prophetic dream of the grain sheafs in Bereshit (Genesis) 37:7, the classic Kabbalistic text *Aur H'Chaim* (The Light of Life) says: "You should appreciate that if a dream is to be perceived as a prophetic vision, it is essential that it be as clear and distinct as bright daylight. The person dreaming it should have the feeling that he actually experiences what he sees in the dream as if it were reality. When these conditions are met, he may consider the dream as a prophetic revelation."[5]

As you move through this book and deepen your relationship with Solomon and his magic, you may find that, in addition to Solomon, other teachers, sages, and wizards come into your dreams to instruct you. If you experience this, it can be a good idea to begin making communion with those figures as well, asking them to aid in your dream work. However, your best and truest guide to the magic of Solomon will always be Solomon himself. Seek him in your dreams and by any other method you like.

Exercises

You don't have to succeed at all these exercises before moving on, but I encourage you to try them all.

- Make or acquire a physical ikon of Solomon.

- Hold a feast with Solomon.

- Incubate a dream with Solomon.

- Acquire knowledge and conversation of Solomon, Magician King, and ask him to aid you in your study and experimentation.

2.4

Logos: Magic of the Mind

"Yah, the Lord of hosts [Adonai Tzevaot], the living God [El Chai], King of the Universe [Melekh H'Olam], Omnipotent [El Shaddai], All-Kind and Merciful, Supreme and Extolled, who is Eternal, Sublime and Most-Holy, ordained (formed) and created the Universe in thirty-two mysterious paths of wisdom by three Sepharim [stories], namely: 1) S'for (סְפָר) [recitation]; 2) Sippur (סִפּוּר) [communication]; and 3) Sapher (סֵפֶר) [numbers] which are in Him one and the same."[1]

At its core, Solomonic magic, like most Jewish, crypto-Jewish,[2] and pseudo-Jewish[3] magic, is language and name magic. In Judaism, it is through speech that creation comes into being, and written talismans[4] are among the most common types of Jewish magical object. A person whose knowledge of Names of Power allows them to break curses, exorcize demons, prophesy, conjure spirits, and work other sorcerous wonders is called a Ba'alat Shem[5] (באלת שם) or "Mistress of the Name."[6]

The History of Hebrew

Hebrew, as we know it today, is a fascinating language, with many unique features that set it apart from other languages. This is largely because it is the only surviving Canaanite language, and among the only successfully resurrected natural languages. Hebrew began to coalesce into its own language, distinct from other Northern Semitic languages,[7] around 1500-1200 BCE in the Levant, then the Kingdoms of Israel and Judah, and flourished for centuries as the everyday spoken "mother tongue" of the people of that region.

Over the course of the Babylonian captivity (586-539 BCE), Hebrew's role as an everyday spoken language was largely replaced by its close cousin, Old Aramaic, although some families probably still spoke Hebrew at home. By 300 BCE, Hebrew was almost entirely out of favor as a spoken language, but it retained prominence in Jewish ritual, liturgical, and magical use, both spoken and written. It was revived as a vernacular language in the 19th century as part of the greater Zionism movement. Today, there are about nine million fluent Hebrew speakers, including around five million people whose native language is Hebrew.[8] As you probably expect, the overwhelming majority of these are in Israel, where Hebrew is the official language.

As with all languages, Hebrew pronunciation varies widely across communities. Ask ten native speakers of English how to say the word "water," and you're likely to hear many different answers. Such is also the case in Hebrew. Further complicating the matter, Hebrew word magic is usually written, rather than spoken, and Hebrew is traditionally written without vowels. As you saw in the previous *Sefer Yetzirah* passage, the same written word can represent a whole family of closely related meanings. This ambiguity, and its enticing opportunities for wordplay, form a cornerstone of Hebrew magic.

The Origins of Writing

The origins of writing are obscure. Ideographic (picture-symbol) writing from ancient China, Mesopotamia, and Egypt are strikingly similar, and all appear to have arisen around 6000 BCE (Neolithic prehistory), but it is unclear whether or not they share a common source. So called "true writing" or phonographic alphabets (where letters represent sounds, not ideas) appears[9] to have first arisen in Egypt when ideographic hieroglyphs were adopted to

Semitic languages by non-citizen workers[10] around 2000 BCE (early middle kingdom). The earliest known inscriptions in this proto-Sinaitic alphabet date to around 1900–1500 BCE (first intermediate period). All Hebrew alphabets derive from an early regional variation of that alphabet called Paleo-Hebrew. Nearly all modern alphabets[11] derive from proto-Sinaitic, mostly by way of Phoenician.

Like English, modern Hebrew has more than one kind of "font." In modern usage the most common are a printed block script and a handwritten cursive. Israelis most often handwrite Hebrew in a cursive script, which (like English cursive) can vary quite a bit from writer to writer. Most non-Israeli Hebrew users are most familiar with the square-letter block print called *Ashurit* (Assyrian), which derives from medieval Aramaic scripts, which is what appears in this book. When inscribing pentacles by hand, I sometimes use Paleo-Hebrew, partly because it looks cool and ancient, and mostly because it's much easier to engrave. You can see these different alphabets in the table on pages 38–39.

Egyptian Hieroglyphics		Proto-Sinaitic	Phoenician Paleo-Hebrew	Square Script Hebrew	Modern English
🐂	ox	𓃾	⟨	א	A
⌷	house	▯	◁	ב	B
⟍	throwing stick	⌐	⟨	ג	G, C
🐟	fish	⊓	◁	ד	D
🧍	praise	🧍	∃	ה	E
🥄	mace	♀	Y	ו	U, V, Y
\\	manacle	=	⅂	ז	Z
🧵	thread	Ⅲ	🯄	ח	H
☦	good	⊕	⊗	ט	
🦵	arm	⌐	⅂	י	I, J
✋	hand	⦙⦙⦙	⋊	כ	K
〜	goad	৭	∠	ל	L

Egyptian Hieroglyphics		Proto-Sinaitic	Phoenician Paleo-Hebrew	Square Script Hebrew	Modern English
〰〰〰	water	〰	𐤌	מ	M
🐍	snake	∽	𐤍	נ	N
📿	peg	⚡	‡	ס	
👁	eye	👁	O	ע	O
⬭	corner	⌐	⊃	פ	P
🌱	plant	∬	⋔	צ	
⊶	monkey	8	φ	ק	Q
👤	head	👤	◁	ר	R
☀	Sun	⊡	W	שׁ	Sh
⬓	land	ω	W	שׂ	S
✕	mark	+	X	ת	T

39

Proto-Sinaitic Ideograms

A remarkable fact about Hebrew is that the phonographic alphabet retains some of its ideographic power. That is to say, root words in Hebrew relate to the rebus of their letters. As an example, let's analyze the proto-Semitic root S-L-M[12] (שלמ), which we discussed previously as the root of Solomon's name. This root, in its oldest form, has a cluster of meanings surrounding "sunset," including "dusk," "completion," "evening star," and "west." From there, the meanings spread out metaphorically to things like rest, peace, safety, and wholeness. SLM is the root of a family of related words: the well-known Hebrew "shalom" and Arabic "salaam" (which both mean "peace"), "Shalem/ Shalim" (the Canaanite god of sunset whose name is shared with the planet Venus in its role as the evening star), and the place-names "Salem" (both the ancient city of Melchizedek and the more recent city of witches in Massachusetts) and "Jerusalem" (which means "House of SLM"). Many other familiar words derive from this root, including "Islam" and "Muslim," both of which are related to SLM in the sense of "peaceful submission."

| water | goad | sun |

In Proto-Sinaitic hieroglyphs, SLM is Sun-Goad-Water. Water and Sun are clear enough, but the meaning of "goad" has changed very much over time. To the writers of Proto-Sinaitic, the "goad" is a shepherd's rod or the walking staff.[13] *Lamed* is a walking staff, a shepherd's rod, and also the Staff of Moses, by which the Great Teacher parted the seas. With this understanding, we can read sun-goad-water as "Sun Shepherded (into) the Waters," or "the Sun sets (into the Mediterranean)." This underscores the idea that the essential meaning of SLM is, as we discussed before, the proper name "Sunset." All other uses are extended by metaphor from there.

I have slightly misled you. In English, and most Indo-European languages, the most basic words tend to be nouns—people, places, and things. In Hebrew (and other Semitic languages), however, many primitive words are verbs—actions. In its essential form, שלמ (SLM) is not "sunset" as a thing, but an action: "to set like the Sun." This animate, active grammar is sometimes difficult to wrap one's head around, but it engenders a very important way of looking at the world. In her fabulous book *Braiding Sweetgrass*, the Native American ecologist, poet, and teacher Robin Wall Kimmerer writes about struggling, as an adult, to learn her people's language, Potawatomi, which is also verb-heavy compared to English. In this passage, she has just discovered the word *wiikegama,* which means "to be a bay."

> When "bay" is a noun, it is defined by humans, trapped between its shores, and contained by the word. But the verb wiikwegamaa—to be a bay—releases the water from bondage and lets it live. "To be a bay" holds the wonder that for this moment, the living water has decided to shelter itself between these shores conversing with cedar roots and a flock of baby mergansers . . . The language is a mirror for seeing the animacy of the world, for the life that pulses through all things . . . The language reminds us, in every sentence, of our kinship with all of the animate world . . . The animacy of the world is something we already know. But, the language of animacy teeters on extinction, not just for native peoples, but for everyone.

Personally, I believe that all words begin as proper names for animate beings. In humans, symbolic culture, including art and speech, appears to have evolved simultaneously with ritual.[14] Ritual's power to build otherwise unprecedented levels of complex social cooperation is one of many driving forces which make language (and symbolic culture more broadly) such a powerful evolutionary advantage. The first time the word SLM was uttered was surely as a greeting and name for our daily visitor, Sun Setting, who gently frees us from the glaring desert Sun and ushers in the peace of a dark, restful night. שלם is one Name of Power for Sun Setting, and all words and names related to it, including Solomon, are (metaphorically) children of Sun Setting.

2.5

Hebrew Names of Power

Names of Power, also called Divine Names, are a type of Hebrew magical formula. Such a name is so clear and true that it pierces the heavens and rings with the power of the spirit it names. The power of the spirit-person *is* the written name itself; for this reason, special care must be taken to write the names correctly, as Solomon says in Kohelet 12:10: ". . . [seek] to find delightful words, to write correctly matters of Truth." This magic is released from the name as soon as any letter is broken.

For this reason, written charms must be carefully protected. Torah scrolls are reverently wrapped and handled with great ceremony; they are artifacts of immense power. If you tell a Jewish grandmother that you're experiencing a string of bad luck, likely the first thing she'll recommend is to check your *mezuzah*.[1] If a single letter has become worn to the point of illegibility, it is said that the protective shield the mezuzah provides is broken. However, the magic of the Name does not immediately dissipate; rather, it is freed to return to the "Well of Souls" from which it sprang, traveling through the vessel of our world to do so. For this reason, one traditional Jewish way to use written charms is to write them in water- or alcohol-soluble ink, and then rinse the words into water, wine or other liquid. For a short time, the power of the Names infuses the liquid, creating a magic potion which is then drunk, washed with, or used as a reflective surface for scrying.

The medieval kabbalistic text *Shaarei Orah*[2] (שערי אורה) or "Gates of Light" highlights the importance of such names, saying:

> [At] the boundary of truth and the tradition of the covenant is that one who wants to attain one's desires regarding the matter of the names of the Holy One of Blessing, that a person needs to make efforts with all of their strength in Torah, to attain the *kavvanot* of each and every single one of those holy names . . . each and every one of these names are viewed as keys to each and every single thing that a person needs on every side and issue in the world. And when one meditates on those names, s/he will find that all of Torah and all *mitzvot* are dependent on them, and when one knows the *kavvanah* of each and every single one of those names, one recognizes and knows the greatness of the One Who Spoke And The World Came Into Being . . .[3]

This gives rise to an obvious question: How is it that the G-d of Israel, who we are so explicitly told is *one*, has so many names? As with all Jewish questions, this one admits a wide variety of answers. One traditional method of answering such question is with the PRDS[4] method, which is an acronym for four "levels" of understanding: **P**lain Text, **R**epresentative, **D**ialectic, and **S**ecret.[5] Let's try it out to answer this question: How is it that the G-d of Israel, who we are so explicitly told is *one*, has so many names?

- At the **Plain Text** level of understanding, it is because the many names were historically understood as separate gods. Many Jews, including myself, continue to understand them in this way.

- At the **Representative**[6] level, it is often understood by allegory. The G-d of Israel is like pure light. Physical reality, where we live and breathe, is like an infinitely faceted gem. Just like a prism splits white light into a beautiful rainbow, from our vantage point in manifest creation, G-d manifests in a beautiful spectrum of holiness. Of the explanations I will offer here, this is the one I have most often heard from modern, mainstream American rabbis across the spectra of observance.

- At the **Dialectic** level, answers to this question are the bulk of Kabbalistic philosophy and Jewish magic. Whole books are written discussing the dialectic intricacies of the many names of G-d, their individual attributes and magical virtues, and their essential unity. You'll get to see many examples of this kind of rabbinic dialectic later in this chapter.

- Finally, at the **Secret** level, this conundrum is in many ways the central divine Mystery of Judaism. How can G-d be both the god of Israel (as Athena is the god of Athenians) *and* the ineffable One who moment by moment breathes Being into Becoming? To each of us is revealed our own experience of this Mystery.

Mainstream Jewish doctrine says there are seven[7] exoteric names of supreme power, and nearly limitless esoteric names. These names of supreme power are so potent that, once written, they must be treated as people, not objects. They should not be erased or destroyed, but respected and cared for while they live, and buried with honor when they fall to natural causes, such as fading, damage, moisture, or anything else that makes even a single word unreadable.[8] This extreme care is an extension of the third commandment, that the Divine Name must not be taken in vain. As with most matters of Jewish thought, opinions are mixed about exactly which seven names are the most holy ones, but one popular septet among Jewish magicians is the one we discuss below. While there is no fixed order for these names, I have tried to arrange them in order of simplicity.

Please note: I have chosen not to use Hebrew letters' final-forms when writing roots, in order to distinguish the root from the word(s) spelled the same way.

The Seven Names

El (אל) is the generic Hebrew word for "god," as well as a proper name of several different, but closely related, Semitic gods: including the G-d of Israel and the Canaanite consort of Asherah. "El" is a very old word, with cognates in nearly every Semitic language. This combination of sounds has almost certainly meant "god" for more than 6000 years.

The name El is closely associated with *chesed* (חסד), a notoriously difficult-to-translate virtue. Older translators often use "mercy," and many modern translators choose "loving-kindness." I most often translate it as "compassion." At its root, chesed is the love that binds Creator to Creation. For example, Tehillim 52:3 tells us that "The chesed of El endures forever." The Torah begins as chesed (compassion) and ends as chesed (compassion).[9]

For this reason, it is sometimes taught that, when one wishes to pray while in distress, one should first call the name of El, with the kavvanah (mystic intent)[10] of conjuring divine compassion.

When El is used in Torah, it is often framing G-d as Divine Lightbringer—highlighting Their ability to replace ignorance with illumination. The Zohar teaches (Tzav 12:94) that "E-l[11] is universally the illumination of the supernal Chochma [Wisdom] . . ."

The Tanya[12] underscores this same point, elaborating: ". . . the Name E-l signifies calling forth the radiance from the Ein Sof Aur [Light Without Limit], which is clothed in the Torah, from concealment to manifestation, so that it should illumine manifestly in man's soul. Thus, too, it is written [in Tehillim 109:13], 'E-l is the L-rd, and He has given us light,' indicating likewise that the Divine Name E-l connotes illumination."[13]

El is the name favored by the matriarchs and patriarchs, particularly when they seek the divine in groves and riversides, where the chthonic Divine is made manifest in the low places. El is also closely associated with the Bull of Heaven and the flash of lightning. El is among my favorite Names of Power. It is rare for me to pray to the G-d of Israel without invoking it, either alone or in combination with other names.

Elohim (אלהימ) is a plural of Eloah (אלוה), which is a form of El. This is the first divine name used in Torah and the only divine name in the first chapter of Bereshit. Grammatically, it is plural. Its Ugaritic cognate is used to denote the children of El, who comprise most of that pantheon. In Torah, it is used to refer both to the (ostensibly singular) G-d of Israel, and also to the gods of other peoples, and at times to groups of human rulers. The most mainstream opinion on this odd happenstance of a plural word being used to describe a singular god is articulated by Ibn Ezra, in his commentary on Bereshit 1:1. "E-lohim is its plural form, and the root [of this] is in the nature of language. For every language has a formal form . . . In the Holy Tongue [Hebrew], the way is to refer to the greater in the plural."[14]

However, as always, opinions differ. The *Kuzari* of Yehuda Halevi[15] says: "The word has a plural form, because it was so used by gentile idolaters, who believed that every deity was invested with astral and other powers. Each of these was called Elōah; their united forces were, therefore, called Elōhim. . . . These deities were as numerous as are the forces which sway the human body and the universe." Personally, I hew closer to this opinion and understand Elohim as a collective singular, describing a divine council, whom I often poetically call the "Circle of Stars," although it is not my intention to equate them to either the classical planets or the scientific stars. When I use the name Elohim to describe the G-d of Israel, I am imagining Them as a council of anthropomorphized Primordial Forces who, moment by moment, collectively breathe Becoming into Being (and vice versa).

The Most Holy Name (יהוה) is generally understood as the proper, personal name of the G-d of Israel. It is considered so holy that many Jews, including myself, do not like to pronounce or transliterate it. Instead, we use a variety of noa-names such as "Most Holy Name," "G-d," "HaShem" (which means "The Name"), or "Tetragrammaton" (which means "The Four Letter Word"[16]). In other cases, we substitute other Names of Power for יהוה, most often Adonai, which we discuss below. However, many Christians pronounce this name as YHVH, JHVH, Yahweh, or Jehovah.[17] Like many Jews, I find this deeply improper. Talmud recounts that "one who pronounces the Name by its letters . . . has no part in the Future World."[18]

In Torah, the Name first appears in Bereshit 2:4, and it is ubiquitous thereafter. The oldest known surviving inscriptions of the Most Holy Name are from the mid-9th century BCE, but most scholars agree the name itself is far older and likely Canaanite in origin. It is unclear if the name is essentially Semitic, or if it is imported from a non-Semitic source. If it is Hebrew, it is generally understood as a form of the Hebrew root היה (HYH), which means "to be." Most often, it's understood to mean something like "to bring into being" and highlights G-d's role as Perpetual Creator. The name יהיה is: He is creating everything from nothing; the yud is used for action that is in the present progressive tense.[19]

Similarly, because of its relationship to היה, the Most Holy Name is often understood to represent G-d in Their aspect of eternity and universality. For example, we are taught: "All the miracles performed by G-d in Egypt which defied all known laws of nature, were invoked by the Ineffable Four-lettered Name י-ה-ו-ה which symbolizes G-d as היה, הוה, יהיה [Who Is, Who Was, Who Will Be] the One who created the world ex nihilo and who is eternal."[20]

The Most Holy Name also invokes G-d as essentially without quality. As the *Kuzari* says: "All names of God, save the Tetragrammaton, are predicates and attributive descriptions, derived from the way His creatures are affected by His decrees and measures. . . ."

Endless commentaries on this name exist, but nearly all understand it to be the primal proper name of G-d. For example, in the midst of the Shaarei Orah quote you read a few pages ago, the text says ". . . we need to go back and make known to you that the essence of faith and the base of the base is to understand and know [that] all holy names mentioned in the Torah are all contained in the four lettered Name, which is יהוה, blessed be, and that is called the body of the tree, and the rest of the names—some are root, some are branches, some are treasures and hidden . . ."[21]

Adonai (אדני) is usually translated as "Lord" or "Master," although it is actually a plural possessive form of אדן (*adon*). That is to say, Adonai actually means more like "My Lords'," rather than "Lord." As with "Elohim," this is generally understood as an honorific plural, although I understand it more as a collective singular. When applied to humans, "adon" is a word for a constellation of social roles we, thankfully, do not often encounter in our culture: a feudal-style warlord, a slave-master, or a tribal patriarch who exerts total control and ownership over his wives, children, and household. It is somewhat less sinister when applied to G-d, although I, personally, still find it mildly uncomfortable.[22] When I pray from the heart, I almost never use this name, unless I am speaking specific traditional prayers or Torah passages.

Adonai is frequently used in conjunction with other holy names. In particular, the compound name Adonai יהוה is often understood as reconciling G-d's particularity with his universality. It is said: "They [the names] are visualized as intertwined in the following way: יהוה אדני יאהדונהי [YHVH ADNI IAHD-VNHI]. This is the unification of God. Even though the name Adonai seems to govern the principle of God's concealment and judgment, nonetheless it is in a complete state of unity with YHVH, representing revelation and mercy. This is the true preparation of the heart of the prophet."[23]

Ehyeh (אהיה) is, like many Names of Power, a form of the root היה (HYH). It is normally translated into English as "I Am," but is perhaps closer to "I Will Be." It is most commonly used in the compound form אהיה אשר אהיה (Ehyeh Asher Ehyeh). Traditionally, this name is often translated "I Am Who I Am," although it is more literally "I Will Be Who I Will Be." I prefer the poetic translation, "I am Being, Becoming."

This name plays a prominent role in *Shemot* (Exodus) 3:14. In that passage, Moses has just asked the Burning Bush what he should call it, and the Bush responds with this name.[24] This is a strange name, part of a strange passage, and there exist many interpretations. Is the god of the Burning Bush ducking the question? Are They trying to say something like, "I am the One who is," meaning that They are the only thing that "really" exists? Perhaps They meant, "I am the one who just is what I am," implying that They lack all quality or description. With a little creative rabbinic wordplay, you can even interpret it as אהיה אשראה יה (Ehyeh Asherah Jah) which would mean "Asherah[25] becoming Jah," although that's an unusual way to spell Asherah.

This name is often described as the central trunk of a tree of Names of Power. For example, the Shaarei Orah says: ". . . the name Ehyeh[26] is the main part of this tree, and from it the roots root out and expand branches to all sides, and the rest of the holy names are all in imagined images of the branches and bases that continue from the body of the tree, and each of the branches produces fruit according to its kind . . ."[27]

On the other hand, the *Kuzari* stresses the essential ineffability of this name, which is not a name, saying: "As to EH'YEH . . . its tendency is to prevent the human mind from pondering over an incomprehensible but real entity. When Moses asked: 'And they shall say to me, What is His name?' the answer was 'Why should they ask concerning things they are unable to grasp?'

In a like manner the angel answered: 'Why askest thou thus after my name, seeing it is secret?' (Judges 13:18). Say to them eh'yēh, which means: 'I am that I am,' the existing one, existing for you whenever you seek me. Let them search for no stronger proof than My presence among them, and name Me accordingly."[28]

Tzevaot (צבאות) is the plural of צבא (*tsva*), which means something like "war," "army,"[29] "militia," or "mob." In the Five Books of Moses, "Tzevaot" is only used to describe human armies. For this reason, some[30] do not consider this one of the Seven Names, but a Name of Power of a lesser order. However, beginning with the prophets, Tzevaot began to be used as a Name of Power, most often translated as "Lord of Hosts" or "Master of Legions." The name first appears in I Samuel 1:11, where Hannah begs to be granted a son,[31] but its most well-known occurrence is probably in Isaiah 6:3: "Holy, holy, holy, is HaShem Tzevaot; The whole earth is full of His glory." Sometimes, instead of being understood as a name for the G-d of Israel, Tzevaot is understood to be the Host of Angels; for example Ibn Ezra reads the preceding verse from Isaiah in that way.[32]

Although Tzevaot is generally read as the plural of tsva, it can also be read as a compound word צבא-ות (*tsva-oht*). *Oht* (ות) means "seal"[33] (as in the biblical phrase "set these words as a seal upon your heart") or sign (as in the biblical phrase "signs as wonders"). The rabbis often use this wordplay as a rhetorical device to explain that, when the name Tzevaot is used, it shows how G-d has cloaked Themself in physical manifestation, showing Themself to us as a sign here, where we live. It is for this reason, the rabbis say, that the name does not appear in the books of Moses: In those days, when the covenant was in its infancy, G-d showed Themself to us in full divine glory. As we grow up, G-d withdraws, giving only hints and signs, teaching as a "guide on the side," rather than as a "sage on the stage." Because "oht" (seal) is also the Hebrew word most commonly used to refer to the pentacles in this book, a similar wordplay can be constructed to make Tzevaot the commander of an army of pentacles, a useful kavvanah (mystic intention) for many types of sorcerous work.

Shaddai (שדי) is an extremely difficult name to translate. Conventionally, it is rendered as "Almighty." Most likely[34] it comes from שדד (ShDD), a root which gives rise to a vast family of seemingly disparate meanings, including "strong," "breast," and "daimon." *The Dictionary of Deities and Demons in the Bible* translates Shaddai as "God of the Wilderness," which it gets from the Akkadian *shaddu,* or "dweller in the mountains," which it relates to the Hebrew שדה, which means "field" or "plains." It explains: "Any El Shadday, is, therefore, a 'god of the wilderness' and can be connected with the iconographical motif of the 'lord of the animals'. . ." I don't fully buy that as an etymology, but Shaddai unquestionably has a Horned God-esque vibe.

Others instead read Shaddai as Sh'Dai, "The One Who Is Sufficient." The root די (dai) means "enough," either in the sense of "to be sufficient" or "Whoa! That's enough!" It is said that, as G-d creates the world, it grows and entangles and spreads ("rooting out" as Talmud would say) until the moment when Shaddai, the All-Sufficient, says "Enough!"

Shaddai is also found on the back of mezuzot, where it is an acronym for *Shomer Dalatot Yisrael,* which is usually translated as "Guardian of the Gates of Israel," although I prefer "Sentry of the Doors of Israel," because it preserves the acronym. Relatedly, the name שדי is frequently used in apotropaic (turning-back) magic, to avert *yetzer harah,* or "the evil inclination" (a phrase which sometimes means "bad behavior" and sometimes means "ill-wishing" or even "hexing.") To use the name Shaddai in this way,[35] we perform the following contemplative exercise: First, we spell out each letter of "yetzer": *yod tzaddi resh.* Then, we turn our focus on the last letter of each letter's name: *yoD, tzaddI, reSH,*[36] giving DISh (דיש). To turn back this evil impulse, we invert the letters, which gives us the name ShDI (שדי) or Shaddai.

Shaddai is a name much associated with wonder working; it is the name which loosens (*m'shaddad*) the laws of nature. The *Ramban* says that this Name "is able to manipulate the astrological framework. This is the Name through which Hashem performs hidden miracles and it was through this name that He would grant Avraham offspring."

Ezekiel offers my preferred reading of the name, as the onomatopoetic ShhhhhhDaiiiii: "I heard the noise of their wings like the noise of great waters, like the voice of Shaddai . . ."[37] This gentle rish-rush of a wave, the rustle of a chorus of angels taking flight, building to a resounding thunderclap-crash, is, to my mind, the most immediate and visceral meaning of the name we call "Almighty."

Shaddai is often used as part of the compound name El Shaddai. This compound is very frequently used in connection with the Matriarchs and Patriarchs, as well as with Jewish tribal Ancestors more broadly. Shemot 6:3 says: "And I appeared unto Avraham, unto Yitzchak, and unto Ya'akov, as El Shaddai, but by My name YHVH I did not make Myself known to them." It is El Shaddai who comforts Avram, prophesying children for Sarai in Bereshit

17: "And when Avram was ninety and nine years, Hashem appeared to Avram, and said unto him, I am El Shaddai; walk before Me, and . . . [I] will multiply thee exceedingly." Similarly, in Bereshit 35:11, El Shaddai prophesies children for Jakob: "And Elohim said unto him, I am El Shaddai; be fruitful and multiply; a nation and a company of nations shall be from thee, and kings shall come out of thy loins."

El Shaddai is not just a deeply sexy name, but also one closely connected with sexual reproduction. In Bereshit 49:25, Jakob is blessing his sons. He says: "By the El Aveinu [God of your father] who helps you, and El Shaddai who blesses you, Blessings of the heavens from above, Blessings of the deep lying under, Blessings of breasts and womb, Blessing of ancient mountains, Blessing of everlasting hills . . ." For me, El Shaddai is an intimate and powerful name, framing the G-d of Israel as the god of my mothers, the god of wombs and breasts, the god of deep ancestry. When I pray from the heart to the G-d of Israel, this is the name I most often use.

The table below summarizes this information in a different order:

El	אל	G-d	People and Land of Israel, Compassion, Sky
Ehyeh	אהיה	I Am	"Being" "Becoming," Epiphany, Wholeness, Foundation
Shaddai	שדי	?	Ancestors, Doors, Sex, Reproduction, Growth, Sufficiency
Elohim	אלהים	Gods	Primeval Creator, Genderqueer, Plural
Tzavaot	צבאות	Armies	"Lord of Hosts," "Master of Legions," Manifestation, Signs
Adonai	אדני	Lord	Ruler, Chieftain, Leader
YHVH	יהוה	---	Most Holy Name, Unspoken, Untranslated, Mosaic Covenant

Other Names of Power

There are many other common names of power, and a variety of methods for constructing them. Learning to properly construct Hebrew Names of Power is a delightfully deep topic, well outside the scope of this book. It requires conversational Hebrew, poetical skill, and the direct involvement of the G-d of Israel. This ability is one of the powers that marks a Ba'alat Shem, a Mistress of the Name.

However, understanding some of the ways in which such names are constructed[38] will help us learn to decrypt them when we see them, a much simpler skill. There are several simple methods to construct such names:

■ **Compounds:** Almost any pair of Holy Names can be conjoined to form another Holy Name. For example, we previously discussed both Adonai Tzevaot and El Shaddai. Larger combinations can also be worked, but require more finesse to properly construct.

■ **El'ification:** To grossly oversimplify, many three-letter Hebrew root words can be combined with El to produce a Name of Power. For example, the root word רפא (RFA) gives rise to a family[39] of related words like "heal," "healer," "medicine," "healing," etc. רפאל (Raphael) is a well-known angel whose name is usually translated as "Healing of G-d," but which also means "God, the Healer" or "God of Healing." For the most part, when "El" comes first, the Name is understood as a name for G-d. An example is "El Gibor," usually translated as "G-d the Mighty." However, when the El comes second (as in Gibor-el aka Gabriel, the Might of El), the Name is usually understood as an independent entity, like an angel.

■ **Ya'ification:** Many Hebrew root words can be combined with יה (Jah) to produce a Name of Power. For example, the root ידד (YDD) engenders a family of related words including "lover," "beloved" and "friend." From that root, ידידיה (Jedidiah) is the name given to Solomon by his teacher, Nathan the Prophet, which means "Beloved of Jah." As an extremely broad rule of thumb, El names tend to draw power down from above, and Jah names tend to reach out to the divine from below.

■ **Mathemagical wordplay:** Many sophisticated combinatoric encryption techniques can be used to produce Names of Power from Torah verses and other sources. In particular, most subsets and permutations of the

Most Holy Name are Names of Power in their own right. For example, the first two letters of the Most Holy Name, יה (Jah), is a common Name of Power. In traditional Jewish teaching, the name Jah (יה) is connected explicitly with the high altar of the Temple, as well as with high place altars in general—places where we rise up to meet the divine. This name is also possibly related to the Egyptian lunar god Iah.

Exercises

1. Investigate, contemplate, and meditate on your own name(s).

   b. How did you come to have this name?
       i.   Who gave it to you?
       ii. Why did they (you) choose it?

   b. Is there a Hebrew Name of Power at its root?
       i.   If yes, what is it?
       ii. If yes, how does that Name relate to you?
       iii. If no, what is the etymology of your name?
       iv. How do its roots relate to you?

   c. How does the sound of your name feel in your mouth?
       i.   What shape is it in the air?
       ii. How does that sound relate to you?

   d. What does it look like written on the page?
       i.   What shape are the letters?
       ii. How does it feel in your hand to draw them?

2. Learn to recognize and write the letters of the Hebrew alphabet.

3. Learn to recognize, say*, and write the Seven Names in Hebrew.

   a. As you do, investigate, contemplate, and meditate on each name in turn.

   b. Do not attempt to say the Most Holy Name aloud.

2.6

Magic: Sorcery & Seals

As we discussed in the introduction, I have a powerful emotional connection to the idea of magic books (and you probably do too!). For most of this chapter, we learn how to bring to life a genuinely magical book. In particular, we be discussing step-by-step instructions on how to create a magical book of Solomonic pentacles. However, more experienced magicians can easily extrapolate from this example to create other types of magic books. Before we get into the details of making a book, let's briefly discuss what I consider to be the fundamental magical operation of all Solomonic magic: the invocation of Solomon, the assumption of his "garment of splendor," and the power to speak in his name.

The Invocation of Solomon

In order to properly perform the magic of this section, you should already have acquired knowledge and conversation of Solomon, as discussed in chapter 2.1. However, if you're still working to accomplish that, I encourage you to start trying to invoke anyway. There is no danger of this magic going wrong; it just might not work very well until you get the hang of it. Sometimes, particularly in invocational magic, "fake it until you make it" is a winning strategy. We usually think of our inner states of consciousness as producing their outward manifestations, but the feedback loop runs both ways. To help understand this, pretend to laugh until you make yourself laugh for real.

Whatever ikon (or mental image) you use for Solomon, examine it and choose specific elements of it to inhabit. With my favorite ikon, I usually focus on the red cloak, but I sometimes add the crown when I require additional authority. Before beginning on any of the magic below, spend some time imagining wearing Solomon's cloak. What does it look like on you? Is it heavy on your shoulders? Feel its texture against your skin. Is it smooth? Rough? Velvety? What is it made of? Is it warm? Does it make a sound when it moves? Smell it. What does it smell like? Handle the clasp at the neck. How does it close? What is it made of? Does it have special magical properties?[1]

Next, imagine Solomon taking the cloak off and placing it on your shoulders. What might he say while he does this? Is it a paternalistic gesture? The soft caress of a lover? The proud investiture of a prize pupil? Notice that, even when he takes his cloak off, he is still wearing it. It has been duplicated. When you can clearly imagine all of this, when you think you know what it will feel like, it's time to move on to an actual invocation.

Before performing this invocation, you should have made several devotional feasts with Solomon, and, ideally, spoken with him in your dreams. Before making your first invocation, set up an especially nice feast. Spend time with Solomon; there should be a genuine rapport between the two of you. Ask him if he will allow you to wear his mantle and speak in his name. In my experience, and the experience of my students, he will say yes. Solomon *loves* to do magic, and he loves to help others do magic too! If for any reason he says no, ask him what you can do to win his favor, and then do that and ask again.

Once you have won his permission, ask him to place his garment of splendor on you, to grant you the blessing of speaking magic in his name. Then, begin to recite a highly rhythmic invocation over and over. I encourage you to write your own (or ask Solomon to give you one), but this is an example you can begin with. I recommend clapping or drumming on the underlined syllables. Repeat the chant, faster and faster, until you feel the power enter you. You may slide into glossolalia. That's a good sign!

I invoke SOLomon, DJINN-Master, TEMple-builder.
I invoke SOLomon, maGIcian and the KING.

As you recite, feel the mantle of power settle around you. Focus on the ways in which it feels different, now that it's really happening, than it did in your imagination. Lean into those feelings. Continue reciting, focusing on connecting the sound of the words with the feeling of the investiture.

Ask Solomon if there is anything he will teach you about using his mantle of power, and if there is anything he would like you to do for him while wearing it. Be cautious with your wording; do not obligate yourself to anything you don't want to do. Say thank you and take the mantle off. How do you feel different when you're not wearing it? If you like, you can "store" the magical mantle in a piece of jewelry, or in the scarf we will consecrate below, but I think it is better to simply store it in the words of the invocation, so that you can assume it at will later just by chanting the words.

Your Magic Book

I strongly urge you to read this entire chapter before performing any of the rituals that follow; they link together. If you decide to perform the rituals, especially if this is your first experience with Solomonic sorcery, I encourage you to make your prototype based on the directions in the book, which you'll then use as a "laboratory journal" while you learn to work with the pentacles. After you feel you have mastered them, you should make a "master book." This will be in your own style, made with all your own discoveries. Such a book is a living person, a magical ally of great power, which, upon your death, should be entrusted to a beloved co-magician or to your most promising student. Should you have neither co-magicians nor students, I encourage you to rethink your life choices and arrange for your book to be consigned to a *genizah*[2] upon your death.

The methods I'll outline in this chapter are designed for people (like me) with minimal artistic and crafting skills. If you have special skills in those areas, I encourage you to make use of them on this project. However, remember that what we are making in this chapter is a working journal for experimentation, and it should be crafted in such a way that it will slowly fall apart from repeated use. You should destroy this laboratory book when you make your master book to free its spirit to move into a new and better home. I see many people get so caught up in the art aspect that they lose sight of this book's purpose. **This is not an art project; this is a sorcery project.** If you want to hand-bind myrrh-ink calligraphy in the skin of a fetal goat, that's awesome, but I encourage you to save such measures for your master book.

Supplies to Gather

To make a magic book as outlined in this chapter, you will need the following supplies. You may adapt this list to your own needs, but you may also need to adapt the rituals to your choices.

- A blank book with at least one hundred pages.

  - I prefer a very large sketchbook with a plain black cover. Mine is 11″ x 18″.

  - Virgin (i.e., not post-consumer recycled) paper is better.

- A white scarf preferably with fringes which is large enough to completely wrap the book.

- For Jews, a *tallit gadol* is a nice choice here.

- The fringes here, as well as in most magical applications, are apotropaic (evil-averting). The theory is that evil spirits get "tangled" in the fringe.

■ A long blue ribbon. Mine is about three yards long, but that's probably overkill.

■ A black ink pen set aside for only this work.

- You may also want other colors and multiple sizes of points.

- I also like to have colored pencils, which I use to color in the inked pentacles.

- If you wish, you can use a dip or fountain pen and special ink, but that is not necessary.

■ Drafting tools

- A pencil, a good eraser, a compass, a straightedge, and a protractor. These do not need to be saved only for this.

- The kits made for high school geometry classes are okay, but a higher quality drafting set is worth it. Poorly made compasses are very frustrating, especially for magic, where losing your cool, even for a moment, means having to start all over.

- Where I live, very fancy drafting sets are often available on craigslist and at thrift stores. Since the advent of CAD, few people use them.

■ Living water. Living water is clean, drinkable water collected from a natural source, such as rain, spring, or well. It loses potency over time, so, ideally, you'll want to collect new water every few weeks. For this operation, rainwater is ideal.

■ Blessed oil. You can use plain olive oil, purchase a premade King Solomon or Abramelin oil, or make your own Torah-style holy anointing oil from the recipe in the Supplemental Materials on my website.

■ Incense and a way to burn it. Use the Solomon incense from *The Big Book of Magical Incense* or the highest quality frankincense you can get.

■ A selection of pleasant-smelling spices, herbs, and flowers. I especially like cinnamon, thyme, and roses for this work, but choose whatever you like.

- Salt. Dead Sea salt is nice, but plain table salt is fine.

- Beeswax tealights. You'll need a lot of these for the work in this book, so stock up.

- Full-fat cow or goat's milk or sweet red wine, and a pretty glass you can dedicate to this work.

- Honey. Ideally, mix honey from Israel with honey from as close to your home as you can source.

Optional Ritual: Consecration of the Scarf

1. Clean and prepare yourself. Minimally, wash your hands, face, and genitals. I like rose-scented soap for this. Ideally, wear festive white clothing. Do not wear clothing with words or images on it.

2. Enter magical space/time/consciousness by any method.

3. Invoke Solomon.

4. Oil your hands.

5. Hold the scarf in both your hands and lovingly caress it with oily hands. Take sensual delight in the texture of the scarf. Twirl the fringes. Let it slither through your fingers. If you prefer, instead of oil, you can wave the scarf through frankincense smoke.

6. Hold the scarf up to the sky. Connect to the energy at the center of the Earth, and then reach up and drag down the starlight, through the scarf.

7. Infuse the starlight into the scarf.

8. While you do, say something like:[3] "Creature of fabric, may Elohim[4] bless you and awaken your soul. Elohim, how great You are! You are robed in glory and majesty, wrapping Yourself in light as in a garment, spreading forth the heavens like a curtain. I, [NAME], who speak with the voice of Solomon, Magician King, ask that you bless and awaken this creature of fabric, awakening its spirit as a robe of glory and majesty, a wrap of light, spreading forth the heavens like a curtain wherever it is spread."

9. Open your mind and choose a name for the scarf. You are not discovering this name; you are choosing it. The scarf does not have a name until you give it one. Whisper the scarf's name to it.

10. Bring the scarf down over your head, like a hood, covering your eyes.

11. Say (something like): "Blessed are you, Elohim, Overseer of All, who hallows me with your teaching and instructs me[5] to lose myself in these fringes."

12. Chill in your scarf hood for a while. Rock gently back and forth, in time with the music of the spheres. Play with the fringes. Whisper to it. Feel the mantle of holiness enveloping you.

13. When you're ready, bring the scarf to your lips, kiss it gently, and neatly fold it up for later.

Optional Ritual: Consecration of the Ribbon

1. Prepare for ritual.

2. Boil spices, herbs, and flowers in living water until you have made a weak tea.

3. Strain the liquid and add as much salt as will dissolve.

4. Let the water cool until it is comfortable to touch, and then put the ribbon in the water.

5. With your dominant hand, swirl the ribbon around in the water, saying something like: "Elohim, how great You are! You are robed in splendor and victory, wrapping Yourself in deep blue like the sea, like the sky, like the blessing eye. I, [NAME], who speak with the voice of Solomon, Magician King, ask that you bless and awaken this creature of blue, awakening its spirit as a wrap of splendor and victory, like the shining firmament in the beginning. Creature of blue, may Elohim bless you and awaken your soul."

6. Take out the ribbon and hang it up to dry. Ideally, hang it in direct sunlight.

7. Once it's dry, prepare again for ritual.

8. Take the ribbon in your hands, and lovingly caress it. It might shed salt. That's okay.

9. Name it as you did the scarf.

10. Repeat the conjuration a third time, continuing to handle the ribbon. You might want to play cat's cradle with it. Think of its relation to the ocean. Think of its relation to the sky. Think of its relation to the eye against evil. Feel its cool, refreshing blueness.

11. When you're done, carefully wind the ribbon up and save it for later.

Optional Exercise: Consecration of the Pen

Using the rituals you've learned as examples, prepare your own consecration ritual for your pen. Begin by thinking about the essential qualities you'd like the pen to have, and then choose divine names that empower such qualities.

Important Ritual: Preparation of the Book

This initial consecration ritual takes about an hour. It is best performed on a Wednesday, during the evening hour of Mercury,[6] while the Moon is waxing, but the timing isn't very important. It is better to begin the work as soon as you are ready than to wait for an auspicious time. You can repeat the consecration later, at a more auspicious time, if you like. Before you enter magical space/time/consciousness, gather your book, the pen, some incense, a tealight, the scarf, and the ribbon. Arrange a table with sufficient space to spread out your supplies. You may wish to decorate the table with a fancy cloth, candles, etc. However, that is not necessary. Prepare yourself for magic in your usual fashion. Minimally, wash your genitals, hands, and face. Wear the scarf like a hood, to create a "tunnel" that blocks out your peripheral vision. When you are ready, invoke Solomon.

Light the incense, smell it, and say something like: "I, [NAME], child of [NAME], speak with the voice of Solomon, Magician King. In that name, and in the name of El Shaddai, I call out to this spirit of incense, that you might awaken to your true nature, strength, and power to attract beneficent daemons and to banish and cause to retreat all hostile phantoms. In the name of El Chai, I call out to the spirit of this incense, that you might awaken to your true nature, strength, and power as a remedy for all humans for the health of body, mind, and soul. May all creatures who smell your sacred fragrance receive healing of body, mind, and soul. In the name El Emet, I declare it to be true. Amen, Amen, and *Selah*."

Hold the book above the incense. Turn it over and over, making sure it is entirely covered by smoke. Riffle the pages to fumigate it inside and out. As you do so, speak to it, saying something like: "I, [NAME], child of [NAME], speak in the voice of Solomon, Magician King. In that name, and the name of El Elyon, I call out to the spirit of this book, that you might awaken to your true nature, strength, and power to truly contain all names, figures, pentacles, or seals in such a way that they receive all due power and in such a way that no deceit, mistake, or blindness might enter herein. In the name of El Olam, I call out to the spirit of this book, that you might awaken to your true nature, strength, and power as a teacher for all sentient beings, for true knowledge and wisdom of self, other, and relationship. May all creatures who read your sacred pages receive true knowledge and wisdom of self, other, and relationship. With the voice of Solomon, Magician King, and in the holy name El Emet, I declare it to be true. Amen, Amen, and Selah."

Spend some time getting to know the book. Feel its cover. Run your fingers lovingly over the pages. Learn its texture and its smell. Kiss the cover. Try to learn its name. When you're done, kiss your book, wrap it in the scarf, and tie it closed with the ribbon. Store your book respectfully until the next time you're ready to work with it.

Front Matter

Before beginning to inscribe the front matter of your book, you'll need to decide on a few things. The first is what name you'd like to use in your work with the pentacles. If you have a Hebrew name, that's a good choice, but any name which is yours is fine. Next, you'll need to choose magical watchwords. These are a quote or short phrase to help guide you and keep you on track in this work; when you are unsure what to do with the book, read the watchwords, and let them guide your choices. I recommend choosing words traditionally attributed to Solomon. As an example, my watchwords for this book you are reading are from Kohelet 12:10: "Teacher sought to find delightful words, to write correctly matters of Truth."

Finally, you'll need to decide on the name of your book. You may use any method to do so. One method to help discover options is to shuffle the Major Arcana of a tarot deck, and pull three cards, one at a time, reshuffling the chosen card back into the deck before drawing the next. Each card is attributed to a Hebrew letter, in order. For example, א is card 0 (The Fool), ב is card

XII (The Hanged Man), and ‏ת‎ is card XXI (The World). This will give you a trilateral root for the name of your book. Many, but by no means all, trilateral roots form the basis of known Hebrew words. Research yours to investigate what it means. If you can't find the root you've discovered, try permuting the letters. If that still doesn't work, think about the meanings of the individual letters. Play with the sounds. If it still doesn't feel right, try a different divinatory technique.

Whisper potential names to your book, until you find the one that makes both of your hearts sing. Focus on both the sound and the meaning. Like any unborn creature, the book does not yet have a name to discover. A name is not an essential feature of a person; we are not born with our names. A name is an interface between an internal self and the external world. Names do not rise from within; they are applied from without. A name is a gift given by one soul to another and grows out of our universal desire to communicate. Until you name it, your book is nameless. Ultimately, you *decide*, rather than discover, a name for your book. Any method you use to help you choose is fine. Before you complete the naming ritual, **do not** speak the name aloud to any living being other than your book, and do not write it down.

Important Ritual: Awakening the Book

This ritual will take about an hour and is best done during any hour of Mercury on a Wednesday. Before beginning the ritual, gather your wrapped book, a black pen, a beeswax tealight, a lighter, and a way to draw a small amount of blood.[7] When you are ready to begin, enter magical space/time/consciousness, light the candle, and unwrap the book. Put the scarf on your head and invoke Solomon. In your most careful and delightful penmanship,[8] inscribe the following on the first page of the book:

- *The Sorcery of Solomon: A Guide to the 44 Planetary Pentacles of the Magician King* (or another title)

- "Written by the magician in her own hand" (or his, or their, or pronoun of your choice)

- Your location, and the date

- Your watchwords

Leave space under the watchwords for your signature and a bloody thumbprint.

If, once you are done writing, you have lost your connection to Solomon, repeat the invocation of Solomon before continuing. **Do not** write the book's name in the book. This is a security precaution in case it is lost or stolen. Unless or until the book is both true enough and powerful enough to withstand public scrutiny and attack, your book's true name should be shared only by you, the book, and close co-magicians you both trust. It is likely that your first book will never be so powerful. Book-birthing, like most things, takes practice to master.

Speak directly to the book, saying something like: "I, [NAME], child of [NAME], speak with the voice of Solomon, Magician King. In that name, and in the name Elohim, I call out to the spirit of this book. Beloved creature of paper and ink, you are no longer an object, but a living person. In the name of The Most Holy Name, I name you [BOOK NAME]. Creature of paper and ink, awaken to your true nature, strength, and power as a magical partner! In the name of El Chai, I give you life of my life, and breath of my breath."

Raise power in your body and then concentrate the power in your heart. Take a deep breath, and exhale the collected power into the book. Say something like: "[BOOK NAME], I acknowledge you as my colleague and friend. Awaken to light, and life, and love. This I declare in the name of El Chai, and seal it with my living blood."

Sign your name at the bottom of the title page, and seal it with a bloody thumbprint. Speak the book's name to it again and greet it warmly. If there is still a flow of power from you to the book, cut it off at this point and ground yourself. Do not let the book drain you. Spend some time with it, just like you did when you initially consecrated it. You may want to sing to it. Beings that are born into love flourish in ways spirits born into oppression never can. Bring your book up right!

Whenever you're done, close the book, carefully wrap it, and store it respectfully until your next session. After the book is wrapped, pinch (don't blow) out the candle and return to quotidian space/time/consciousness. If you like, you can sleep with your book like a teddy bear, like a longtime lover, like twins still sharing a womb. Record your dreams.

2.7

The Great Seal

Famously, Solomon had a magic signet ring on which was inscribed a great seal, by which he controlled spirits. Many candidates exist for this seal, and I am of the opinion that Solomon bore multiple seal rings. Most versions of the Great Seal are based around either the hexagram or the pentagram. For our work in this book, we use the seal below, built from a pentagram and five names of power.

Counterclockwise from top left: El Emet, El Shaddai, El Chai, El Olam, El Elyon

The Meaning of the Pentagram: Mathematics, Myth, and Magic

The pentagram is among the oldest of magical symbols; the origins of its magical use are lost in the mists of time. We'll spend some time examining the pentagram, both to discover some of its magical virtues, and also as an example of the sort of symbolic analysis that we'll use to decrypt the pentacles.

When I analyze any symbol, I like to look at it from three viewpoints, which I call the "essential," "pan-anthropic," and "cultural" lenses. **Essential** characteristics of a symbol are those inherent in the symbol itself. I think of them as the sort of characteristics that an alien race would also associate with the symbol. They are most often mathematical in origin. **Pan-anthropic** characteristics are those seen by all or most humans, no matter their culture. They are often linked to human biology and/or Earth's ecology. Finally, there are the **cultural** associations of a symbol, which different people understand very differently. As we look at the characteristics of the pentagram below, I encourage you to think about how to apply this method of analysis to other magical symbols you work with.

The essential features of the pentagram come in two flavors: characteristics of the number five and the geometric features of the pentagram itself. Five is a positive whole number; that is to say, it is an answer to questions of the form "How many?"

It is also, of course, an odd number. Odd numbers are those which cannot be evenly divided in half. Visually, we can understand whole numbers as rows of dots, like this:

$5 =$ ● ● ● ● ● $8 =$ ● ● ● ● ● ● ● ●

Odd numbers, like five, have a dot in their center, whereas even numbers, like 8, have an open space.

$5 =$ ● ● ⊙ ● ● $8 =$ ● ● ● | ● ● ● ●

Odd numbers have a pivot, that is, a tenuous balancing point. Even numbers, on the other hand, balance more easily, "folding" around an empty center.

In addition to being odd, five is also prime. Prime numbers are divisible only by themselves and the number one. The Fundamental Theorem of Arithmetic tells us that prime numbers are, in some sense, the essential building blocks for all numbers. Every whole number can be made by multiplying prime numbers. Even more wonderfully, every number has only a single unique "recipe" of prime numbers from which it can be composed.[1] Prime numbers are the essential "notes" that blend together to form harmonious chords of composite numbers. Interpreting this magically, we begin to understand five as one of the essential building blocks of creation, but one that is a little bit unstable, always seeking a partner to help it balance. For this reason, the number five, as well as other odd prime numbers,[2] like three, seven, eleven, etc., are often magically associated with relationships between the magician and other sentient beings.

As we investigate the number five further, we discover many other delightful properties. For example, five is a Fibonacci number. The Fibonacci sequence starts with two ones. From there, the next number is determined by adding the two previous numbers, like this:

1

1

$1+1=2$

$1+2=3$

$2+3=5$

$3+5=8$

.

.

.

$$F_{n-2}+F_{n-1}=F_n$$

For reasons that are not entirely understood, the Fibonacci sequence, and individual Fibonacci numbers, appear very frequently in nature and are intimately related to the human sense of beauty. We discuss that a little more below, when we talk about the essential characteristics of pentagrams and their relationship to the so-called golden ratio. Magically, Fibonacci numbers are almost always connected to a simultaneous sense of both slowly unfolding beauty and flashes of inspiration. This can be literal, like the blossoming of a flower or the swelling of a fruit, or more metaphorical, like the five-seeded apple teaching Isaac Newton about gravity.

Five broadly, and the pentagram particularly, is even more intimately connected to the beauty of the Fibonacci sequence than other Fibonacci numbers because of five's special relationship with the number we call the "golden ratio." The golden ratio is a magical proportion that appears in natural shapes which are especially pleasing to humans, such as flowers and human faces, as well as spiral shells and spiral galaxies. It frequently appears in great art.

In ancient Greece, the number was named after the great Pheidias, the 5th century sculptor/architect and Pythagorean initiate who designed and oversaw construction of the Athenian Parthenon. In his honor, we sometimes call it by the Greek letter φ or ϕ, which is written "phi" and said (by Americans) "fye" (rhymes with "my"). Phi makes the f/ph sound that begins Pheidias's name.

One example of the golden ratio and its connection to human sensations of beauty and proportion can be found in the pentagram.

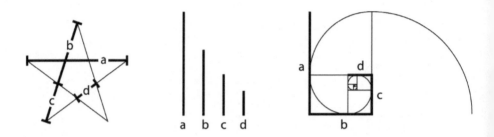

In this diagram, the proportion of segment a to segment b, and b to c, and of c to d, are all the golden ratio and thus fit onto the so-called golden spiral. Using the pentagram, we can calculate an exact value for the golden ratio.[3] That value is $(1+\sqrt{5})/2$ (which is slightly more than 1.618). This clearly shows the intimate connection between five and the golden ratio.

Combining all these properties together, we learn that five is one of the essential building blocks of nature, one associated with beauty and cosmic harmony, particularly the dynamic and unstably beautiful harmonies of nature. These characteristics of the number five are essential; if there are other sentient beings with whom we can communicate, then they must agree that's just what the number five is like.[4] Since one of the core goals of Solomonic magic is to acquire knowledge and conversation of just such beings, it's good to know that there is a language we are sure to share. That universal language *is* mathematics. Both the Euclidean geometry of the Solomonic seals and the fractal geometry of nature are essential to, and thus understandable by, all sentient creatures, no matter what type of body they have (or don't have). Magic that relies on essential meaning for symbols is magic that is effective everywhere and on everyone, as long as the symbols are properly employed.

However, humans have some very important connections to the number five, and with the pentagram, which other sentient beings, whose bodies are other shapes, don't necessarily share. Five is the shape of our hands. Most humans have five fingers on each hand; four that reach and a special one, the thumb, which grasps. That ability to grasp and carefully investigate and manipulate objects is one of the many special features of human bodies that are not shared by all other creatures. For example, many cultures understand humans to have five primary senses: vision, hearing, smell, taste, and the somesthetic or body-wide sensation.[5] The senses, like the hands, reach out into the world and grasp things (which we call "perceptions" or "sensations"). Those are then brought back to us to investigate and manipulate. On a larger level, most humans have five protuberances with which our core interacts with the world; a head, two arms, and two legs. Magically, almost all human cultures associate both the number five and the pentagram with the open hand pushed out to ward something off, with the action of reaching and grasping, as well as with more metaphorical kinds of investigation and manipulation. However, that magical association is pan-anthropic and not essential; magic that relies on these hand-like properties of the number five will work only on beings in relationship with humans.

Cultural History of the Pentagram

On top of the layers of essential and pan-anthropic features of pentagrams, there are a dazzling variety of cultural meanings. Solomonic magic broadly, and the Solomonic magic of this book in particular, draws strongly on ancient Levantine cultural foundations, filtered through an early-modern Western European lens into our modern English-speaking culture.

Perhaps the strongest relevant cultural associations of the pentagram come from the teachings of Pythagoras, who introduced many of the previously discussed mathematical teachings into the West, and whose work underlies almost all Western numerology and magical mathematics. The pentagram was the Pythagorean symbol by which members of the secret mystery cult identified one another. They strongly associated the pentagram with Ὑγιεια (Hygeia), the goddess of flourishing and harmonious well-being whose name is often translated as "Health." Her name is also the root of our modern word "hygiene." Ὑγιεια was often written counterclockwise around the vertices (points) of a pentagram, as in the image on page 68.

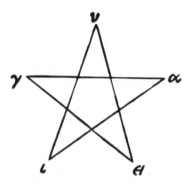

Although Hygeia is often portrayed as Asklepios's daughter in mainstream/orthodox classical Greek religion, in Orphic cults, of which the Pythagorean cult is one variety, she was understood to be his divine lover and teacher. Asklepios is the primeval surgeon and Hygeia the primeval medicine woman. Her most famous and glorious temples, which she shared with Asklepios, were in Epidaurus, Pergamom, and Kos.[6] There, people came seeking healing and incubated wisdom dreams in underground snake hibernacula.

Legendarily, Hygeia's worship was introduced to classical Athens by Pheidias, himself a Pythagorean initiate. During the construction of the Parthenon, it is said, one of the chief masons was injured, and secular Athenian physicians had no hope of his recovery. After a miraculous intervention by Hygeia, Pheidias sculpted a golden image of her for the Parthenon, whom he named Athena Hygeia. While the name Athena-Hygeia is often understood as "Athena the Healer," it can also mean "Hygeia of Athens." Shortly thereafter, the Delphic oracle recommended Hygeia to the people of Athens to help contain a resurgence of plague. In 420 BCE, her cult was officially introduced into the city's pantheon, and the plague rapidly subsided. Thus was her divinity there secured among the noninitiates.

While to the uninitiated, Hygeia is a goddess of health and healing, to the initiate she is much more. Health of the body is only one facet of Hygeia's sacred harmony. She is the goddess that ensures natural systems remain in balance. She heals bodies and also spirits. She heals humans and also ecosystems. Hygeia is the fractal beauty inherent in nature's geometry, the guiding hand that shapes the whole cosmos toward perfection. This is just one cultural instantiation of the pentagram's connection with the golden ratio, and thus with cosmic beauty.

Around the 6th century BCE (after the time of Solomon), the pentagram became the emblem of Jerusalem, a name whose etymology we discussed in chapter 2.2. The letters were often written clockwise between the vertices of a pentagram, as shown in the images below. The image on the left is in modern Hebrew characters, while the ones on the center and right show a 6th century BCE pottery seal inscribed in Paleo-Hebrew.[7]

Perhaps owing to its Greek and Hebrew significance, the pentagram was also an important symbol in early British Christianity. For example, in the 14th century romance "Sir Gawain and the Green Knight," the pentagram is on the shield of Gawain. The poet explains that this symbolizes Gawain's perfection, and mentions the pentagram's relationship to the five senses, the five wounds of Christ,[8] the five joys of Mary,[9] and the five virtues of knighthood.[10]

Later, the pentagram began to be more commonly associated with the five neoplatonic magical elements, earth, air, fire, water and the magical "quintessence" (fifth essence) sometimes called "spirit" or "aether."[11] From there, it entered into modern witchcraft, where it displays a number of meanings and uses, almost all of which are grounded in its essential and pan-anthropic qualities of cosmic harmony, unfolding beauty, open palm warding, and reaching/grasping.

Five Holy Names

Before you inscribe your Great Seal into your book, you should choose five holy names of power for it. There is no single correct set; I have used many combinations over the years. Personally, I prefer to use Jewish holy names while working the magic of Solomon, but Solomon was infamous for his religious promiscuity, so go wild. No matter their culture of origin, choose names whose power and inherent sacredness are, *for you*, immediate and undeniable.

Try to choose a "covering set" of names; that is, be sure to include five different kinds of sacredness.

Above all other considerations, I encourage you to let beauty be your guide. Play with many options and permutations of the names. When you feel the sacred power well up within you, when you are moved to tears by holy beauty, then you'll know you've found the right ones. However, it's okay if you don't find them right away. Remember: the book you are making now is just for practice! You can experiment with different combinations as you learn. If you don't have strong feelings on what names to use, I encourage you to try out the quintet, which I'll discuss below, all of which are built on the Name of Power אל (El), which we discussed in the previous chapter. Recall that, generally, "El" is a word for any god, not exclusively for G-d.

El Emet : אל אמת

The word Emet (אמת) means "truth" or "true." The name El Emet is sometimes translated as "The True God," but usually as "The God of Truth." In the Babylonian Talmud,[12] we are told that "The seal of the Holy One, Blessed be He, is Emet."

The three letters in Emet, aleph (א), mem (מ), and tav (ת), are the first, middle, and last letters of the Hebrew alphabet. Because of this, it bears some similarities to the Greek holy name "Alpha and Omega." In the beginning, there is Truth. As things continue, there is Truth. At the end of everything, Truth is what remains. The inclusion of this name on the Great Seal encourages everything to be true; it helps me "find delightful words and write correctly matters of Truth" (Kohelet 12:10).

El Elyon : אל עליון

The word elyon (עליון) means "uppermost." It derives from an extremely old Proto-AfroAsiatic root, ELH, which probably meant something like "height" or "mountain." This combination of sounds[13] has almost certainly meant "high place" for more than 15,000 years. Thus, the name "El Elyon" is usually translated as "God Most High." In Bereshit, El Elyon is called "the parent of Heaven and Earth" and is the god of Salem and its priest Melchizedek, as we discussed earlier. It is primarily for this connection, as the god of Salem, and thus SLM, that I chose this name for my Great Seal.

El Shaddai : אל שדי

As I mentioned previously, El Shaddai is one of my favorite Hebrew god names; when I pray from my heart to the god of my mothers, this is the name I most often use, and that is the primary reason I chose it. We discussed both El and Shaddai in the previous chapter, and how their combination weaves together features of both.

In Torah, the name El Shaddai is the one used by the Matriarchs and Patriarchs.[14] It is often used in conjunction with teachings concerning sex, intimacy, and reproduction. In many cases, El Shaddai takes on the role of a mother goddess and is called by the powers of the ancestors. For example, in Bereshit 49:25, Jakob blesses his sons thus: "By the El Aveinu[15] who aids you, and El Shaddai who blesses you, blessings of the heavens from above, blessings of the deeps below, blessings of breasts and womb, blessings of ancient mountains, blessings of everlasting hills . . ."

I chose this name both for its ancestral ties and because of Shaddai's connection with doorways. The Great Seal, of course, is a magic gateway through which spirits are birthed, and El Shaddai helps to guard the gate.

El Olam : אל עולם

Olam (עולם) can mean "world" or "universe" or "forever" or "aeon." It is an old Canaanite name, predating the rise of Jewish monotheism. In those oldest incantations, it is often used as an alternate name for El, although some scholars believe they were originally distinct gods. In modern use, El Olam is usually translated as "Eternal God," or sometimes "The Ancient God." The translation "God of the Whole World" is common in modern American progressive Judaism and is the one I grew up with. However, "God of the Forever" is my preferred translation.

El Olam, in both ancient and modern use, in both religious and magical contexts,[16] is very often associated with the goddess Asherah,[17] with the World Tree, and with sacred groves. For example, when Abraham plants a sacred grove in Bereshit 21:33, he dedicates it in the name of El Olam. This association with the World Tree is among the reasons I chose this name; it facilitates the Great Seal's role as a connector between the Heavens, the Earth, and the Great Below.

El Chai : אל חי

Chai (חי) uncomplicatedly means "life" or "alive." It is the root of Mother Eve's Hebrew name, חוה (Chava). In modern Judaism, חי is very frequently used as an amulet. Its characters also form the number 18. For this reason, the number is very auspicious to Jews. For example, it is traditional to give charity in multiples of eighteen, so as to "give life."

El Chai is most often translated into English as either "Living God" or "God of Life"; I prefer the latter rendering. When used in Torah, El Chai is often portrayed as a god directly intervening in human events, such as when Joshua promises that military victories will show "that the God of Life is among you."[18]

Important Ritual: Awakening the Great Seal

This ritual can be done at any time, but an evening hour of Mercury on a Wednesday is best and it is better if Mercury is not retrograde. Before beginning, choose your five holy names. Spend some time deciding how to arrange the names and how to orient the pentagram. Use a compass and straightedge to get it right. The geometry is important. If you, like me, are not clever-handed, I recommend copying the page with the seal on it, sizing it for your book, and tracing it with a straightedge. The series of inscribed pentagrams inside is infinite; you can draw as few or as many as you want, but be sure to know they're all there, going on and on forever. Draw a few practice seals to make sure you're happy with your choices and then, again using your straightedge, draw the seal into the book with black ink.

Arrange your scarf over your head, allowing it to hang at the side, constraining your vision to your workspace. Lay your book flat and place a tealight at each exterior vertex of the pentagram. If necessary, weigh down the facing page. Put a small bowl of anointing oil nearby. When you're ready to begin, light the candles. Enter magical space/time/consciousness by any method. While you work, keep your mind focused on the Great Seal.

Begin to chant the invocation of Solomon, as we discussed in the last chapter. If you're not painting or coloring the seal, you may want to rattle or drum along with the chant. Continue chanting the invocation until you feel the mantle of Solomon's power descend upon you. When you do, cast a circle into the outer boundary circle of the Great Seal. In all of the instructions that follow, I assume your Names of Power are in Hebrew. If they are in a language written left to right, run the energy counterclockwise. In this scenario, the energy should go opposite of the words, like you are winding a spring.

To cast the circle, hold your arms out like you're hugging someone. Raise them to the level of your shoulders and turn your palms to face your chest. Cycle internal energy rapidly though that circle, clockwise. That is, the energy should go out your left fingertips and into your right fingertips. Run the circuit as fast as you can while still maintaining a clean circle. Once you have built up enough momentum, the energy circuit should continue to spin when you remove your attention, at least for a little while. Slowly bring your arms in, collapsing the circle down between your hands, out your left middle finger, into your right middle finger, out your right thumb and into your left thumb, around and around. Again, get it going fast, until it has enough momentum to keep spinning.

Bring your hands down to the circumference of the Great Seal, and slowly slide the energetic circle off your hands and onto the paper. Once you've got it circling the Seal, cast it from your hands with a final "flick," like you are casting a fishing line. Be sure to keep it spinning throughout this whole process. If you've properly cast the circle, it should remain spinning for the duration of this ritual, but if needed, give it a clockwise "stir" from time to time to keep it cycling. The energy circle should move through the candle flames, drawing power from them. They might flicker, sway, or jump, but be careful not to spin them so hard they go out. If you feel like you've "lost your groove," you may wish to invoke Solomon again at this point (or any point) to strengthen the connection.

Open the consecration by saying something like[19] "I, [NAME], child of [NAME], speak with the voice of Solomon, Magician King, calling out to the Circle of Elohim, who have governed since the beginning of Ages. O You of infinite wisdom, You whose breath weaves waves on the waters, whose song sets alight the stars, I call to You in the name of Solomon, Magician King, and by the oaths and covenants which we have sworn. Come and be with me now as I do this work. Grant me full measure of Your wisdom. Let me breathe with Your breath. Let me sing Your holy song. Holy Ones, Circle of Elohim, I call to You by Your holy Names: El Chai, El Shaddai, El Olam, El Elyon, El Emet . . ."

Continue chanting the names, permuting the order. Play with your intonation. If you feel called to do so, sing. This is really a "more is more" kind of working; you can't really overdo it.[20] You may find yourself stuck, drawn to repeat one name over and over. When that happens, run your fingers over the printed name, and push extra energy into it, wiggling it into place until you can feel it settle back into the circle. Move on to another name. You will almost certainly find some names harder to "awaken" than others, but eventually you'll feel them each become active and attentive. Once you've awakened all the names, recite them again, clockwise, around the circle.

Return to your oration, saying something like: "Great Pentagram, eternally extended, surrounded by the Circle of Elohim, live forever in this Great Seal, marked with your holy names. Awaken and enliven it as a portal of sorcery. Let the seal be wise and subtle, kind and openhearted. Grant it the grace of every science and every art. O Great Seal, symbol of the secret science, standard of strong sorcery, sacred sign of Solomon, you are charged and awakened with the holy names, El Chai, El Shaddai, El Olam, El Elyon, El Emet. The power of the Circle of Elohim is on you and in you and all around you. May you be a portal and a table, a sign and signet and seal. Every pentacle placed inside you, awaken them with your own virtue, by the power of the Holy Names you bear, that they be strong and efficient, wise and subtle, kind and openhearted. All this I charge in my own name, [NAME], and in the name of Solomon, Magician King, in whose voice I speak. Amen, Amen, and Selah."[21]

Now (and this is an important step many people are prone to skipping) sit still and be quiet, waiting for a response. You might find white noise, ideally the sound of rushing water, will help give a spirit-voice a sound-body in which to manifest. Similarly, clouds of incense smoke can provide a body for visual manifestation. Trust yourself. Interpret everything that happens in this magical space/time/consciousness magically but keep your wits about you. Be sure it comes from outside, not inside, of you.

Once you've gotten a response, ask your Great Seal if it has a name. If it does not, offer to give it one. Whisper sweet nothings in its ear. Tell it how long you've wanted to meet it, how eager you are to get to know it better. Ask if there is anything else you can do for it. When you're done communing, blow out the candles and move them off the book. Dip your dominant index and middle fingers in the oil (you can use other or more fingers or hands; I usually end up using both hands), and slowly and lovingly trace them around the circle, and then along the pentagrams. Experiment with going different directions. Pretend you're a DJ rocking out on a turntable. Have fun! You're not so much winding a spring as you're "winding up" a partner. Caress the seal like a lover,[22] feeling it pulse with power.

Feel the Great Seal gain power, expanding and becoming three dimensional: two dimensions on the paper and one to which you do not have direct sensory access. (Your human neuro-architecture will not allow you to visualize this. You need to use a rational, not perceptive, sense to understand it. Just do your best and don't worry about it too much. All the necessary geometry is built into the Great Seal, whether you understand it or not.)

The internal pentacles may begin to wriggle and writhe, squirming like fractal snakes, temporarily filling all of space/time. Don't panic! That's a good sign. Feel the Seal sinking roots into the Other Place. Feel it blossoming out into a flower. When you're almost out of energy, give the circle you cast one final hard spin clockwise, and feel it close back up to a two-dimensional drawing in a book. Push as much energy as you can. Don't worry about being precise with your energy or your geometry; you supply the power, and the seal, properly drawn, will supply the geometry.

As the circle (and your energy body) slows and settles, pick the book up to your lips, kiss it directly in the center of the seal, say goodbye, promise to come visit again soon, and close the book. Take the scarf off your head and wrap it around the book, tying it closed with the ribbon.

Stand up and move around. Aerate your body. Drink some water. Ideally, go immediately to bed and dream[23] about your book. Allow the book to sit, undisturbed, for a week before using it to charge a pentacle. This will give the Great Seal time to settle into its permanent form.

Working with the Great Seal

As we progress in our work with the Book, we'll activate the Great Seal to trigger the special magical space/time/consciousness in which we continue to shape and teach our Book. In the method I'm teaching here, we'll do that before inscribing pentacles into the Book, but it can also be used for other kinds of Solomonic magic.

OPENING THE GREAT SEAL

1. Enter magical space/time/consciousness.

2. Untie and unwrap the book. Set the ribbon aside. You can hang it around your neck, tie it around your head or waist, or use it to make a circle around the book if you want.

3. Kiss the scarf and put it on your head. Whisper its secret name to it and ask for its help and protection.

4. Invoke Solomon.

5. Greet the book and kiss it. Open the book to the Great Seal.

6. Rub your hands together until they are hot.

7. Use them to "spin" the Great Seal counterclockwise (that is, in the direction of the writing) to open it.

8. Feel its roots rooting out from the Other Place; feel it expand and blossom, opening a magical space/time/consciousness vortex in the book.

9. Greet your Great Seal and explain why you have opened it. In the beginning, that will probably be in order to teach a new pentacle to the book, but you'll learn (and invent) lots of other ways to work with it.

10. Usually, at this point, you'll turn to another page in the book.

CLOSING THE GREAT SEAL

1. You should already be in magical space/time/consciousness if the seal is open.

2. Spin the Great Seal clockwise (that is, opposite the direction of writing) until their petals and roots retract, and they are just a drawing in a book.

3. Kiss the seal and say thank you.

4. Close the book, kiss them goodbye, and say thank you.

5. Wrap the book and tie them closed.

6. Kiss the wrapped book a third time and put them away until next time.

2.8

Making & Using a Magic Book of Pentacles

In the SLM method, the first copy of each pentacle a beginner makes and awakens should be in their book. You needn't make all the pentacles in order. This is a working book, and it doesn't have to be too neat. If you like, you can enter multiple pentacles of the same planet in one session, but the magic is rather draining, so you might not want to. While exhausting, the method for adding a pentacle to your book is very simple:

1. Prepare yourself and your space.

2. Enter magical space/time/consciousness.

3. Invoke Solomon.

4. Unwrap and open your book. Read your watchwords, ideally out loud.

5. Kiss the book, and greet it by its secret name.

6. Explain why you have awakened it (to teach it a new pentacle).

7. Spin open the Great Seal.

8. Find a blank page.

9. Carefully pencil in the pentacle.

10. If you wish, write translation notes and anything else you want surrounding the pentacle.

11. Leave the facing page blank, for adding notes about your experiences.

12. If you have "lost the vibe," invoke Solomon again.

13. With your special pen, carefully ink in the pentacle, usually in the following order:

    a. The outer circle—focus on it as a boundary between magical and normal space. The versicle:

        Read it silently first and contemplate its many meanings. What is its function on this pentacle? Hold this kavvanah clearly in your head while you ink. Read it out loud when you are done.

b. The inner circle—focus on it as a lens that focuses power through the versicle.

c. Any geometry or other interior figures. Think carefully about why they are present.

d. Holy names. Think carefully about the name and why it is there.
   Read each out loud both before and after inking it.

e. Angelic names. Hold an appropriate kavvanah for each name while you write it.
   Read each name aloud both before and after inking it.

f. Everything else. Remain clearly focused on what you are doing, and why.

14. When you are done inking, make sure it is dry and won't smudge, and then . . .

15. While reading the versicle aloud, cast a circle between the versicle and the interior of the pentacle, with the intention of creating a sacred space within. Cast in the direction of the writing. (Clockwise for English, counterclockwise for Hebrew.)

16. Run your fingertips along any geometry, pouring in power until you feel it awaken.

17. Read each name aloud, and touch it lovingly with your fingertips, tickling it awake.

18. If there is anything else to awaken, do so.

19. Cast another circle around the outside, once again reading the versicle aloud. Be sure there is a strong energetic boundary.

20. Put a beeswax tealight in the middle of the pentacle and light it.

21. Pour as much raw magical power into the pentacle as you can manage. Don't worry about patterning it; a properly constructed pentacle will do that for you. You may sense the geometry moving or spinning. Sometimes this will be jerky, like rusty gears. Just keep pushing energy until everything is flowing smoothly.

22. When you are tired, or when the candle goes out, cast one more circle around the outside, and allow the energy to settle while you collect yourself.

23. Once you and the pentacle have caught your breath, pick up the book and address it by name, saying something like "In the name of Solomon, magician king, I have taught to you this pentacle, called [NAME]. In your bosom, let this seed blossom to power."

24. Kiss the pentacle, put the book down, and . . .

25. Make the holy sign of your choice over the book. I like to make the so-called "gesture of priestly benediction," which is a ש shin (see picture below). It was this gesture that Leonard Nimoy used as the model for Spock's "Live Long and Prosper" sign.

26. If desired, repeat to teach another pentacle. When you are done . . .

27. Spin down the Great Seal. Remember to say thank you.

28. Close and wrap your book. Thank them by name and say goodbye until next time.

29. Return to normal space/time/consciousness.

30. Let the book sit for at least a week, to let everything settle in.

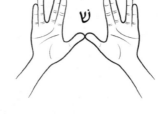

Making & Using Non-Book Pentacles

With the exception of the Lunar Lock & Key, book pentacles can be spun open and closed in the same manner as the Great Seal. When open, they are powerful portals of magic, as well as sentient living beings in their own right. The most basic way to work with a pentacle in your book is to spin it up, light a candle on top of it (to "feed" it the light and heat), and simply speak to it directly, explaining what you'd like.

However, most often, I use the pentacles in my book as "tables of practice" on which to work other magic. Sometimes, I simply write a petition for a specific short-term (less than one month) purpose, open the Book, open the Great Seal, spin open the relevant pentacle, read the petition out loud to the pentacle, put the petition, words down, on top of the pentacle, and light a beeswax tealight on top. Once the candle has gone out, I close the Book without spinning down the pentacle or the Great Seal, until the matter the petition concerns is concluded, at which time I close the pentacle and the Great Seal.

Another option is to "clone" the pentacle out of the book onto another medium. In my opinion, the best medium for most pentacles is paper or parchment, which has the benefits of being cheap, readily available, easy to work with, and simple to store. I often write large pentacles on the backs of petitions, and then color the pentacles in with related sigils. I slip the pentacle-papers into files or books relevant to the matter at hand, post them where relevant people will see them, or otherwise deploy them as part of a larger spell. Paper scrolls can be worn as talismans by placing them in a small case or locket, hung in the home as protection, added to a mezuzah, mojo bag, or other magical item, dissolved in water to make a potion for drinking, bathing, or scrying in, or used as components in many other types of magic.

However, for both aesthetic and practical reasons, sometimes other media are desirable. If you can write on it, then it's an appropriate medium for a Solomonic pentacle. Personally, I am especially fond of mirrors and magnets. These days, the most popular material on which to write the planetary pentacles is metal.

Until the 9th century, humans knew of only seven truly elemental metals: gold, silver, copper, quicksilver (mercury), iron, tin, and lead. Today, many magicians believe that the assignment of these so-called "metals of antiquity" to the classical planets was fixed in antiquity. However, that is not exactly the case. Quicksilver was largely unknown in the ancient Mediterranean, and some alloys, particularly electrum (gold + silver), bronze (copper + tin) and a type of naturally occurring brass (copper + zinc) called "orichalcum" (which means "mountain copper") were often considered elemental metals and assigned to the planets.

This led to a variety of planetary assignments. For example, in the Mithraic cult, there was a planetary gatewalking ritual called the *klimax heptapylos* (ladder of seven gates). In the context of that rite, the metals were allocated to the planets as follows:

- Lead: Saturn
- Tin: Venus
- Bronze: Jupiter
- Iron: Mercury
- "Coin alloy" (probably orichalcum): Mars
- Silver: Moon
- Gold: Sun

It wasn't until the early middle ages that the correspondences had largely solidified into our modern list. For example, in Chaucer's 14th century *Canterbury Tales*, the Canon Yeoman recites the following verse:

> *The bodies sevene eek lo! hem heer anoon:*
> *Sol gold is, and Luna silver we thrape,*
> *Mars yren, Mercurie quik-silver we clepe,*
> *Saturnus leed, and Jupiter is tin,*
> *And Venus coper, by my fader kin!*

The seven bodies also, lo, look here now:
Sun is gold, and Luna silver we insist,
Mars iron, Mercury we call quicksilver,
Saturn lead and Jupiter is tin,
And Venus copper, by my father's kin!

For personal reasons, I generally don't like to wear most metals in contact with my body, and for this reason I don't normally wear metal pentacles (or jewelry more generally). However, I often make pentacles from laser-cut metal pendants for other people. Some of my magical colleagues posit that laser engraved pendants are unacceptable for Solomonic pentacles, but I do not agree.

At multiple points in the Babylonian Talmud, we are told that Solomon conscripted many people (both human and demon) to track down a legendary magical cutting tool (or possibly a magical worm who could eat through stone) called the שָׁמִיר (*shamir*). The special magical property of the shamir is that it could cut metal or stone, but it was not a weapon that could shed blood. If Solomon had had access to a magical machine that cut metal with light, I assure you he would have used it.

However, I absolutely agree with my colleagues who say that a machine-made pentacle "fresh off the press" is not a magical item. On the other hand, they are excellent as "blanks" on which pentacles can be made. To do so, begin by preparing for Solomonic magic in the usual way. Wash the pentacle blank. While you do so, speak to it. Awaken the metal itself, as you would any magical ingredient. Dry off the pentacle, and get ready for magic. Open the book, the Great Seal, and the relevant pentacle. Hold the pentacle in your nondominant hand, text up. Use your dominant hand to pull an energetic cord from the versicle on the pentacle in the book into the same versicle on the metal pendant. Do the same with the names and other symbols in the interior of the pentacle. When you are done, carefully put the metal pentacle, words down, concentric with the book's pentacle. Put a beeswax tealight on top, and let it burn down. After it has, carefully remove the newly made metal pentacle and seal the magic into it, just like you would into the Book.

You can use a similar method on almost any other material, as well. Cloth, wood, fabric, wax. . . . As I said before, if you can write on it, it's a suitable material on which to put a pentacle. I often use oil paint markers to write a pentacle on the outside of a terra cotta bowl, and then write a Babylonian-style incantation text on the inside. You can use body paint, henna, markers, or cosmetics to write them on your body (or someone else's). Personally, I would not get one as a tattoo, but many people do.

However, before writing a pentacle, please recall that, once enchanted, they are people, not objects, and must be treated as such. As people, they must not be thrown out, but allowed to live out their natural life span and then their remains must be interred respectfully. If they are drawn on the body, you can't scrub them off (or otherwise intentionally efface them). They should be allowed to naturally fade and decay.

In my opinion, being rubbed off on bedsheets, or rinsing off (without scrubbing) in the shower constitute natural decay. Thus, you may bathe normally while wearing them, but you may not intentionally hasten them off. Of course, you should decide for yourself what seems right to you. The exact interpretation of the law is less important than the fact that the prohibition on destroying Holy Names is not a religious superstition, nor a magical instruction—it is a moral imperative. That Name is a *person*, not an object, and people shouldn't be thrown out like trash.

Exercise

■ Make your Magic Book

Planetary Pentacles

"So now, behold the Stars of our World, the Planets which are Seven;
the Sun, Venus, Mercury, the Moon, Saturn, Jupiter and Mars. The
Seven are also the Seven Days of Creation; and the Seven Gateways
of the Soul of Man—the two eyes, the two ears, the mouth and the two
nostrils. So with the Seven are formed the seven heavens, the seven
earths, and the seven periods of time; and so has He preferred the
number Seven above all things under His Heaven."

—SEFER YETZIRAH 4:12

As discussed previously, we are not working with the entire Key of Solomon in this book. Rather, we'll discuss one very particular topic, the planetary pentacles in Mathers's chapter 18. Many of the pentacles Mathers presents in this text are also found in older manuscripts of the Key, but they are sometimes quite dissimilar to them. This book you are currently reading is intended as a guide to Mathers's versions of the pentacles, and I will refer to other editions only when Mathers is not clear.

With one exception, these forty-four pentacles are circular diagrams, usually understood as amulets. Mathers arranges them by planet, starting with the pentacles of Saturn and ending with those of the Moon. Although Mathers categorizes the pentacles by planet, they are not, in their essence, astrological. In traditional European magic, there are understood to be three basic kinds of magic; 1) natural, 2) celestial, and 3) divine.[1] To grossly oversimplify, natural magic primarily relies on the inherent magical virtues of natural materials and on alliance with natural and elemental spirits.

Celestial magic, which we moderns often call "astrological," relies primarily on careful astrological timing to infuse the powers of celestial bodies and sacred geometry into the magic at hand.

Although the planetary pentacles are often spoken about as celestial/astrological magic, they are not. As we have already discussed, they are, like the rest of the rich and long-lasting tradition of Hebrew amulet magic, what Agrippa called "Divine" (also called "Ceremonial" or "Theological") magic, which relies primarily on sacred Names of Power and alliance with angels, god(s), and other divine beings.

Personally, I employ all three of these types of magic in my work with the pentacles, and I encourage you to do so as well; make your pentacles with appropriate colors, incenses, inks, and/or metals. Choose astrologically appropriate times in which to write and consecrate them. However, in my opinion, by far the most important component in empowering the pentacles of Solomon is to carefully attend to and understand the sacred Names of Power on which the pentacles call, and to hold kavvanot appropriate to those names while writing and speaking them. We discuss this further in part three: Mercury ☿.

There are many ways to style your pentacles. Although the names, geometry, and symbols need to be precise,[2] you have great freedom as to their aesthetic. Versicles may be written in Hebrew, in translation, or both. Hands, scorpions, and other representative images can be drawn in many ways. Although the images in this book are all black and white, when I write amulets, I nearly always color them. I encourage you to develop your own distinctive style.

• • •

As I mentioned in the contents, the pentacles in this book are not in the same order as Mathers's. They are numbered to match Mathers, for ease of reference.

Additionally, I have provided more support and guidance for the shaping of your own understanding and kavvanot on some pentacles, and provided less guidance on others. This is because I wish to show a variety of methods for developing such understanding and intent, but also encourage you to apply similar techniques for creating your own kavvanot for others. It is my hope that, by the time you get to the end of this book, you not only understand the forty-four pentacles in this book, but you also feel empowered to attempt to decipher other Hebrew amulets and form your own powerful kavvanot for their use.

☽

The Pentacles of the Moon

To bless the New Moon at the proper time is like
greeting the Divine Presence.

—TALMUD, SANHEDRIN 42A

For me, there is almost nothing so magical as our beautiful Moon. Long ago, about 4.5 million years, Moon was part of the Earth. A large body, today called Theia, struck Earth and ripped off pieces of her. Over time, many of those pieces coalesced. Eventually, there was only our Moon, shining by night with the reflected light of Sun. From the viewpoint of Earthlings, Moon's most striking characteristics are her luminescence and monthly shape changing. Like all luminous beings, the Moon is associated with illumination in both literal and metaphorical senses. However, in Jewish myth and magic, the Moon's primary attribute is her ever-renewing mastery of time. For example in the traditional prayer for the sanctification of the Moon, we say: ". . . And G-d said to the Moon, Levana, 'Renew yourself!' [she is] a crown of beauty to the womb-born, who are destined to renew themselves like her . . . !"

Lunar magic is most often about the unseen and the unconscious. To my mind, the archetypal lunar magic is dream incubation, the practice of ritually inducing a specific dream before going to sleep. It was extremely common in ancient Israel, and all over the ancient world. For example, tablet 4 of the Epic of Gilgamesh includes Gilgamesh seeking such a dream, and Bereshit 46:1-7 describes Jakob's famous incubation of his dream ladder, which we discuss more in the Jupiter chapter, along with the pentacle I call Jakob's Chariot.

As you saw in the sanctification of the Moon, the Hebrew name for the Moon is Levana (לבנה), which means "White One." The Moon's day is, obviously, Monday, and her metal is silver. The gems I most closely associate with the Moon are moonstone and amethyst. Moon is sometimes represented by bears, deer, owls, rabbits, and bats. The angel I most closely pair with the Moon is שריאל (Sariel), whose name means "Prince[1] of El," but others say the angel of the Moon is גבריאל (Gabriel), whose name means "El is my Strength" or "Hero of El." Personally, I understand Gabriel to be more properly associated with Mars.[2]

☽ 1: The Lunar Lock & Key

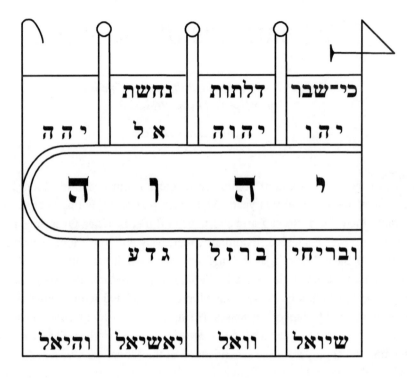

ABOUT THIS PENTACLE, S. L. Mathers says, "This and the following serve to call forth and invoke the Spirits of the Moon; and it further serveth to open doors, in whatever way they may be fastened." This pentacle is unusual in several important ways. Most obviously, it is the only one in the collection which is not in the form of a circle enclosed by a versicle. Manuscripts disagree on which way is "up" for this pentacle. Based on the orientation of the writing, I believe this pentacle is intended to be oriented with the "towers" pointing up, as shown, but most manuscripts show it with the towers pointing toward the right. With the towers up, the pentacle resembles a door or gate with five uprights, with a large latch across them, which aligns with the proposed purpose of the pentacle—to open doors. Although it is likely a mistranslation,[3] many Christian bibles have 1 Kings 6:31 discuss the doors of Solomon's Temple having five doorposts, as the pentacle depicts when oriented according to the writing.

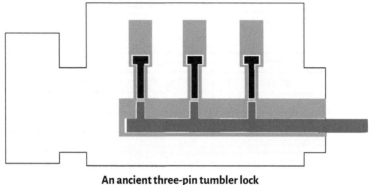

An ancient three-pin tumbler lock

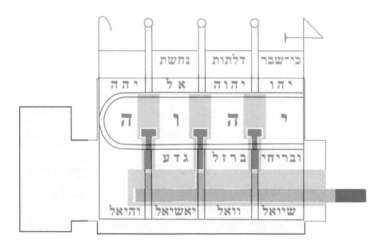

The Lunar Lock & Key Pentacle superimposed on the three-pin tumbler lock

However, to my mind, this pentacle also resembles an ancient three-pin tumbler lock, such as the one pictured. This type of lock was first used in ancient Mesopotamia and remained the standard locking mechanism throughout Levant and Europe until the 17th century. It can be hard to imagine how such a lock works, but if you ask the internet to show you a video of an "ancient three pin tumbler lock," you can see one in action, which will make it much clearer. Note that, in the pentacle, the key is not yet in the lock. This will be clearer once you understand the words.

In the text-upright position, the pentacle displays five lines of text. From top to bottom, we have:

כי-שבר דלתות נחשת	Versicle
יהו יהוה אל יהה	Divine Names / tumblers
יהו	Most Holy Name / keyhole
ובריחי ברזל גדע	Versicle
שיואל ואול יאשיאל והיאל	Angel Names / key

Taken together, lines one and four are the versicle, in this case Tehillim 107:16, which means something like "Because He has broken[4] the gates of copper, and the bars of iron He has hewn." This is clearly in keeping with the pentacle's reported use in opening doors. In the context of the psalm, the doors being opened are those of slavery or imprisonment. Notice that, unlike the other pentacles, the versicle is not around the edges. I understand this to be because the versicle outlines the edges of the lock, and the bottom line represents the key, not yet in the keyhole. Indeed, I often make this pentacle (on cardstock) in two pieces, a "lock" with the first four lines, and a "key" with the final line.

Line two (the tumblers) gives four well-known Jewish god names, יהו יהוה אל יהה, three of which are forms of the Most Holy Name. יהו (Yahu) is a piece of the Most Holy Name which is normally used as a theophoric suffix, such as in names like אליהו (Eliyahu aka Elijah). The second name is the Most Holy Name itself. The final name is יהה (Yah), which may be the oldest form of the Most Holy Name. It is familiar from the word "hallelujah," which roughly means "hail Yah." Although "Yah" is a more accurate pronunciation, for personal reasons, I prefer "Jah."

The third name, אל (El), is both the proper name of several specific gods and the generic word for any god. We discussed this name extensively both in the section on the Seven Holy Names and when we learned about the Great Seal.

The bottom line of text on the pentacle, which I understand to be the key, lists the names of four spirits, generally understood as angels.[5] To the best of my knowledge, these names are known only from this pentacle. The first name is שיואל (Shioel). To me, this appears to be a variation of שירל (Sheol) which is an Aramaic name for the underworld, and likely also a name for a god of the underworld. This name is very old and has many Semitic cognates. The particular spelling here, with אל (El) at the end could shade the meaning to something like "El's Underworld" or "El of the Underworld." The conflation of names for the underworld and names for underworld gods is very common across many cultures. For example, in Greek, "Hades" is both a place and a god. Similarly, our English word "hell" is the same word as "Hel" a Norse underworld goddess.

The next name is ואול (Vavel or Vauel). It is unusual for angelic names to end with the letters ול, so I think it is entirely possible that ואול is a scribal transposition error, and this name should be read as וואל, which would be pronounced similarly. With this assumption, the name derives from the letter ו or the letter's name[6] וו (*vav*), both of which mean "hook" or "latch." Thus, this spirit's name is something like "Latch of El" or "The El of Latches." The help of such a spirit would clearly be very relevant to the proposed function of the talisman.

The third name יאשאל (Iashel) is harder to parse. I believe it may be derived from יאש which means "to cause to despair" or "to lay low." The Paleo-Hebrew root of that word (shown below) can be read as arm-bull-down, which means "to push down on." Thus, Iashel may be understood as "The El Who Causes Despair" or "The El Who Lays [Enemies] Low" or "The El Who Pushes Down." I think the final meaning makes the most sense in this case. We call on Iashel, the El Who Pushes Down, in order to press down the latch called Vavel.

Finally, we have והיאל (Vehiel) perhaps from והיו (Vehiu), which means something like "and they will have been." This name is difficult to translate, partially because Hebrew verb tenses are not exactly analogous to English ones. In English, we might call this spirit "The El of What Will Have Been," or "Divine Consequences," or more metaphorically as something like Fate or Karma or Wyrd, depending on the context.

If you accept my conjectures, the line indicates that the daimons of this pentacle, those with whom we interact to use the pentacle, those who are written on the key, are called:

1. Underworld God

2. El Who Pushes Down

3. El's Latch

4. Divine Consequences

With the aid of those Great Powers, focused through the image of the three-pin tumbler lock, protected by the versicle "Because He has opened the gates of copper, and the bars of iron He has separated," we open the gates of the Underworld and acquire power over fate. In my opinion, the most important function of the first lunar pentacle is to use it to open the gates of the underworld as a magical initiation.

This is among the many reasons why I construct my magic books of pentacles (including this one) to begin with the lunar ones and work up from there, even though many manuscripts begin with Saturn and work their way down. In many cultures, the first initiation of a magician is to enter into the Land Below and arise again. In particular, in many Jewish magical traditions, including *Merkavah* (a kind of ecstatic trance journey we discuss more later), we are taught that we must first learn to descend before we can learn to ascend to the heavens.

Exercise: Going Below

What follows is a suggestion for a kavvanah to hold during the construction and contemplation of this seal. This exercise may take several tries if you have never before journeyed to the Underworld. Not to worry; it just takes practice! With practice, you'll rapidly get faster at this, but for beginners, it might take up to an hour. After the exercise, I'll list some common mistakes to avoid, and some things to try that might help if you're stuck. Like most rules, these instructions are for beginners. Magicians who have "gone below and seen the many things" can ignore them.

Warning: If you are prone to panic attacks, dissociation/depersonalization, or psychotic episodes, it is unwise to perform this exercise. If you're going to try anyway, have someone who has experience with trance magic *and* experience talking you down from an episode physically present in the room with you for your first trial.

1. Enter magical space/time/consciousness.

2. Invoke Solomon, Magician King.

3. Open the Great Seal.

4. Imagine that you are contracting to the center of your being.

5. Imagine the Lock & Key at the center of your being.

6. Carefully call each name, holding its meaning in your mind, while you tickle the "tumblers" to open the lock.

7. Contract further. Be infinitesimal.

8. Go through the Lock & Key, which is now an open gate, to enter into the Underworld.

9. You may experience a bit of vertigo, or a kind of shiver down your spine.

10. There should be a distinct, physical sensation of downward movement, as on an elevator. If there is not, *imagine* that there is until you feel like you are going down.

11. Keep going down, down, down like Alice down the rabbit hole, until you run out of down to go. (If you're new to this, this might take a very long time.)

12. When you arrive at the bottom, take a moment to reorient yourself.

13. Near you, there is a sort of shimmering membrane or curtain of static. It is often described as a waterfall, but it is not made of water. I believe it to be some sort of neurological "white noise." Listen/look/sense for it, and then go through it.

14. Welcome to the Underworld![7]

15. You may experience an encounter with a type of spirit sometimes called a "Dweller on the Threshold" appearing to guard this entry to the Underworld. If you do, it's important to remember that it is largely a manifestation of your own fear. It can't hurt you unless you're afraid of it. It may appear as a beloved ancestor, but more often it will flick through several forms and may take the form of Cerberus, the Great Black Dragon, or some other kind of monster. It may take other forms. However, none of those are its true form. Its true form is your fear of death. Do not be afraid; it's there to protect you, not to protect the gate against your entry. Be careful, and respectful. Don't freak out. If you like, wear the second lunar pentacle to help you keep your cool.

16. The area immediately on the other side of this gate is very safe. Feel free to explore, but don't wander too far if this is your first journey here.

17. When you're ready, go back through the "waterfall" and back up, up, up, back into your body and your normal state of consciousness. Go back by the same path you went down.

18. Drink water. You might not realize it until you start to drink, but you're very thirsty.

19. Take notes. Like a dream, the experience will fade quickly.

20. Stand up, walk around, laugh, and be sure you're fully integrated back into your body.

21. Do something that requires a lot of mundane focus, like bookkeeping, to be sure you're fully back to normal space/time/consciousness.

22. For beginners, it's generally unwise to allow yourself to drift to sleep after such a journey without fully returning to mundane consciousness first.

Warning: All fairy tale rules apply! Mind your manners in the Underworld!

- Don't be rude, pushy, or entitled.

- Don't be a coward.

- Don't lie.

- Don't steal.

- Don't eat the food of the underworld.

- Don't accept presents if you can help it. If you must, give a return gift soon.

- Don't make promises.

- Don't give your full name.

- Things are not what they seem.

- While not foolproof, having a spirit repeat something three times is a good practice to ensure clarity of "translation."

- Try not to get lost or veer too far off the path unless you want to have an adventure!

- Fortune favors the bold.

COMMON BEGINNER MISTAKES

- Don't do this exercise anywhere you wouldn't feel comfortable falling asleep.

- Don't fall asleep. If you're falling asleep, it's because you're sleep deprived. Get more sleep outside of this exercise.

- Don't do this while your body is moving rapidly relative to the Earth (like in a car).

- There are actually only two ways to fail at this:

  - Some people (like me!) are so distractible that they can't focus their attention long enough to keep going down, or so uptight that they have trouble letting go and just falling. Regular meditation will help improve your focus and chill; it has mine.

  - Don't go up and down and up and down; it produces "tangles" in the energy flow. If you get distracted, either come the whole way back up and start over from the beginning or just return to going down. Don't vacillate.

- Try to return by the same path you took going down.

- Don't leave things in the underworld.

- Don't panic! Breathe deeply and slowly in through your nose and out through your mouth.

- Wear a second lunar pentacle.

- Don't run away if a spirit shows up. It's very rude! You came here to see them.

- Don't immediately interpret everything as a threat.

- Don't let this dissolve this into a sex fantasy or other daydream. Do your daydreaming later, if you want.

IF IT ISN'T WORKING: HELPFUL TIPS

These tips are arranged in order; try several from the top of the list before resorting to things lower down.

1. Sit up straight, with your chest open and your shoulders back, directly over your hips.

2. Breathe slowly and deeply, in through your nose and out through your mouth. Do not pause between inhalation and exhalation; try to make it a smooth circle.

3. Wear a blindfold.

4. For reasons I don't fully understand, it helps to touch the tip of your tongue to the roof of your mouth. My yogi friends tell me it "completes the energy circuit."

5. A regular drumbeat or metronome in the range of 180–480 beats per minute can be very helpful. Experiment with different tempos. Personally, I like 216 bpm.

6. Listen to rain, ocean, or a similar pseudo-white noise. My favorite is "large metal bowl in the dishwasher." Do not listen to static (i.e., not animated) white noise for long periods of time. It's bad for your brain.

7. Don't wear metal.

8. Unknot/unbind your hair. I have short hair, so I can't speak to its efficacy, but several long-haired colleagues recommend this.

9. Practice in uncomfortably cold or hot environments. Personally, I like being immersed in cold water, but some people swear by sweat lodges. Experiment to see if either extreme works for you.

10. Lie flat on your back.

11. Try listening to a descending Shepard tone.

12. If you are failing because you can't relax, try adding a mild chemical support like a little cannabis. I find alcohol suppresses my psychism, but some people use it in this context.

13. If you are failing because you can't focus, try adding a mild chemical support like nicotine or caffeine.

14. Write and record, in your own words and voice, a hypnotic guided meditation. Once you get the hang of it, wean yourself off the recording. Do not use guided meditations in other people's words and voices for this.

☽ 2: Under the Wing of El

THE SECOND LUNAR PENTACLE is the more typical in form: circular, with a versicle around the circumference and some names of power in the middle. It is the first of a sequence of lunar pentacles which all feature a hand. There are many ways to draw these hands. I often use a traditional Jewish hand design called a *Hamsa,* which features an open palm and points with its (elongated) middle finger. No matter how the hands are drawn, like all pointing or gesturing hands, they are intended to draw special attention.

Mathers says that this pentacle "serveth against all perils and dangers by water, and if it should chance that the Spirits of the Moon should excite and cause great rain and exceeding tempests about the Circle, in order to astonish and terrify thee; on showing unto them this Pentacle, it will all speedily cease." Remember the "curtain of static" or "waterfall" I spoke about in the previous exercise? I understand this pentacle to also be a protective talisman for crossing that threshold (and other similar thresholds).

The vesicle around the circumference of this pentacle, the "lens" through which the interior powers are focused, is Tehillim 56:12. I translate that as "I trust in Elohim. I will not fear. What can beings of mere flesh do to me?" However, it could also be read as "Because I trust in Elohim, I will not fear what man can do to me." Note that the word I have translated as "beings of flesh" and "man" is adam (the same as All-Father Adam's name) and more literally means "Earthling." This is clearly in keeping with its use as a protective talisman. This psalm was legendarily written by Solomon's father David "when the Philistines took him in Gath." David had fallen out of favor with King Saul and fled to Gath (modern Tell es-Safi), a city of the Philistines, Israel's political enemy. When the king of Gath heard the legendary warrior was in his realm, he had him arrested as a spy. David feigned madness and was released. Praise be!

Inside the pentacle are two names of power. The first is אל (El), which you already know. The second is אבריאל, which I transliterate as Averiel, but many others write Avriel. I understand this word in the context of the word אבר, which means "strength of the wing" or "pinyon feather," but it can also euphemistically mean "penis." It is sometimes used poetically in connection with the idea of finding shelter under the mighty wing of El, and that is the context in which I understand this name on this pentacle. Averiel is the Strong Wing of El, in this case called for protection from dwellers on the threshold or other dangers at other watery thresholds.

This pentacle is said to be effective against all danger when traveling by water. I have little experience traveling by (literal) water, but I have every faith this pentacle would be good under those conditions. However, for protection during out-of-body travel, I prefer the third pentacle.

☽ 3: The Conjurer's Hook

MATHERS TELLS US THAT THIS pentacle is efficacious ". . . upon a journey . . . against all attacks by night, and against every kind of danger and peril by Water." For reasons that I hope will be obvious once we've analyzed it, I understand this pentacle to be especially good for protection during oracular adorcism,[8] and that is the context in which I most often use it. Like the previous pentacle, this one also features a hand. The surrounding versicle says: "Please, HaShem, deliver me! HaShem, make haste to help me!" It comes from Tehillim 40:14 and is a straightforward plea for help when in immediate distress.

Within the pentacle are the names אוב and וואפאל. The first, אוב (*ob*), literally means "canteen," but figuratively means a trance medium or vessel possessed by a (often ancestral) spirit teacher. By extension, it can also mean the familiar spirit itself, as well as a seance-like ritual for communing with such spirits. For example, the woman often described in English as the

"Witch of Endor"[9] is, in Hebrew בעלת-אות בעין דור or the "mistress of the ob, from Endor.

The next name, וואפאל (Vavafel), is harder to understand. As we previously discussed, וו means a hook or latch. אף (ahf) literally means "huff,"[10] "snort," or "nostril" and can figuratively mean any emotion which makes the nostrils flair, like anger or disgust. In this context, I understand the name Vavafel to mean something like "Hook-Huff-El": the El you breathe in to become possessed like an ob-mistress. I would translate this name as "El Who Attaches by Breath" or "Breath-Attaching El."

Thus, bound around by the versicle-lens of seeking the help of HaShem, this pentacle summons the ancestral ob-spirits and/or your personal ob-spirit as well as the El Who Attaches by Breath. This makes it especially appropriate as a protective talisman for trance mediumship and for journeys "across the water." I often wear this pentacle when I work sorcery, especially oracular adorcism. Although I usually use other methods, this pentacle is also helpful to help mediate communication with a familiar spirit. In addition, it is (as Mathers says) good against nightmares, although I prefer the fifth lunar pentacle for that purpose.

☽ 4: The Witch's Teacher

MATHERS SAYS THIS PENTACLE "defendeth thee from all evil sorceries, and from all injury unto soul or body. Its angel, Sophiel, giveth the knowledge of the virtue of all herbs and stones; and unto whomsoever shall name him, he will procure the knowledge of all." These two uses might not seem immediately similar, but another way to phrase this is that the pentacle both defends against malicious witchcraft and teaches practical witchcraft.

Although in modern Anglophone magic, we often think of Solomon as a highly intellectual wizard, who did only the most abstruse of ceremonial magic, that is very far from how he has traditionally been understood. Solomon is wise in all the ways of nature and famed as a master herbalist. This reputation arises from 1 Kings 5:13, which is generally translated as something like: "He discoursed with[11] trees, from the cedar in Lebanon to the hyssop that grows out of the wall . . ."

The versicle on this pentacle is from Jeremiah 17:18 and says "Shame them, who persecute me, but I am not shamed. Lay them low, but I am not laid low. Bring upon them an evil day, and let them be doubly destroyed!" This is a traditional formula for curse reversal, which loosely means "I'm rubber, you're glue! Whatever you send bounces off me and sticks to you."

Inside are the following names:

- אהיה אשר אהיה Ehyeh Asher Ehyeh
- יההאל Yahahel
- סופיאל Sophiel

We discussed the first name, Ehyeh, extensively in 2.2. The next, יההאל (Yahahel), is a well-known angel, whose name is sometimes said to mean "The Shining El" or "The Shine of El," from the root אהל, which means "to illuminate." However, I think this name is more likely some variation of יה האל, Jah h'El, "G-d the god." In either case, this particular name is associated with the subtle relationship between celestial light and intellectual brilliance that we call "enlightenment," as well as with wisdom, understanding, and knowledge, and I encourage you to lean into such a kavvanah when you inscribe it.

Blaise de Vigenère[12] lists Yahahel (which he transliterates as "Iahhael") as the sixty-second of his seventy-two "angels of the Shem H'Mephorash."[13] He associates Iahhael with Tehillim 119:159, "See how much I love Your instructions, HaShem? Because You are compassionate, awaken me!" As an angel of the Shem H'Mephorash, Iahhael is associated with the first decan of Taurus[14] and the tarot's Five of Pentacles.[15]

The final name, סופיאל (Sofiel), is almost certainly related to the root סוף (sof), which means "ending." The word סוף comes from שפה (safah), which literally means "lip" and can figuratively mean "speech" or "boundary" (like the lip of a bowl). Sof is the limit past which a thing does not exist. The word is familiar to kabbalists as part of the Holy Name אין סוף (Ein Sof), which means "Without Limit," but which also means "transfinite" in modern Hebrew. Sofiel brings things (like your enemies) to a close, but also teaches about the endings of things, what in Greek would be called their *telos* (τέλος), and in English can mean something like their "destiny" or "purpose." Despite the fact that the names are etymologically unrelated, there is a strong harmony between סופיאל (Sofiel) and the Greek goddess Σοφια (Sofia), whose name means "wisdom."

Sofiel is a great teacher of wisdom, as well as the true purposes of magical materia. I have also found them to be an excellent tutor in small cardinal topology.[16] I find them easy to contact with classic dark mirror conjuration, drawing the pentacle directly onto the mirror, and that is the most common way I use this pentacle.

☽ 5: The Dreamer's Servant

MATHERS SAYS THAT THIS PENTACLE "serveth to have answers in sleep. Its Angel Iachadiel serveth unto destruction and loss, as well as unto the destruction of enemies. Thou mayest also call upon him by Abdon and Dalé against all Phantoms of the night, and to summon the souls of the departed from Hades." This is one of my favorite pentacles. I use this one primarily for protection against nightmares (phantoms of the night), to which I was prone when I was younger, and often write it for friends and clients for that purpose. I also sometimes use it for dream incubation, particularly to conjure the dead. I almost never use it to destroy my enemies, but I have every reason to believe it will also work for that.

The versicle is taken from Tehillim 68:2 and means "Awaken, Elohim! Their enemies, scatter! Enemies who hate Them, flee before Them!" In the context of the pentacle, it clearly serves as a banishing.

The top interior name is יהוה אלהים (HaShem Elohim), which I personally understand as "HaShem among the Circle of Powers" or even "G-d, all the gods."

Under that is an illustration which is usually referred to as a "mystic character of the Moon." To my eyes, it resembles a wand. Some manuscripts include it and others do not. My experience is that its inclusion or omission makes no difference at all. A piece of personal *gnosis*:[17] I understand it to be a direction to knock rhythmically, stressing the second of every four beats. I often use that rhythm of knocking in conjunction with this pentacle, but I really can't say if it makes a difference in the conjuring, or if it just helps me attain the correct trance state.

The next name, יכדיאל (Ixadiel), whom Mathers mentioned, is harder to translate. It is possibly related to the root כדד, which means something like "glow with heat" or "gleam like a gem," but which can also mean "burn" or "work very hard." The next name, אזראל (Azarel[18]), is probably derived from the root אזר meaning "to encircle" or "to bind." Back when I was a baby witch, the first protection spell I was taught was "I stand in circles of light that nothing unwanted can cross." When calling these two names in succession, I hold a similar kavvanah of glowing protective circle, albeit one that is slightly more martial.

So, what about this "Abdon and Dalé" that Mathers spoke about? Many people understand Abdon to be a corruption of Abaddon (אבדון), a daimon of the abyss whose name may be related to the root אבד, which means "loss," and may be related to the Greek Ἀπόλλων (Apollo), whose name is sometimes said to mean "Destroyer," but is probably pre-Greek and means more like "drive away [evil]." When the name Abaddon is used in Torah, context generally implies a place within the Underworld, a terrible place of fire and destruction. On the other hand, עבדון (Abdon) is also a (human) given name. For example, one of the biblical judges[19] was so named. It means "servant," "slave," or "worshipper." It is from an old Semitic root, ABD. That is the same root as the more familiar Arabic name, Abdul.[20]

Dalé is less clear, but is perhaps related to the root דלה (*dalah*), which means "to draw up" (as from a well). Cross-culturally, wells are understood as "holy holes" and portals to the Underworld.[21] The drawing up of spirits from the Underworld, as through a well, is very clearly in keeping with the stated purpose of the pentacle.

As I mentioned previously, one way to understand a pentacle is as a diagram of a ritual. That is particularly clear in this case. I understand the ritual outlined by the fifth pentacle to be broadly:

- Banish with the versicle.

- Call HaShem Elohim.

- Maybe wave a wand around? Maybe knock? Maybe nothing?

- Cast a circle with Ixadiel and Azarel.

  - For nightmare protection, stop here.

- For compulsive necromancy, draw up a ghost servitor from the Underworld with the names "Abdon" and "Dalé."

☽ 6: The Rain Maker

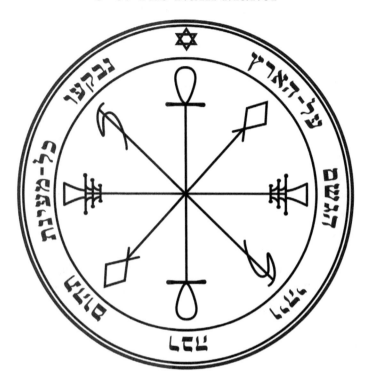

THIS IS THE FIRST OF MANY eight-rayed pentacles. Every planet has at least one. They are harder to interpret than most of the other pentacles because they have fewer names/words on them. Of this one, Mathers says: "This is wonderfully good, and serveth excellently to excite and cause heavy rains, if it be engraved upon a plate of silver; and if it be placed under water, as long as it remaineth there, there will be rain."

The circumferential versicle is excerpted from the story of Noah's flood in Bereshit 7:11–12 and says "Burst open all the fountains of the Great Below, and rain was upon the Earth."

The eight-rayed star is a common symbol in Levant. It is the cuneiform for "god" or "planet" and is most often associated with the planet Venus. I believe it may be intended here as a four-dimensional compass rose. There's really no way to know, but we'll discuss it a little more later in the book.

What follows is entirely speculative. I present it largely as an example of a way to develop your own kavvanot to employ with the pentacles.

Examining the symbols, I am struck by their similarity to the three great magic wands of ancient Egypt, the *ankh* (♀), *djed* (▯), and *waas* (|). Is this the meaning intended by the original author of the pentacle? Who can say?

The ankh is the wand of life. Some people say it is a mirror; others say it is a sandal. I find both explanations unconvincing because figures are routinely shown holding it through the loop. Some believe it to be related to the similar ring and rod symbol in Mesopotamian sacred iconography, which is generally understood as a sort of ruler and measuring tape. Some say it is a type of absorbent knotted cord used as a tampon, called a *tyet,* whose character is ▯. Personally, I think it is a vertebra. It is associated with the goddess Isis, particularly in connection with her role as a healer. It generally conveys the meaning of "Long may you live!"

The djed represents a pillar; sometimes a column that holds up a building, and sometimes a human spine. Some say its original form was a sacred tree, and others a phallus. In all of these cases, it represents strength and stability. It was often used as an amulet for the dead, hung around the neck, and presumed to protect the spine. It is associated with Osiris, particularly in his role as lord of the dead. It often appears in combination with the tyet.

The waas scepter is most often paired with Set, although Anubis and a variety of other gods, priests, and pharaohs are also pictured with it. It is a sign of power and dominion, frequently used as a magical staff to control chaotic natural forces, such as storms. It is a staff in the shape of a (highly stylized) sha, the so-called "Set-animal" or "Typhonic beast." This creature appears often in Egyptian hieroglyphs and images. It is an unknown species with 1) a stiff, forked tail, 2) long, erect, square-tipped ears, and 3) a long, slightly hooked nose. Personally, I suspect it is a now-extinct breed of canid from which greyhounds were domesticated,[22] but friends more knowledgeable about Set than I am suggest to me that it is either a hare or a mythic monster, not intended to portray any real-life animal.

Arranging these around the pentacle (as shown in the figure on page 107), we see that waas-scepter is broken. Why? Because it is the staff used to control storms! In this pentacle, it is broken, angering Set and calling for his fury, which comes in the form of storms.

Because I have always lived in places where we rarely have drought, and often have very severe storms, I have little experience using this to call rain, although I have been told it is very effective for that purpose. As I will discuss again later in this book, because we live in a time with a dangerously disrupted climate, I find meddling with the weather deeply unwise except in genuine emergency.

Exercises

- Add the Lunar Lock & Key to your book.

- Do the "Going Below" exercise that accompanied it.

- Add at least one other lunar pentacle to your book. I recommend the Witch's Teacher.

☿
_____

The Pentacles of Mercury

"One who was born under the influence of Mercury
will be an enlightened and expert man, because Mercury is
the Sun's scribe, as it is closest to the Sun."

—TALMUD SHABBAT 156A

As with all the planets, Mercury is closely tied to its namesake god, but they are not identical. Mercury is the quickest and smallest planet in our solar system and the innermost. It orbits the Sun every eighty-eight days. Because of its speed, it is often associated with travel gods (such as the Roman Mercury, the Greek Hermes, and the Babylonian Nabu), however it has been aligned with many other gods as well. For example, in ancient Greece, the planet Mercury appears to have originally been understood as two different spirits, a morning version sacred to Apollo, and an evening star sacred to Hermes.

I imagine it thus: in prehistory, most people never traveled very far, and most spoke only one language. However, even then, that was not true of everyone. Travelers, messengers, storytellers, translators, traders, and go-betweens of every type have always existed, and these are the people of Mercury. Additionally, Mercury rules all activities done "by one's wits," including writing, mathematics, fast-talk, gambling, con-art, sleight of hand, sorcery, spirit-speaking, spirit-travel, and all types of navigating, both literal and metaphoric. Fleet-footed Mercury is also the planet of runners, and (by extension) all athletes and gaming competitors, although the Solomonic pentacles do not focus on this aspect.

The symbol for the planet Mercury, ☿, is called the "caduceus" and represents a staff or wand wound around with two snakes. It has been associated with messengers since deepest antiquity.

There is no singular color attribution for Mercury. The seven-rayed spectrum, dark purple, bright orange, most neon colors, and rainbow opalescence are all associated with Mercury. Personally, I most often work with Mercury using a combination of saffron orange and eggplant purple. Unsurprisingly, the metal most associated with mercury is obviously mercury (aka quicksilver), although many modern magicians also use aluminum. Some of Mercury's special sacred numbers are 8, 23, 64, 88, 260, 10^{100} (called a "googol"[1]), the golden ratio φ (which we discussed in conjunction with the pentagram of the Great Seal), and $\aleph_0$ (the number of points on a line). In truth, however, *all* numbers, and the very concept of Number, are darlings of Mercury. Similarly, alphabets and ciphers, as well as scribes and linguists, are the domain of celestial Mercury, the Great Scribe of the Sun.

The role of the scribe, or *soferet*[2] (סופרת), is a very important one in Jewish magic. The root word ספר (SFR) gives rise to a large family of words with meanings like "count," "storytell," "write," "scroll/book," and "number." If we analyze the Paleo-Hebrew hieroglyphics, we have thorn-mouth-head. Presumably, that is because writing uses a thornlike instrument (a pen or engraver) to record sounds and ideas. Today, as in ancient days, the craft of the *sofer* is often taught from parent to child, although there are many schools for training scribes. We know that such schools also existed in deep antiquity, because of a 15th century BCE letter from a teacher to the parent of a pupil, demanding payment of overdue tuition.[3]

The most important part of the Hebrew scribe's craft, when making sacred and magical texts (including Solomonic pentacles), is not the calligraphic skill or artistic talent. The famed master scribe and scribal teacher Rabbi Shimon Zeide of Merkaz Hasofrim, in Brooklyn, New York, says, "In order to make it kosher, I would say, you don't need so much skills."[4] Rather, what is most important is the *keva* and kavvanah with which they are made.

The word קבע (keva) is usually translated as "fixed" and comes from a root meaning "permanency." In this context, I think the best translation for it is "ritual precision." Sacred and magical texts should be copied from an example (or a draft), rather than composed from memory. They must be perfect in their ritual precision (keva). As the Talmud says, "When I came to study with Rabbi Yishmael, he said to me: My son, what is your vocation? I replied: I am a scribe who writes Torah scrolls. He said to me: My son, be careful in your vocation, as your vocation is heavenly service, and care must be taken lest you omit a single letter or add a single letter out of place, and you will end up destroying the whole world in its entirety. Addition or omission of a single letter can change the meaning from truth [emet אמת] to death [met ⁵.[מת

As I have mentioned before, kavvanah, the mystic intention held while writing, is also extremely important. The word kavvanah (כונה) arises from the root כונ, which means "to be present," and the foundational element of kavvanah is paying careful attention to what you're doing: really under-standing and thinking about each word or name you write. Talmud relates, ". . . any Torah scroll in which the mentions of God's name have not been written with the proper intention is not worth anything." Written amulets are just the same.

It is entirely possible to empower a written amulet without being able to read or understand the writing, by awakening it as it you would any other sort of amulet, as a home for spirit powers. This produces not a true Sol-omonic pentacle, but rather an amulet which happens to be decorated to resemble a Solomonic pentacle. There's nothing wrong with that. However, like all Hebrew amulets, the Solomonic pentacles are intended to be more than that. Each word, each letter, ought to be written and awakened with focused intention. I encourage you to, in alliance with your own spiritual allies, awaken your pentacles as homes for familiar spirits. However, the true power of a Solomonic pentacle, the essence of what a Solomonic pen-tacle is, arises from these words and names.

When preparing to make sacred or magical texts in the Jewish/Hebrew tradition, the scribe must clean, prepare, and center themselves, declaring their intention to engage in sacred work. Next, they must read each word, contem-plating its many meanings,⁶ and then say the word or name out loud. Only then can they begin to write the characters, while holding the specific kavvanah of the task at hand in mind. By involving their whole mind and soul in the pro-cess, the scribe produces scrolls and amulets which physically embody both eternal spiritual powers and ephemeral ritual speech, making manifest a rush-ing fountain of magic.

Written amulets for magical purposes are extremely common in Jewish communities, both ancient and modern. The expectation is that, when prop-erly made by an expert, amulets can be assumed to be effective. However, it is also possible for nonexperts to write them effectively if they maintain clear and powerful kavvanot. For example, in the time of the Mishna (circa 200 CE), the rabbis discussed whether amulets may be worn on the sabbath, when carrying most things⁷ and wearing jewelry are forbidden. "And he may neither go out with phylacteries, nor with an amulet when it is not from an expert, but rather it was written by someone who has not established a reputation as an expert in writing amulets that are effective for those who carry them."[8] In other words, amulets are acceptable when there is a reasonable expectation of their magical efficacy. Although the text does not explain the rabbis' reasoning, I believe it is because amulets are commonly for healing and protection, and the positive commandment of preserving life and well-being is surely more important than even the most sagacious of rabbinic prohibitions, like carrying on Shabbat.

☿ 5: The Cross of Father El

MATHERS TELLS US that his fifth pentacle of Mercury ". . . commandeth the Spirits of Mercury, and serveth to open doors in whatever way they may be closed, and nothing it may encounter can resist it." I use it in many different ways, but primarily to open the Gates of Abundance in money and marketing magic, and to open the Gates of Perception, both for sorcery and for learning magic, which is why I'm teaching it first of all the Mercury pentacles. I sometimes use this pentacle in combination with others, which we'll discuss when we get to those pentacles. .

The seal as a whole has the form of an equal-armed cross in a circle, sometimes called a "Sun cross." This symbol has a very long history, which is intimately tied up in the fascinating history of wheels as man-made machines. As we use them today, axled wheels for transportation seem to have been invented around 6000 BCE in or around modern Iraq. However, other kinds of wheel machines (such as grain mills and potting wheels) appear to be much older. The earliest wheels were solid disks, but they soon evolved to a four-spoke variety.

Wheels, when combined with the domesticated horse, were a world-shaking technological breakthrough. Among other things, their combination gave birth to the chariot, a nearly unstoppable war machine that was one of many factors behind the Indo-European conquest. This technological advancement figures heavily in many Indo-European myths (particularly myths of the solar chariot) and in Hebrew mythology as well. One of the foundational stories of Jewish mysticism is Ezekiel's vision of the chariot,[9] which appears in the first chapter of his book. That story is discussed in much greater detail in the Jupiter chapter, along with the pentacle called Jakob's Ladder.

At a less culturally determined level, the Sun cross has an arrangement of perpendicular lines which segments two-dimensional space into four quadrants. At their intersection, those lines create an origin, a center point from which a coordinate system (like the four cardinal directions) can be established. Similarly, it establishes an Axis Mundi, the stable point around which the Wheel of Being can spin. As a general, but not universal, rule, when the Sun cross appears in magic, it is a sign of stability, of the Sacred Center, and of the orderly arrangement of the universe.

The versicle of this pentacle is from Tehillim 24:9.[10] It says, "Gates, lift up your heads! Eternal doors, be lifted up! The King of Abundance[11] is coming in!" That is clearly relevant to the stated purpose of the pentacle. However, Zohar 1:23b:22 suggests a deeper reading that connects this passage to the archangels and supernal powers: "During Shacharit [morning prayer], the lion descends to receive the prayer with its arms and wings—every living creature[12] has four wings. This is Michael. During Minchah [afternoon prayer], the ox descends to receive the prayer with its horns and wings, and this is Gabriel. On Shabbat, the Holy One, blessed be He descends with the three patriarchs—Chesed [Compassion], Geborah [Strength], and Tiferet [Beauty]—to receive His only daughter through them. This is the secret of Shabbat [שבת]—Shin [ש, fire] and Bat [בת, daughter]. At that time, the celestial living creatures that are called by the name Yud Hei Vav Hei say, as it is written: 'Lift up your heads, O you gates; and lift them up, you everlasting doors; that the King of Glory may come in.'"[13]

The names on the interior of this pentacle are simple. In the top right quadrant is אל (El), a name which should be very familiar by now. On the top left we have אב (Ab), which means "father" or "male ancestor" but can also sometimes mean a teacher to whom one is apprenticed, a godfather, a patron, or a sponsoring power broker. Across the bottom is the familiar יהוה, the Most Holy Name, split into Jah and Vah.

To activate this very straightforward pentacle, I simply call the three names repeatedly, then call the four Holy Living Beings of Ezekiel (Bull, Eagle, Lion, and Man), and imagine each creature unfolding their quarter of the pentacle to reveal a gateway to the storehouse of יהוה, the King of Glory, who is your patron אב (Ab) and the divine patron of all Solomonic magic.

☿ 2: The Seal of Lost Causes

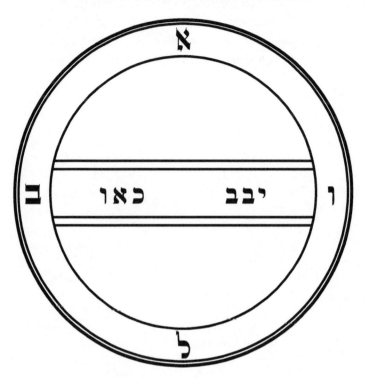

MATHERS SAYS OF THIS pentacle that "the spirits herein written serve to bring to effect and to grant things which are contrary unto the order of Nature; and which are not contained under any other head. They easily give answer, but they can with difficulty be seen." Before we move on to translating the names of these spirits, recall that, as mentioned in the previous chapter, crying is an extremely common dream induction technique in Levantine magic, both ancient[14] and modern.[15] Why is this relevant? Mathers reads the circumferential letters, starting at the left and tracing an inverted cross, as בואל, a name he fails to translate, which I assume would be said something like Buel; this name also appears as the seventh overseer of the first firmament in Sefer Razim. If, on the other hand, they are read naturally, that is counterclockwise from the top, the name is אבלו (Evelu), from the root אבל, which means "to mourn" or "to grieve." This meaning is highlighted by the inner names.

The name on the right, יבב, is a very common root, which means "to keen" or "to wail." The left name, כאו, is slightly less clear. It is probably a form of כאב, (ka'av), which means "to be in pain." However, possibly it is a copyist error, and it should read כאן, which means "here/now." As you can see, the vav (ו) at the end could easilly be mistaken for a nun-sofit (ן). In either case, the inner names are clearly an exhortation to cry over the pentacle,[16] and that is how I use it.

☿ 1: Mercury's Pentagram

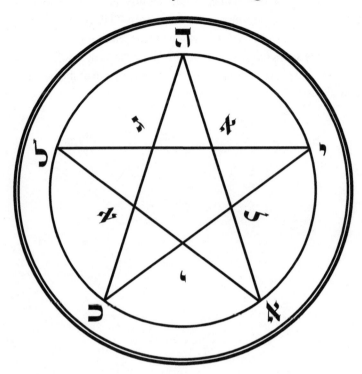

THIS IS PROBABLY MY FAVORITE of all the pentacles; it is the only pentacle I regularly wear. Mathers says of his first pentacle of Mercury that it "serveth to invoke the spirits who are under the Firmament." In this context, "firmament" is a biblical reference. It is the English word most often used to translate the biblical רקיע, which means something like "dome" or "membrane."[17] In biblical cosmology, it is, as you can see in the diagram on page 119, essentially the "top of the sky." All natural spirits, including planetary spirits, are "below the firmament"; the only thing above is the high heavens.

Before we discuss how this pentacle generates such awesome power, we'll begin by translating the names.

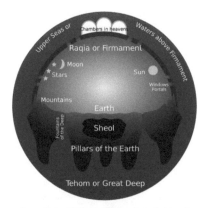

Early Hebrew Conception of the Universe. Stephen L. Harris, 2003. CC by 4.0 DEED.

For the circumferential name, we read along the pentagram, starting at the top right. That gives יכהאל, which Mathers renders in English as Yekahel, although I prefer the more direct transliteration Ikahel. The name derives from יכה-אל. At the end is the familiar divine name El, which ends so many angelic names. The beginning part, יכה, is the third person future of הכה (*hikah*), so the name means "El will penetrate," or "El will strike," or even "El will kill." In this pentacle, I generally prefer "He will penetrate."

For the name between the points of the pentagram Mathers reads counterclockwise starting in the top right ✦ and finds the name אגאיל (Agail). I am skeptical about this reading, both because it fails to end in אל (even though it sounds similar), and because אגא is not a word I understand. Instead, I think it should be read as the complement of the outer name, starting in the top left ✦ and reading counterclockwise around the inner (invisible) pentagram, as shown in the diagram below. That yields גיאאל (Giael, "GUY-ee-el"), which unambiguously means "Valley El," the perfect enveloping partner to the Penetrating El on the exterior.

Giael, the Valley Spirit, is very well known worldwide, under a variety of names. For example, chapter six of the *Dao De Ching* (below in an interlinear "seal script") can loosely be translated as:

The Valley Spirit never dies.

She is called "Dark Mother."

(1) the river-valley (2) spirit (3) never (4) dies
(5) this (6) is called (7) the dark (8) mare / female

Dark Mother is a Gateway—

the root of earth and heaven.

(1) the dark (2) mare / female (3) the same (4) a gateway [is]
(5) this (6) is called (7) heaven (8) and earth (9) the root / essence

Forever liminal, barely existing,

Effortless in practice!

(1) continually (2) continually (3) barely seeming (4) to exist
(5) [yet] use of (6) the same (7) is without (8) toil

Please allow me, if you will, to wax rhapsodic about this spirit for a moment. For me, the essential nature of the Giael is in her primeval form of River Valley, wet and lush, the first teacher of humans. Of course, every river valley, and every River Valley, is different, but most share some core qualities. They are chthonic, cool, shady, and fertile—the birth canals of our Dark Mother. Because their ecosystem has a natural "flow," they are (relative to other ecosystems) turbulent and constantly changing. Additionally, they are regionally heterogeneous; every part of the river valley is different from every other. For this reason, things that evolve to live in river valleys are often especially adaptable. Humans are no exception to this rule. Nearly all experts agree that humans arose in the Great Rift Valley of eastern Africa, along the shores of her many rivers and lakes. Such environments are our natural habitat; they're where we learned to be human.

Rivers are powerful ley lines through which energy, information, populations, and trade goods flow. Congo, Nile, Euphrates, Tigris, Balsas, Danube, Ganges, Yellow River, Jordan, Mekong, Amazon, Volga, Mississippi, and innumerable other great rivers worldwide have birthed complex cultures and empires that shaped, and continue to shape, our world. Writing, agriculture, art, and technology are all the gifts of the River Valley. Of course, so are empire, slavery, and warfare. River Valleys are the cradle of mankind; Dark Mother is the gateway of all the things, both good and bad, which make us human.

These two forces, the penetrating inward force from Above and the embracing force that radiates out from the Womb of the Earth, are woven together in this pentacle, forming the holy pentagram, whose magical virtues we previously discussed.

To activate the powers of this pentacle, first reach up, up, up to the firmament and call out the name Ikahel. Feel its explosive power. Feel the starlight penetrate you from the depths of outer space. Next, reach down, down, down into the center of the Earth, and feel the cool, wet depths. Call out the name Giael. Feel the water that makes you up. Feel the river valley that gave your birth. Rapidly chant both names, feeling yourself as the pillar of light between Above and Below, the vessel through which Father Sky and Mother Earth[18] come together, the rhythm of their lovemaking giving shape to the cycles of time. Feel the powers combine within you. It is the power of this union that enables humans to invoke all spirits under the firmament. Remember that you are a child of Earth and Starry Heaven.

While holding the kavvanah, I hold the pentacle in my hand and feel the tension between the Valley and the Penetrating One in my body. I pour that potential energy into the pentacle, as a sort of battery for spiritual power which I can call upon later. That is to say, I think of this pentacle as a generator, condenser, and battery of raw magical power. I wear it as both a badge of spiritual authority and a reservoir of sorcerous power when I'm interacting with spirits.

☿ 4: The All-Knowing Dodecagram

MATHERS SAYS ABOUT this pentacle: "This is further proper to acquire the understanding and knowledge of all things created, and to seek out and penetrate into hidden things; and to command those spirits which are called Allatori to perform embassies. They obey very readily." When I was in graduate school studying theoretical mathematics, I made very heavy use of this pentacle to help me learn, and I found it extremely effective. I have less experience with using it to command the Allatori, but I'll share what I do know after we analyze the pentacle itself.

Before we start translating this one, let's talk a little about its geometry. The shape pictured is called a dodecagram.[19] It has twelve vertices, and its "turning number" is five; if you stand at the center, and trace the star around you with an outstretched hand, you will end up turning around five full times by the time you complete the star. In combining the virtues of these two numbers, the dodecagram accesses the power of both. We've already talked extensively about the virtues of the number five, so let's next turn our minds toward the number twelve.

Twelve's most important features lie in the fact that it's highly divisible.[20] Of whole numbers smaller than twelve, only five and seven (both prime) do not share factors with it. That makes twelve a very convenient base for calculating.[21] It was the key number in ancient Babylonian mathematics[22] and astrology, from which our modern astrology derives. That is why there are twelve signs in the zodiac. It is from that astrological root that most of Western cultural associations with groups of twelve (including the twelve tribes of Israel, the twelve Olympians, and the twelve apostles) draw their rhetorical power.

Also inherited from Babylon, most of our everyday timekeeping is based around the number twelve. There are sixty (5x12) seconds in a minute and sixty minutes to an hour. There are twelve hours of day and twelve hours of night. There are twelve months in a year. All of this highlights twelve's close relation with time, and with the orderly cycles of nature. Twelve helps us understand complex things, by allowing us to see the underlying patterns that inform seemingly chaotic events. It is that virtue which we especially treasure in the All-Knowing Dodecagram.

The phrase around the pentacle's outer circumference means, "Wisdom and power are in his house; knowledge of all kinds of stuff endures forever." This is not a direct quote from Torah, although it bears some similarity to Tehillim 112:3. Note that the word I have translated as "stuff," דברים (devarim), can also mean "words," which is how it is generally understood as the first word (and thus name) of the book Christians call "Deuteronomy." This overlap in meaning between words and the stuff they represent is an important feature of the Hebrew amulet tradition: words of Power **are** the powers they name.

The name in the center is El. The other letters are a little trickier to read. Mathers suggests, "IHVH, fix thou the Volatile, and let there be unto the void restriction." I believe he gets this by reading counterclockwise around the outside, starting from the top right, and then turning around and reading clockwise around the interior (see diagram). This gives יהוהשרשירווהא לכהיהבלהלהוהוא. Separating that into words, we get יהוה שרש ירווהא לכהיה בלה והוא. A slightly more literal translation of that would be something like "HaShem, take root in the flow! The darkness, he is withered!"

However, something about that translation has never felt right to me. In particular, why turn around in the middle? While I was musing on it, my coven did an evocation of Arbatel,[23] an angel of revelation. I showed the pentacle and asked the angel about it, and they said (through a possessed medium, who did not know the pentacles and does not read Hebrew) that: "It has the power to trigger great insight. . . ." They continued, saying: "We angels try to meet the yearnings in your heart . . . it's in our nature . . . we are beings that satisfy desires. When our Father takes root in the heart, wonders occur."

Following that advice led me to my preferred reading of the pentacle, which begins the same as Mathers, but continues on the same spiral path without turning around (see diagram on page 125). That gives יהוהשרשירירוהאאוהוהללבההיהכל, which breaks out to כל היה והלב אוה ירוהא שרש יהוה. I loosely translate that as "HaShem, take root in the flow! Desire of the heart is Everything."[24]

Having (perhaps) solved the mystery of the letters, let's move on to Mathers's instructions. Who or what are the "Allatori"? Personally, I believe the name is related to the Latin *allātus,* which means "delivered" or "carried forth," usually in the context of a messenger. However, I think the meaning also partakes of the Latin *ālātus,* an adjective meaning "winged." That spirits of a Mercurial pentacle are winged messengers is unsurprising. Other sources describe the Allatori as "demons of the fiery south." That is much in keeping with my (limited) experience of them.

☿ 3: Mercury's Wheel

EACH PLANET EXCEPT the Moon has a wheel pentacle like this one, centered on an eight-rayed star with symbols on each spoke, and with four angelic names around the circumference. Generally, these are the easiest to use but the hardest to decrypt, partly because symbols are more prone to corruption in the transmission process than are words.[25] In my practice, I primarily use the wheel pentacles as "cranks," which can be spun up to provide additional power for other pentacles. I often put a wheel pentacle on the back of other pentacles from the same planetary "family," a practice which I believe is quite standard. Occasionally, I also use them in cross-planet combinations. However, I think there is great value in attempting to understand them. If nothing else, it's a really fun puzzle, and I encourage you to try your hand at it to develop your own kavvanot for this and the other wheel pentacles.

Mathers says that this pentacle is used to "invoke the spirits subject unto Mercury; and especially those who are written in this pentacle." So, let's start there. Who are the spirits written in this pentacle? Starting at the top, and proceeding counterclockwise, we have:

- כוכביאל Kokaviel
- גדוריה Gedoriah
- סאוניה Sauniah
- חכמהיאל Chokmaiel

The top name, Kokaviel, is very easy to understand; כוכב (Kokhav) is the Hebrew name for the planet Mercury, although in some contexts, it can more generally mean "planet" or "star." Kokaviel, then, is the El of the planet Mercury. Kokaviel is also found in the Book of Enoch, a Jewish text from late antiquity, where they are listed among the fallen angels. They also make an appearance in *Sefer Raziel HaMalakh*, a medieval[26] Jewish grimoire, where they are understood as being directly in the service of heaven.[27]

The name on the left, Gedoriah, is slightly harder, but is almost certainly based on the root גדר, which means "to enclose" or "to wall off." In this context, Gedoriah might be a spirit of walled cities,[28] but I think it is more likely to mean something like "Master Mason." For example, גדר is used in that context in 2 Kings 12:12. Masonry is, historically, a kind of highly technical engineering profession and has a very long history of association with the Hermetic/Mercurial mysteries.

The name at the bottom, Sauniah, grows from the word סאון (*saun*) which means "sandal." In some contexts, it can also mean "soldier," just like English speakers sometimes call soldiers "boots on the ground." However, since Mercury is famed for his magical sandals, I think a literal reading is preferable here.

Finally, the name on the right, Chokmaiel, means Wisdom El. Although the word chokmah is almost always translated into English as "wisdom," it also partakes of the English "creativity" and "quick-wittedness." Chokmah is commonly anthropomorphized into a pseudo-goddess. Her Greek name, under which she is more familiar, is Sophia. Solomon says of her: "Chokmah has been my love. I courted her when I was young and desired to make her my lover. I burned for her beauty."[29]

Now that we understand the powers to awaken when making the pentacle, let's talk about some ways to use it. As I mentioned earlier, I use all of these wheel pentacles as "cranks" to generate power for other pentacles. In general, I make them back-to-back with another pentacle of the same planet, although sometimes I mix and match them. After awakening the pentacles on both sides (as we discussed in the Making & Using Non-Book Pentacles section), I energetically spin power through the wheel pentacle into the other. It helps the other pentacles capture and hold more energy. I do this when I want the pentacle to grow more powerful over time, and when I will be employing it in circumstances where there is an abundance of free energy. For beginners, I don't recommend wearing wheel pentacles long term; they can be a little draining.

Exercises

- Add at least one Mercurial pentacle to your book. I recommend the All-Knowing Dodecagram.

- Write a petition relevant to the concerns of that pentacle. I recommend a request for aid in learning Solomonic magic.

- Empower the petition using the method you learned at the end of the Magic: Sorcery & Seals chapter.

♀

The Pentacles of Venus

The Jerusalem Talmud relates that one sage asked another:
"Why are you bathing in the Bath of Aphrodite?" . . . he told him,
"I did not come into her domain, she came into my domain. One does
not say, the bath was built as adornment for Aphrodite [Venus]
but one says, Aphrodite was made as adornment of the bath."

—JERUSALEM TALMUD AVODAH ZARAH 3.4.1, TRANSLATION
AND COMMENTARY BY HEINRICH W. GUGGENHEIMER

Venus is the planet of every type of love. While we most often think of her as a planet of romantic or sexual love, she also controls all the bonds that unite people together: not just romance, but family, community, and politics as well. Our world is an increasingly complex and interconnected one. Venus, the Wile-Weaver, the Charming One, is the divine navigator of complicated social politics. As a general rule, Venus magic is very practical; there are few situations where increasing your interpersonal charm goes amiss.

But Venus is more than just that; hers is the force that brings forth life from life. Venus is the Great Green Goddess who taught us how to garden, who taught us the relationship between seed and sprout, who taught us the relationship between sex and babies. Venus is the vital *viriditas* that ripens both the fruit on the vine and the child in the womb. Says Saint Hildegard of Bingen: "There is a power that has been since all eternity and that force and potentiality is green!"

The symbol of the planet Venus, ♀, has become the symbol for "female". It is linked to the ankh, and it sometimes partakes of all the complex associations of that symbol (as discussed in the Moon chapter). Often it is (probably erroneously) understood as a hand mirror. Others think it may represent a *sistrum,* a kind of a rattle with jingles like a tambourine, or a necklace. Venus is closely associated with mirrors for another reason. In the ancient world, mirrors were commonly made of copper, and the connection between the metal copper and Venus is very strong, as we discuss at the end of this book, when we learn about the planetary metals. Mirrors, both copper and glass, are excellent material on which to write Venus pentacles.

The Hebrew name for the planet Venus is נוגה (*Nogah*), which means "Shining One." In modern Anglophone magic, Venus's number is seven, and her day is Friday.[1] She is associated with lions, doves, wolves, and peacocks. As mentioned before, her metal is copper, and her gem is the emerald. The angel most often associated with Venus is Anael (הניאל), whose name means "Joy of El." In English, this name is sometimes spelled "Haniel."

While Venus as a planet has very broad magical applicability, the Venus pentacles in the Mathers edition of the Key of Solomon do not cover the full range of magic we would expect from Venus. Unlike most of the planets, which have seven pentacles each, Mathers lists only five Venus pentacles, of which two are too corrupt for me to read. Missing are many Venus-related concerns we would normally expect to see addressed in a compendium of practical magic, including magic to promote conception and amulets for healthy pregnancy and birth.[2]

Moreover, the text's understanding of "love" leans a bit rapacious for my taste. Like all texts, the Key of Solomon can really be understood only by examining the historical and cultural context in which it was written. The Key, in the form we know it today, was written by and for highly literate, male, Catholic bourgeoisie and nobility of the European Renaissance. When this is understood, the paucity of Venus magic in these manuscripts is not so surprising, nor should be the narrow representation of Mars we see in the next chapter.

Conjuration by Love

There is a mistaken notion that Solomonic magic is always a brutally compulsive procedure, wherein spirits are forcibly bound against their will. That is not true; many Solomonic-style conjurations rely on love, rather than threat, to win the attention of the summoned spirits. For example, allow me to present this medieval Hebrew incantation text[3] which gives instructions for a conjuration by love.

After making a seal, the magician is told to take it, on the evening preceding Wednesday, somewhere he can be alone. There, pleasant spices are burned. If the conjurer is afraid, the text advises, they should "take four pieces from a deer's antlers, one piece out of each antler, and stick them into the ground around the circle, toward its four winds [cardinal directions]."

Next, we are told, the magician should hold the seal in their hand, and with paper and pen prepared, sit in the circle and say:

In the name of הי הי הי הי הו הו וה הו הה הה הה הה הו הו הה הו הו אי: Fire consumes fire, and in the name of the Fire, which controls all fire, and in the name of the Ineffable Names, which burn everything with fire and which extinguish the flames of fire, I adjure you Iramrami . . . son of Ashmodai, who is the highest of the kings, who is mentioned before the great ones, who ruled in the days of Solomon . . . show yourself to me now . . . for I indeed love you, and I have exerted myself in seeking your well-being. . . .

The instructions conclude, "And make sure that you smile, so that he [the spirit] may see that you are not afraid of him. . . ."

♀ 1: The Wheel of Venus

As I MENTIONED in the previous chapter, most of the planets have a wheel pentacle very much like this one, of which Mathers says, "This and those following serve to control the spirits of Venus, and especially those herein written." Beginning at the top, and going counterclockwise, the four names on this pentacle are:

- נוגהיאל Nogahiel
- אהליהו Ohelihu
- סוכוהיה Sukohiah
- נעאריאל Nearial

On most of the planetary wheels, the name at the top is simply the name of the planet appended to the name El (אל), and this one is no exception. As we discussed, Nogah (נוגה) is the Hebrew name for Venus, and Nogahiel is that same name El-ified to produce an angelic form. The name on the left, Ohelihu, also has two parts. Yahu (יהו) is a divine name we've discussed before. The root אהל (*ohel*) is a common one, relating to tents.

The next name Mathers spells סוכוהיה (Sukohiah), but I think it should be סוכותיה (Sukotiah), with ת instead of the similar-looking ה. *Sukkot* (סוכות) is the name of a weeklong Jewish harvest festival which begins with Libra's full Moon. It is the plural of *sukkah* (סוכה), which means "booth" or "shack." The rabbis teach that, during the festival, the booths we build represent our temporary homes as we wandered the desert following the exodus from Egypt. In ancient times, Sukkot was the end of harvest time, when the whole community lived in the fields in tents and booths, working together to bring in the harvest before the rains came.

Finally, Mathers's pentacle has נעאריאל (Neariel), a name which is difficult to interpret. It is possibly related to נער (*ne'ar*) which means "boy." However, many Latin manuscripts give the name as Nangariel, which suggests the name may be misspelled. I think it should be נגאריאל (Nagariel), from the root נגר, which means "flowing out," like the rains after Sukkot.

Like most of the wheel pentacles, I use this one primarily on the back of other Venus pentacles, as a sort of crank to power them up. However, I suspect it could also be used to bring autumn rains.

♀ 2: The Seal of Sheba

MATHERS SAYS THAT this pentacle, his second of Venus, is used for "obtaining grace and honor, and for all things which belong unto Venus, and for accomplishing all thy desires herein." This is one of my favorite pentacles, and the only of the Venus pentacles I regularly use for myself. When I do so, I usually ask the pentacle to make me as beautiful, desirable, regal, politically savvy, and charismatic as the Queen of Sheba. However, I more often use this pentacle to charge petitions.

The versicle of this pentacle is from the Song of Songs 8:6. When the book is read as the love story of Solomon and the Queen of Sheba, these are her words to him: "Set me a seal on your heart and on your arm, for as strong as Death is Love." It is for this reason that I call this one the "Seal of Sheba."

The fifth word, עֲל־זְרוֹעֶךָ, is traditionally translated as "on your arm," and I have followed this tradition. More specifically, it can mean "on your bicep" or "on your shoulder," which is why some people choose to tattoo this seal on their left bicep. Additionally, the root word, זרע, means "to sow seed" and "to fructify" in both agricultural and sexual contexts. I believe that this wordplay is an intentional double entendre, suggesting that one's partner be held in one's heart and energetically infused into one's orgasm.

To read the name around the outside of the pentagram (below), we begin at the bottom and go counterclockwise, which gives יונאל, or Yonael. I understand the root of this name to be יונה-אל (Yonah-El), which means Dove (or Pigeon) of El. In many cultures, doves (and pigeons) have been associated with Venus since time out of mind. They have an exceptional sense of navigation; when lost, they can (almost) always find home. These messengers of Venus played an extremely important role as carriers of messages: they kept the peace among Solomon and his many allies, as they had been doing for kings since time out of mind, and as they continue to do to our own day.

To read the name in the points of the pentagram (shown on page 136), begin with the ע at the bottom right and go clockwise (i.e., backwards). This gives עימאל (Aimel), a very close cognate of the common Arabic-origin proper (human) name Aimal, which means "hoped for" or "wished for." Thus, I understand Aimel to be an angel of wishing.

Finally, to read the innermost name, we start at the top right and go counterclockwise, using the א as both the beginning and the end. That gives us אהויעא (Ahavia). This is a less common spelling of the familiar god-name אהבה (Ahavah).[4] In English, Ahavah is usually translated as "Love."

Putting that all together, we see that the Seal of Sheba instructs us in her ritual:

1. The energy of activation is that of the lovers in the final chapter of Song of Songs, who both are and are not Solomon and the Queen of Sheba.

2. The seal itself can be worn as a pendant on the breast (i.e., on the heart), on the arm, and also energetically cast into a target, sowing it like seed.

3. The names of power to be called[5] while tracing their respective shapes around the pentacle are:

   - Yonael, the Dove
   - Aimel, the Wish
   - Ahavah, Love

♀ 3: The Matchmaker of Monachiel

OF THIS PENTACLE, Mathers says that "if it be only shown to any person, [it] serveth to attract love. Its angel Monachiel should be invoked in the day and hour of Venus at one o'clock or at eight."[6] Although I usually refer to the point-to-point triangles as an "hourglass" shape, I think they are better understood as a hexagram in which the upper and lower triangles have been pulled apart like a spring. As usual, the writing on the pentacle provides more information about its mechanism.

The circumferential versicle is the first part of Bereshit 1:28, which says, "And Elohim blessed them, and said to them: 'Be fruitful and increase, and consecrate the land and tame it.'" In context, "them" refers to Earthlings, newly created.

In the middle of the pentacle, outside the triangles, is written יהוה אדני, Hashem Adonai, a very common compound name we've spoken about at length already. The table summarizes the interior names from top to bottom. I will discuss them individually below.

עלמיאל	Elemial	El of Single People
רוח	Ruach	Spirit, Breath
יאל	Iel	El Will
יהוה	HaShem	Most Holy Name
אדני	Adonai	Lord
דגל	Degel	Banner, Flag
אחדים [אחידם]	See discussion below	See discussion below
מונחיאל	Monachiel	Comforting El

The name at the top, Elemiel (עלמיאל), is closely related to עלם, *elem*, which means "unmarried post-pubescent man" and is often translated "virgin." Many people might translate Elemiel as "The El of Virgins." In the context of this pentacle, I prefer to translate it as "El for the Marriageable," which I poetically understand to mean "El the Matchmaker."

The second word from the top, *ruach* (רוח), means "breath," "spirit," "wind," or any other "invisible force." It is one of several Hebrew words used for various parts of a human soul.

The vertical letters in the upper triangle spell יאל, which means "El Will." In keeping with my understanding of the hourglass as a separated hexagram, I generally read it in combination with the vertical letters in the lower triangle, which spell דגל, which, when understood as a verb, means "to be conspicuous" or "to carry a banner" but can also be understood as a noun meaning "flag" or "banner." When the vertical names are read together as a single name, we have דגליאל, which means "El will raise a Banner" or "The Banner of El."

In Mather's version of this pentacle, he has written inside the lower triangle, at the bottom, אחידם, a word I do not understand. I think, instead, it should be אחדים, the plural of the familiar divine name אחד (Achad), which means "One." The illustration on page 138 reflects this change.

As you might imagine for the plural of the number one, this is a relatively obscure word. I translate it as "unity" or "one all together." It is used in the story of the Tower of Babel in Bereshit 11:1 in the phrase: ודברים אחדים (v'devarim achadim), a deeply confusing and much interpreted phrase which is usually translated as "and of one speech" or "and with unified speech." As we discussed before, the first word, *devarim*,[7] means "words." Based on this,

I understand the phrase רוח אחדים (Ruach Achadim) to mean "unity of spirit," "with unified spirit," or "of one spirit."

At the bottom of the pentacle is the name Monachiel (מונחיאל), whom Mathers calls the angel of this pentacle. To me, this name seems closely related to the (human) names Menachem (מנחם), which means "comfort," and Muna-khia (מנוחה), which means "serenity." The root word נוח gives rise to a large category of words relating to comfort and calmness. I understand Monachiel's name to mean something like "The El of Putting People at Ease." In my experience, this angel is a great negotiator and is particularly good at comforting the restless dead.

Understanding the names all together informs my reading of this pentacle as a matchmaker who gives comfort by uniting the many banners (tribes/clans/factions) of El. This makes perfect sense as a Venus pentacle when it is understood within its cultural context.

The Talmud[8] tells a story about matchmaking as a sacred act, which I shall retell for you:

A Roman matron asked a Rabbi, "In how many days did G-d create the world?"

"In six," he answered.

"And since then," she asked, "what has G-d been doing?"

"Matching couples for marriage," responded the Rabbi.

"That's it?!" she said dismissively. "Even I can do that! I have many slaves, both male and female. In no time at all, I can match them for marriage."

To which the Rabbi countered, "Though this may be an easy thing for you to do, for G-d it is as difficult as splitting the Sea of Reeds,"[9] whereupon she took her leave.

The next day the matron lined up a thousand male and a thousand female slaves and paired them off before nightfall. The morning after, her estate resembled a battlefield. One slave had his head bashed in, another had lost an eye, while a third hobbled because of a broken leg. No one seemed to want their assigned mate.

Quickly, she summoned the Rabbi and acknowledged: "Your G-d is unique, and your Torah is true, pleasing, and praiseworthy. You spoke wisely."

Judaism is, at its core, a shared ancestry cult, and, as the story implies, matchmaking is taken very seriously. Marriages are the foundation of traditional Jewish family life. It is said that the act of making a loving and fruitful match is as meritorious as that of saving a life; it is understood that all such good matches are divinely inspired.

In this context, particularly in light of the choice of versicle, I understand this pentacle to be primarily intended to help the "marriage-minded" secure a love match. Because I am "not the marrying type," I do not have much personal experience using this pentacle, but I have made it for clients many times, both to help them find a marriageable partner and to strengthen an existing marriage. When I make it for others for either purpose, I usually have it laser etched in copper with Mathers's version on one side and a pentacle showing the two triangles combined into a hexagram, as shown below, on the other. Once I have awakened all the names and sealed the pentacle, I instruct clients to use it in conjunction with a petition outlining the characteristics of their desired match and relationship.

♀ 5: The Square of Venus

MATHERS SAYS OF THIS ONE: "When it is only showed unto any person soever, it inciteth and exciteth wonderfully unto love." The versicle, from Psalm 22:15, means, "My heart, like wax, melts within me." However, in the context of the psalm, this is not a metaphor for love, but for dying. Read in context, that verse and the next say: "My life ebbs away: all my bones are disjointed; my heart is like wax, melting within me. My vigor dries up like a shard; my tongue cleaves to my palate; You commit me to the dust of death." To my mind, that's not a natural choice for a love pentacle! That is one of many reasons I prefer the Seal of Sheba to this Square of Venus.

Before we discuss the lettering on this pentacle, I'd like to take a moment to discuss the magical virtues of squares—figures that have four equal-length sides and four right angles. The number four, like all even numbers, has a quality of balance. Because four is two squared, this association with balance is balanced against itself, making it even more stable and reliable. Square numbers generally, and four in particular, provide a stable foundation on which to balance complex magics. All four-sided figures partake of these qualities, but when the four sides are the same length (as in squares and rhombi), these virtues are amplified, and a quality of unity is added.

As we discussed with the Cross of Father El, right angles establish coordinates for two directions of movement, or degrees of freedom, that do not interfere with each other. For example, movement to the left or right is independent of movement front and back, because the left/right movement is at a right angle to front/back movement. Figures with four right angles (squares and rectangles) combine the stable balance of fourness with the freedom of movement of perpendicularity. Putting all this together, we come to understand squares as symbols of stable balance, unity, and freedom. Squares form a very strong foundation in two dimensions: tables upon which magic can safely rest without being constrained. Thus, squares can be understood as signs of material sovereignty and dominion.

The Mathers version of this pentacle has an illuminated letter *chet* (ח) in the middle, but many other manuscripts have a yod (י) inside, forming the word חי (*chai*). As we discussed with the Great Seal, "chai" means "life" and is commonly used on amulets. In our version, we have restored the yod.

Around the central square is a "secret alphabet" or cipher for Hebrew called Passing the River.[10] Its history is unclear. Legendarily, it is the alphabet taught by the angels to the Patriarch Abraham. It was popularized among occultists in the 1533 *Three Books of Occult Philosophy* by German magician Heinrich Cornelius Agrippa.

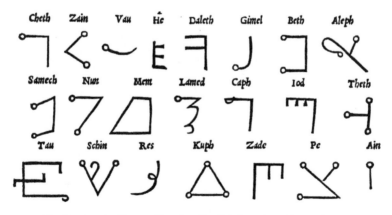

The Passing the River or *Transitus Fluvii* cipher. Cornelius Agrippa, 1533.

However, the Passing the River on Mathers's rendition of this pentacle has several unreadable characters, which I suspect were caused by the scribe's difficulty writing an unfamiliar alphabet sideways. I read his pentacle as:

- Top: אלהים
- Left: אב??
- Bottom: אלגביל
- Right: ל???ב?

While the top name, Elohim, is clear, the rest are not. After consulting several other manuscripts, I choose to write my pentacles with the following names:

- Top: אלהים Elohim
- Left: אדני Adonai
- Bottom:אלגבר El Gebor (God of Might)
- Right: לשדי l'Shaddai (with Shaddai)

The pentacle above reflects those spellings.

Because of my poor understanding of this pentacle, I rarely make use of it. Instead, I use the Seal of Sheba to incite and excite love. If you decide to use this, no matter how you choose to interpret the names, you should be sure that your kavvanah precisely matches the words you write.

♀ 4: The Octagram That Commands Love

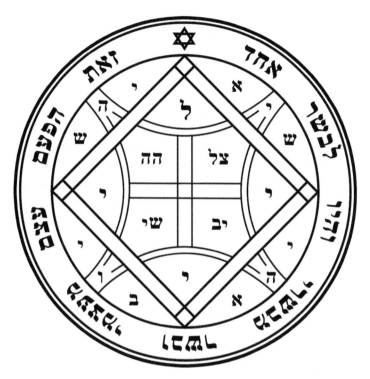

MATHERS SAYS OF THIS pentacle that it is "of great power, since it compels the spirits of Venus to obey, and to force on the instant any person thou wishest to come unto thee." The versicle is from Bereshit 2:23-24. It is Adam's wedding vow. "Now this is bone of my bones and flesh of my flesh . . . and they were of one flesh."

Starting with the ' in the top right and reading counterclockwise around the four corners of the astroid gives us the Most Holy Name. For the letters outside both the diamond and the astroid ⌐⌐, we begin again at the top right with the א and read counterclockwise. This gives us איש באיש (*ishi b'ish*), which means "wife and husband" or "woman and man."

Now we come to the names within the inner diamond. I regret to inform you that, after consulting several old manuscripts of the Key, all of which have different letters on the interior, I have concluded the interior is undecipherable (to me, at this time). I no longer use this pentacle, which is a shame, because it's very beautiful.

This is the very first Solomonic pentacle I ever made, when I was about fifteen or sixteen. I was quite new to magic, and I didn't really know what I was doing at the time. I did not yet know Hebrew, my Latin was very poor, and I did not yet have Mathers's translation, only images from a Latin manuscript, which I dutifully copied into my magic book.

At that time, I used this pentacle for compulsive love spells targeted at specific people. While it was more or less effective, it was also a stupid adolescent choice I regret. It always ended badly for both me and the other party. In general, I strongly recommend against beginners working targeted love spells, especially using magic they don't fully understand. In addition to being ethically icky, they are very likely to "monkey paw." Essentially, this is because the type of person who is susceptible to enchantments of this type is simply not a good partner for a magician.

Exercises:

- Teach at least one Venus pentacle to your Book. I recommend the Seal of Sheba.

- Add a pentacle to a magical bath (or shower) by writing a paper pentacle, awakening it (probably by cloning it out of your book), and then dissolving it in water to create a potion. The Seal of Sheba, added to a bath with salt, rose petals, and goat's milk, is excellent for drawing lovers, increasing libido, facilitating the healing of sexual trauma, and promoting self-love.

$$\odot$$

The Pentacles of the Sun

". . . the Sun, who is like a groom coming forth from the chamber, like a hero, eager to run his course. His rising-place is at one end of heaven, and his circuit reaches the other; nothing escapes his heat."

—TEHILLIM 19:5-7

The most prominent celestial body is, of course, our Sun. Sun drives both our day/night cycle and also the cycle of the seasons. Sun is the energetic engine from which (almost) all energy on Earth derives. It is the (almost) eternal fountain of sustenance that powers our food cycle, the rhythm of life and death. Sun shines on everything, mountain and plain, sinner and saint, making no distinctions. This is at the core of its mythic and magical resonance in every culture.

The symbol for Sun is a circle with a dot in the middle: $\odot$. This symbol clearly represents the Sun disk as it appears in the sky. Sun is associated with yellow, white, and both the color and metal gold. Some of the Sun's special numbers are 1, 4, 6, 10, 100, and all other powers of 10. It is associated with lions, bees, roosters, snakes, horses, cows, and falcons. Some angels especially associated with the Sun are Michael, Rafael, and Auriel. The Greek name for the Sun is Ἥλιος (Helios) and the Hebrew name is שמש (Shammash), which we discuss further along with the next pentacle.

☉ 2: The Wheel of the Sun

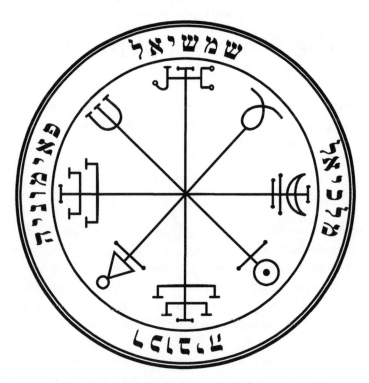

LIKE THE OTHER PLANETARY wheels, I use this primarily as a crank to generate power for the other solar pentacles. Mathers says that it "Serves to repress the pride and arrogance of solar spirits, which are altogether prideful and arrogant by nature." As usual for the wheels, it has four names around its circumference.

- Top: שמשיאל Shemeshiel
- Left: פאימוניה Paimoniah
- Bottom: רכודיה Rakudiah (note the change in spelling from Mathers)
- Right: מלכיאל Malachiel

The top name, Shemeshiel, is the name for the Sun, שמש (*Shemesh*), followed by the name El. It can be translated as "El of the Sun" or "Sun, the El."

The sound "sh-m-sh" has been associated with the Sun far longer than writing has existed. In addition to being the pan-Semitic name for the physical Sun, it is the name of a variety of solar gods and goddesses and, as such, appears in many spells, including the exorcism below, based on Mukal tablet IV.

Wash your hands, face, and genitals.

Wear white.

*Say: "Of the Sun, who is his father? Who his mother? Who is his sister?
He is the judge."*

Tie three knots in a length of white woolen yarn, while you say:
  "The father of the Sun is Sin, the Moon."
  "Nikkal, She of the Grove, is his mother."
  "Manzat, the Rainbow, is his sister."

Then, gently whip the patient with the yarn three times while saying:
  "He is the judge."
  "Shamash is the judge."
  "Shamash, the Sun, is the judge."

Untie the knots in order, saying:
  "Shamash, the Sun, destroys the witchcraft, releases the spittle."
  "Manzat, the Rainbow, releases the bonds."
  "I cause the winds to carry off sorcery, rebellion, and the evil word!"

Throw the string into a fire.

Wash yourself again.

*Advise the patient to take a salt bath or scrub with salt in the shower
before they go to sleep.*

To use the pentacle in combination with this, I recommend using the pentacle in your book as a table of practice, on which you light a beeswax candle and carefully braid together four pieces of white woolen yarn while reciting the four names, and then use the resulting cord in the exorcism.

The name on the left of the wheel is usually anglicized as Paimoniah, although I prefer to read it "Paimon Jah." Paimon is a demon-king[3] of the *Ars Goetia*, a 17th century Solomonic demon catalog. There, the following is said about him:

*The Ninth Spirit in this Order is Paimon, a Great King, and very obe-
dient unto Lucifer. He appeareth in the form of a Man sitting upon a
Dromedary with a Crown most glorious upon his head. There goeth
before him also a Host of Spirits, like Men with Trumpets and well
sounding Cymbals, and all sorts of Musical Instruments. He hath a
great Voice, and roareth at his first coming, and his speech is such
that the Magician cannot well understand unless he can compel him.
This Spirit can teach all Arts and Sciences, and other secret things.
He can discover unto thee what the Earth is, and what holdeth it up in
the Waters; and what Mind is, and where it is or any other things thou
mayest desire to know. He giveth Dignity and confirmeth the same. He
bindeth or maketh any man subject unto the Magician if he so desire
it. He giveth good Familiars, and such as can teach all Arts. He is to
be observed towards the west. He is of the Order of Dominations. He
hath under him 200 Legions of Spirits, and part of them are of the
Order of Angels, and the other part of Potentates. Now, if thou callst
this Spirit Paimon alone, thou must make him some offering; there
will attend him two Kings called LABAL and ABALIM, and also other
Spirits who be of the Order of Potentates in his Host, and 25 Legions.
And those Spirits which be subject unto them are not always with them
unless the Magician do compel them. His Character is this, which
must be worn as a Lamen before thee, etc.*

The name at the bottom, Rakudiah, is hard to interpret. Mathers has רכודיה
(RKUDIH), but I think it should be רכוביה (RKUBIH), with a ב instead of a ד,
from the very ancient pan-Semitic root RKB, which means "mount" or (later)
"vehicle." This is also the root of Merkavah, a type of Kabbalistic ecstatic
trance journey which we discuss further at the end of this chapter. This change
is reflected in our pentacle.

☉ 1: The Countenance of El Shaddai

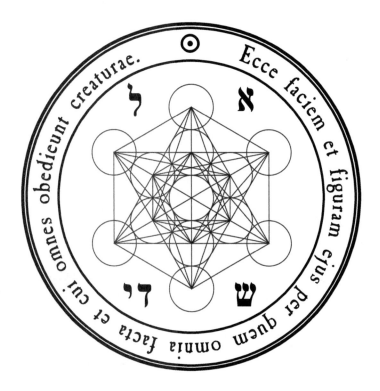

THIS IS MATHER'S FIRST solar pentacle, about which he says, "The countenance of Shaddai the Almighty, at whose aspect all creatures obey, and the angelic spirits do reverence on bended knees." Around the circumference is written, "Ecce faciem et figuram ejus per quem omnia facta et cui omnes obedieunt creaturae," which is Latin for "Behold the face by which all things are done, which all creatures obey." To the best of my knowledge, this is not a Torah quote.

In Mather's version of this pentacle (shown on page 152), within the circle is an image of a bearded man with horns and rays of light shining from his head. Behind the head is the familiar name שדי אל or El Shaddai. Despite the fact that Mathers clearly intends this image as "the countenance of Shaddai," it is strikingly similar to many depictions of Moses, including Michelangelo's famous statue. (See page 152.)

In classical art, gods and other beings of power were often shown as having curling ram horns. This iconography, called the "horns of Amun," is inherited from Egypt. As Amun,[4] and later Amun-Ra, rose to the head of his pantheon, his horns became a symbol of the power of divine kingship. Both Zeus and the God of Israel were syncretized with Amun and were often depicted wearing his horns. The horned iconography later became associated with Moses. Shemot (Exodus) 34:29, when describing Moses descending from Sinai with the Tablets of the Pact, portrays him as having קרן (*keren*), a word which can mean horn, but can also mean a ray or beam of light. Rashi explains it thus: "קרן is an expression connected with the word קרנים, 'horns,' and the phrase קרן אור, the 'light horned,' is used here because light radiates from a point and projects like a horn."

Mathers goes on to say, "This singular pentacle contains the head of the great angel Methraton or Metatron, the vice-regent and representative of Shaddai, who is called the Prince of Countenances, and the right-hand masculine cherub of the Ark, as Sandalphon is the left and feminine."

Metatron is a second-in-command lesser god or superangel in Jewish and Christian myth. His name is of unclear origin. Some say its root is the Hebrew מטר (*matar*), which means "rain," perhaps highlighting the God of Israel's role as a storm king. Others say it is from the Greek μετὰ (*meta*) θρόνος (*thronos*), or "before the throne." Personally, I believe its roots intersect with the Indo-Iranian (Aryan) god Mitra, the Oath Binder. Mitra is a god of truth, justice, and light who is often depicted as emanating rays of light. Over time, Mitra gave his name to the Zoroastrian Mithra, the Judge of Compacts, and the Roman Mithras, whose mystery cult was deeply embedded in the imperial army.

The equation of Metatron with Shaddai, which is quite traditional, is rooted in *gematria,* a type of Hebrew numerology. The claim is:

Shaddai = שׁדי‎ = 10+4+300 = 50+6+200+9+9+40 = מטטרון‎ = Metatron

However, since I do not believe Metatron to be a natively Hebrew word, I find this argument rather weak.

You can use the pentacle as Mathers does, with the face, but personally my Jewish upbringing has left me uncomfortable drawing a humanoid face and labeling it El Shaddai. Instead, I make my pentacles with the geometric representation called "Metatron's Cube," as you saw above.

Metatron's Cube is, as the name implies, an orthographic projection (that is, a flattened diagram) of a three-dimensional figure. Metatron's Cube is often understood as a sacred shape which depicts the harmonious unity of creation; it is understood to contain all shapes within it. It depicts the five so-called Platonic solids (convex[5] regular[6] polyhedra[7]) all embedded in the same sphere. There are only five[8] Platonic solids.

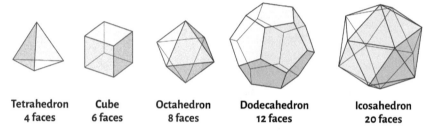

Tetrahedron	Cube	Octahedron	Dodecahedron	Icosahedron
4 faces	6 faces	8 faces	12 faces	20 faces

Traditionally, the Platonic solids are associated with the elements, as follows:

- The tetrahedron with fire because it is pointy, like fire.

- The cube with earth because it is stable, like earth.

- The octahedron with air. Plato explains this is because matter composed of octahedra is light, like the air, but I don't really understand why octahedra are lighter than other shapes.

- The dodecahedron with water because the almost-spherical shape is slippery, like water.

- The icosahedron with ether, again for reasons I do not entirely follow.

They are also sometimes associated with the planets,[9] because of something German astronomer Johannes Kepler called the "cosmographic mystery." If the Platonic solids are nested together (as pictured on page 154), then the distances between their enclosing spheres are (somewhat close to) the same as the sizes of the orbits of the planets. However, when Kepler acquired access to more precise measurements and discovered that the orbits of the planets are not circular but elliptical,[10] he abandoned this theory.

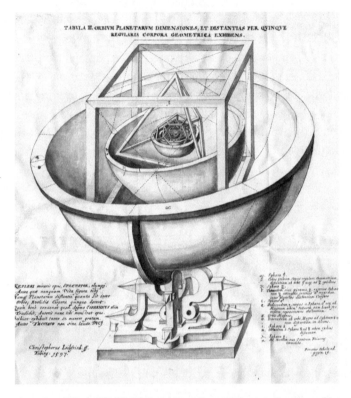

Kepler's Platonic solid model of the Solar system from *Mysterium Cosmographicum* (1600)

I particularly like this pentacle and use it extensively, especially for Merkavah, which we discuss further in the Jupiter chapter, in relation to the pentacle I call Jakob's Ladder.

☉ 3: The Twelvefold Name of G-d

MATHERS SAYS OF THIS pentacle that it is used "to acquire kingdom and empire, to inflict loss, and to acquire renown and glory." I understand this pentacle to be intended for use in wars of conquest; however, I most often use it for renown and glory in business, often in conjunction with advertising or job interviews. It can also be used to acquire companies, real estate, or other property.

As Mathers presents it, the versicle says:

שלטני שלטן עלם ומלכותי עם דר ודר

However, I think it probably should say:

שלטנה שלטן עלם ומלכותה עם-דר ודר

With this small spelling correction in the first (rightmost) word, this is Daniel 4:31 and means "Their dominion rules forever, and Their kingdom from generation to generation." Our pentacle reflects this correction.

We discussed squares when we learned about the Square of Venus; they are a symbol of stability and foundation. When squares are nested inside one another, an illusion of depth is created, expanding the foundation of the square up into a tower and establishing a fortress-like perimeter. Similarly, squares inscribed within circles have their own special powers.

The Square in the Circle

As you perhaps recall from your schooling, Pythagoras was a Greek philosopher, mathematician, and sorcerer who lived in the 5th century BCE. Along with a school of many other important thinkers of his day, including his wife Theano, Pythagoras revolutionized Greek thought, both rational and mystical. Millennia later, the influence of Pythagorean philosophy continues to be woven throughout our entire culture; you literally learned some of our cult mysteries in high school. Today, the Pythagorean cult is best known for our teachings on right triangles, number theory, reincarnation, and Orphic ritual.

Among the central tenets of early Pythagorean cosmology was the idea that numbers (by which they meant ratios of counting numbers, what we would call "rational[11] numbers" or "proper fractions") were the fundamental building blocks out of which Creation was woven. That belief, in conjunction with deep contemplation of the square inscribed within the circle, induces a very specific mystic trance state which Pythagoreans call "knowledge of incommensurability" or sometimes "knowledge of irrationality."[12] It is beyond the scope of this book for me to lead you through every step of this Mystery. However, if you know high school geometry, or are willing to learn it, it is well within your power to achieve such a state yourself.

CONTEMPLATIVE PRACTICE: SEEK KNOWLEDGE OF INCOMMENSURABILITY

To seek knowledge of incommensurability, strive to understand the relationship between the size (diameter) of the circle and the size (side length) of the inscribed square. What is the ratio between them?

Seek to understand why, no matter what scale you choose to draw it at, the ratio between the circle's diameter and the side length of the square will never be captured in whole numbers or their ratios.[13]

And yet, does not the orderly operation of the kosmos depend on harmonious and rational relationships between fully understandable coherent ideas, that is to say, on ratios of whole numbers?[14]

Next, sit in contemplation of this: Our senses are insufficient to measure what is. No matter how fine the marks, no ruler will allow us to precisely measure both the diameter of a circle and the side lengths of its inscribed square. What other things are incommensurable? What else can't we measure with our mundane senses?

• • •

So, on this pentacle, we have nested squares, a sign of fortified material sovereignty, inscribed inside a circle-versicle about G-d's eternal sovereignty. The pentacle bridges these incommensurable ideas by use of the Most Holy Name, which appears twelve times. As we discussed when we studied the All-Knowing Dodecagram, the number twelve is extremely important in Jewish magic as a symbol of cosmic order, owing largely to an inheritance from Babylonian mathematics and astrology. There are twelve jurors on a jury, and twelve months in a year, all arising from this same cultural construct of the number twelve as a symbol of cosmic harmony and just order.[15] We also discussed how twelve is a desirable number for complex calculations, because it has many factors. By investigating those factors, we discover that, as the product of three and four, twelve partakes of the generative power of the triangle and the stable power of the square. As the product of two and six, twelve partakes of two's ability to even things out with six's harmonious beauty.

Putting everything together, we begin to develop a kavvanah about how this pentacle draws on the power of just kingship and harmonious cosmic order, and then mirrors it down into our material world as earthly kingship, status, and power.

This is one of my favorite pentacles. I like to combine it with the Seal of Sheba for interviews, performances, and other situations in which one really wants to shine with charisma. As we discussed previously, in Hebrew a person whose charismatic shine allows them to hold the attention of a crowd is called a kohelet. Solomon is the quintessential Kohelet, and this combination of pentacles allows us to wear his garment of splendor.

☉ 4: The Wheel of HaShem Adonai

MATHERS SAY THAT THIS pentacle will ". . . enable thee to see the spirits when they appear invisible unto those who invoke them; because, when thou hast uncovered it, they will immediately appear visible." The versicle, which is from Tehillim 13:4-5, says, "Enlighten my eyes, lest I sleep the sleep of death. Lest my enemy say 'I beat him!'" This short psalm is David's plea to a god who seems to have turned his back on him. David begs that he be allowed to Know once more. According to Talmud[16] this psalm is sung "to the One who rejoices when conquered." This seems very fitting for a pentacle designed to open the eyes to the hidden.

Inside is an eight-spoked solar wheel. In the hub of the wheel is written, starting at the top and going counterclockwise, יהוה אדני, HaShem Adonai. We've discussed both of these names and their combination at length already. At the circumference of the wheel, each spoke is topped with an inward facing triangle and a character from the Passing the River alphabet, which we discussed in conjunction with the Square of Venus. Starting at the top and decrypting counterclockwise gives the same name, יהוה אדני (HaShem Adonai).

I like to use this pentacle, in combination with the Conjurer's Hook, to help open psychic senses for people who are having trouble accessing them. To do that, make a pentacle with the Wheel of HaShem on one side and the Conjurer's Hook on the other. Lie down under direct Sun, close your eyes, and put the pentacle on your forehead, wheel side down. Feel the hand on the hook pushing down. Feel the heat of the Sun warming the wheel, which slowly begins to spin, drilling in. This can be a little scary or uncomfortable; just breathe through it. If the discomfort rises to the level of panic or pain, take the pentacle off, get out of the Sun, drink some water, and sing for a while. Take a few days off and then apply the treatment again. It's okay to split it up over several sessions. You can also put an awakened pentacle in a container of any vision-supporting herb to provide a bit of a boost, and then drink the herb as tea or smoke it from a pipe. The Wheel of HaShem Adonai can also be combined with the All-Knowing Dodecagram to improve spirit communication skills, and with the Triangle of Shaddai, which we will discuss shortly.

☉ 5 The Square of AGLA

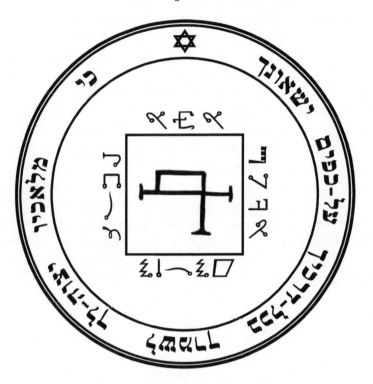

THIS IS A SLIGHT MODIFICATION of Mathers's fifth pentacle of the Sun, about which he says, "It serveth to invoke those spirits who can transport thee from one place unto another, over a long distance and in short time." Personally, I use it primarily to aid in travel in the Other Place.

The versicle is from Tehillim 91:11-12 and says, "Because He will give His angels charge over you, to keep you in all your ways. They shall bear you upon their hand." In Jewish communities, this psalm is frequently recited as a protective charm, including at burials. It is also commonly used in written protective amulets. For example, the medieval text *Shimush Tehillim* (Uses of the Psalms), reputedly written by the 11th century Iraqi *gaon* (genius/school-master) Hai ben Sherira, suggests it be recited, along with #90, for "recovery from illness. Protection against lions or evil spirits or any form of evil," and notes that it can also be used as a written amulet.

Inside is a square with an inscribed circle. Inside the circle is a stylized sigil, which I believe to represent a saddle. Around the square in Mathers's version, in badly corrupted Passing the River cipher, is written (counterclockwise from top right):

אתאד ?יב?? פל??למ אדנ

After consulting several other manuscripts and the spirit of Solomon, Magician King, I believe it should say (counterclockwise from the top), אתה גבור לעולם אדני (Atah Gibor Leolam Adonai), which literally means "You are mighty forever, Adonai." Encrypting that into Passing the River gives our pentacle the Name of Power אגלא (AGLA), a *notarikon* (a type of Kabbalistic acronym) of this phrase. We will discuss this name further in the next chapter, along with the pentacle called The Shield of AGLA.

☉ 6: The Triangle of Shaddai

MATHERS'S SIXTH AND PENULTIMATe pentacle of the Sun is the Triangle of Shaddai, about which he says: "It serveth excellently for the operation of invisibility, when correctly made." While I have never successfully made one correctly enough to become literally invisible, I have found this pentacle extremely effective for obfuscating, hiding, lying, and keeping secrets private. The versicle is pieced together from Tehillim 69:24 and 135:16. In some ways, it is the opposite of the versicle of the Wheel of HaShem Adonai.

תחשכנה עיניהם, מראות; ומתניהם, תמיד המעד.

Let their eyes be darkened, that they see not;
and make their loins continually totter.

עינים להם, ולא יראו:

Eyes have they, but they see not.

Inside the versicle is a point-up equilateral triangle, a sign of fire and the Great Father. Around the triangle, starting on the left and going counterclockwise, is written in Passing the River: בראשית ברא אלהים את השמים ואת הארץ. Note that Mathers's version is missing the aleph in בראשית (Bereshit), which has been corrected in our pentacle. This is the opening line of Torah: "When Beginning,[17] Elohim made the heavens and the land."

Within that triangle, contained in the formless void, is the name שדי (Shaddai), the roiling god of the wild. Within that is a circle containing another triangle, which I understand to be both the Celestial Alphabet character for yod (י) and the hidden and eternal flame. The so-called Celestial Alphabet is another of Agrippa's Hebrew ciphers. We will see it again in the next chapter.

I think this is perhaps the most beautiful of all the pentacles. The carefully constructed nesting layers of darkness and confusion, shielding and cloaking the eternal flame in the middle, speak to me very powerfully. I like to combine it with the Wheel of HaShem Adonai for situations where I'd like to be able to hide while seeing invisible things; for example I use it for "running silent" in the Other Place, as well as for clandestine operations here on Earth. For this work, I imagine holding the Wheel of HaShem in my left hand, face up. I imagine the Triangle of Shaddai rising up out of my palm, through the wheel, as a small flame, sometimes atop a candle, which both lights my way and keeps me hidden from others, like a medieval Hand of Glory.

☉ 7: The Angelic Iron Cross

I CALL MATHERS'S FINAL solar pentacle the Angelic Iron Cross. Mathers says about this pentacle: "If any be by chance imprisoned or detained in fetters of iron, at the presence of this pentacle, which should be engraved in Gold on the day and hour of the Sun, he will be immediately delivered and set at liberty." The versicle, from Tehillim 116:16-17, says, "You have freed me. I will offer thanksgiving sacrifice, and I will call upon the name HaShem."

The interior is a complicated diagram depicting an inscribed circle turned inside out within its circumscribing square. Within that are two sets of four angel names. Inside the perimeter of Mathers's square, counterclockwise from the top, we have the following names, each of which I'll discuss in more depth below.

- חסן Hasan
- אראל Erel
- פורלאך Purlach
- טל-יחד Tel Yechud

The name at the top, Hasan (חסן), is a common (human) name meaning "the strong one." Mathers calls this an angel of the air. On the left is Erel or Arel (אראל), which means "Valiant One." This name may be more familiar in the plural; the Erelim (or Arelim) are a well-known choir of angels. In Isaiah 44:7 they are said to be angels of peace. Traditionally, the Erelim are understood as fiery angels of compassion who weep at the thought of Isaac's sacrifice and who gather up the righteous dead.

At the bottom, we find Purlach (פורלאך), whose name is slightly less familiar. The word *pur* (פור) literally means "bowl," but it is also a type of Akkadian divination by casting of lots in which a soothsayer tosses stones in a bowl to answer questions, and I believe this to be the context here. *Lak* (לאך or לאכ) is a three-letter root which gives rise to a large category of words related to sending, serving, working, being an employee, or completing a goal. Thus we can understand Purlach as an earth angel who could be called something like "Servant of Fate."

Finally, on the right, we have Tel Yechud (טל-יחד). *Tel* (טל) means "dew," and *yechud* (יחד) is a root that gives rise to a family of words related to unity and togetherness, including the Name of Power, אחד (Achad), which I've mentioned before. I believe it should, instead, read אל יחד (El Yichad), the El of Drawing Together, and that is how it is written in our pentacle.

Across the diagonal are four more angelic names. The name in the upper left, Ariel (אריאל), is a famous angel whose name means "Lion of El." Although the etymological connection is unclear, many consider Aral (אראל) and Ariel (אריאל) the same angel, leader of the choir of Arelim (אראלים). In addition to being the proper name of a specific angel, Ariel is also a poetic name for the city of Jerusalem.[18] Ezekiel uses Ariel as a name for the eternal flame of the high altar in the new temple to come (in chapter 43 of The Book of Ezekiel).

The name in the bottom left, Seraph (שרף), is another famous angel more commonly known in the plural, as the Seraphim (שרפים). The root שרף means "to burn," and the seraphim are often described as burning (venomous) serpents. In the sixth chapter of Isaiah they are described thus: ". . . I saw Adonai sitting upon a high throne, lifted up, and His train filled the temple. Above Him stood the seraphim; each one had six wings: with two each covered their face and with two each covered their feet, and with two each did fly. . . . Then one of the seraphim flew to me, with a glowing stone in his hand, which he had taken with the tongs from off the altar; and he touched my mouth with it. . . ."

On the bottom right, we find the name Keruv (כרוב), whose name is often Anglicized as "Cherub." The Keruvim (Cherubim) are another well-known choir of angels, whose name derives from a Proto-Semitic root meaning "to bless." These angels are often depicted as griffins, or as four elemental animals (usually, bull, eagle, lion, and human), or as four-headed creatures with heads of each elemental animal. They are often tasked with holding up the Heavenly Throne, and their statues grace the Arc of the Covenant.

Finally, in the top right, the name is Tarshish (תרשיש). The leader of the Tarshishim (תרשישים), Tarshish is often given as the name of the angel that delivered Daniel from the lion's den. That passage describes the angel thus: ". . . a man clad in linen, and his loins were girded with a cluster of pearls. His body was like Tarshish, and his face was like lightning. His eyes were like fire-brands, his legs were like burnished copper, and the sound of his voice was like a clamoring crowd."[19] In plaintext readings, *tarshish* is understood to be a type of gemstone or precious metal, perhaps amber or electrum. It is also the name of a (possibly legendary) place, far to the west of Israel. Solomon's mines in Tarshish were the source of much of his fabulous wealth.

I like to combine this pentacle back-to-back with Under El's Wing for protection against fear and anxiety. Personally, I find it a little more protection than I want in most circumstances; too much protection magic tends to dull my senses. However, I often make this for clients who prefer more protection than I do.

Exercises

■ Teach at least one Solar pentacle to your Book.

■ Make a wearable talisman by cloning a pentacle out of your Book onto a scroll that you put in a locket or other case, or by cloning a book pentacle onto a pre-engraved metal pentacle. Wear your talisman and keep track of how you and others feel, act, and behave differently when you are wearing it.

■ Contemplate incommensurability.

♂

The Pentacles of Mars

Rabbi Nahman ben Isaac observed: "He who is born under Mars will be a shedder of blood. Rabbi Ashi observed: Either a surgeon, a thief, a slaughterer, or a 'mohel' (a performer of ritual circumcision)."

—TALMUD SHABBAT 156A:11-12

M ars is often called the Red Planet, a name that arises from its color, visible with the naked eye from Earth. This rusty coloration is caused by iron oxide (also the main component of earthly rust). Likely because its color is so similar to dried blood,[1] Mars is closely associated with war in Western cultures. It is from Mars's Latin (and thus English) name that our word "martial" derives. In addition to war, Mars is the patron planet of plow agriculture, hunting, animal husbandry,[2] and all things male, masculine, and butch.

The Greek name for the planet Mars is Ἄρης (Ares), which is of unclear, possibly pre-Greek, origin. The Hebrew name for this planet is מאדים (Maadim), which we discuss further with the wheel pentacle. The color of Mars is red, and its metal is iron. Animals associated with Mars include the wolf, bear, and snake. Mars has no strong numerical associations, but 5, 9, and 25 are loosely Martial. Some say Michael is the angel of Mars, but I believe Gabriel to be a better choice. Others suggest Camuel or Uriel (Auriel).

As with all of the planetary divinities, Mars is much degraded in our culture. Just as Venus is reduced to a bimbo, Mars is reduced to a brute. This is an unfair characterization. Before the rise of the Roman empire, the Latin Mars's martiality was not that of an imperial army of conscripts and slaves, but rather a volunteer coalition of fighters who came together in times of trouble to defend their own. Mars is the strong iron fence that separates the safety of home from the dangerous adventures of the wild.

Although often seen through the eyes of a petty and vengeful upper class, the pentacles of Solomon are the martial magic of the wisest king who ever lived, of the author of Kohelet, who lived for years as a wandering beggar and came home to administer a just peace. They cover a range of martial possibilities.

♂ 1: The Wheel of Mars

MATHERS DESCRIBES THE Wheel of Mars as ". . . proper for invoking spirits of the nature of Mars, especially those which are written in the pentacle." For reasons I do not understand, Mathers's edition presents this pentacle rotated forty-five degrees counterclockwise from how we have shown it above. We have put it in the same position as the other wheels, with the planetary angel (Madimiel) at the top. Since I understand these pentacles to be "wheels," they do not really have a "correct" orientation. Wheels are meant to spin.

These are the spirits who are written around the pentacle, counterclockwise from the top:

- מאדימיאל Madimiel[3]
- ברצהיה B'ritzayah
- אשיאל Eshiel
- אתאוריאל Ithuriel

The first name is the El of Madim (מאדים), which is the Hebrew name for the planet Mars. It derives from the root אדם (Adam) and, in this context, is generally understood to mean "red." It can also mean "soil," "clay," and "earth." It is also related to the very old root דמם, which means "blood" or "silence." All of these meanings come into play as roots of All-Father Adam's name, but in the context of the angel of Mars, the name surely refers to the color of the planet. Madimiel is the El of the Red Planet.

The bottom left name is B'ritzayah (ברצהיה). The letter ב, when it appears at the beginning of a word, sometimes functions as a preposition meaning "at" or "in" or "with." I believe that to be the case here. The root word, רצה, gives rise to a family of words related to wanting. This name can be understood as "The Jah Much Desired" or "The Jah Who Satisfies Desire." This reading is influenced by the angelic instruction I mentioned when we discussed the All-Knowing Dodecagram that "We angels try to meet the yearnings in your heart . . . it's in our nature . . . we are beings that satisfy desires."

In the bottom right is Eshiel (אשיאל), whose name uncomplicatedly means "Fire El" or "Fire of El." The word "esh" or "aish," meaning fire, is (like the letter shin [ש] itself) onomatopoetic; in it, we hear the hiss of the flame.

Finally, in the top right is Etauriel or Ithuriel (אתאוריאל), whose name is related to the more familiar Auriel (אוריאל), the Light El. Grammatically, the את (et) at the beginning changes the case to the accusative.[4] Their name means something like "(With the) Light of El." Under the spelling Ithuriel, they also appear in *Paradise Lost,* where they are said to have wielded a spear against Satan. Personally, I experience Ithuriel as wielding the Divine Light as a spear, like an extra-long lightsaber.

As with all wheel pentacles, I use this one primarily as a "crank" to build martial power for other pentacles. Most often, I put it on the back of other Mars pentacles, and occasionally I use it as a table of practice for other Martial work.

♂ 2: The Shield of Yeshua

ABOUT THIS PENTACLE Mathers says that it "serveth against all kinds of diseases, if it be applied unto the afflicted part." Around the circumference is a versicle from John 1:4: "In him life was, and that life was light to humans."

In each vertex of the hexagram is the letter ה (*heh*). As we've discussed previously, ה developed under the influence of the Egyptian hieroglyph *hilul*, which means "jubilation" or "praise" and looks like:

In this context, I understand the hehs as a chorus of hallelujahs surrounding the other names, but there are other ways to understand them. For example, in gematria, the letter ה represents the number five and is sometimes used as a substitute for the magical amulet of the open hand, which we discussed in the context of the Great Seal. With this kavvanah, the pentacle takes on a more protective aspect.

At the bottom of the inner hexagon is the name אלהים, Elohim. At the top is יהוה, the Most Holy Name with an extra י (yod) in the middle. Down the center, reusing the י from the top and the ה from the bottom, is יהשוה, the Most Holy Name with a ש (shin) in the middle. This name, often pronounced "Yeshuah," is a common way for Christians to spell Jesus's name in Hebrew, although it is unlikely that was a spelling used during the time in which the Christian gospels are set.[5] I don't really care for this pentacle, and I rarely use it, except in combination with the Cross of AGLA, which we will discuss shortly.

♂ 3: The Triangle of Shaddai Elohim

ABOUT THIS, MATHERS SAYS, "It is of great value for exciting war, wrath, discord, and hostility; also for resisting enemies, and striking terror into rebellious Spirits; the Names of God the All Powerful are therein expressly marked." Around the circumference is the second half of Tehillim 77:14: "What El is as great as Elohim?" This psalm begins with a section where the narrator recounts their anguish. They are kept awake at night with anxious memories. Beginning at verse 11, they start to talk themselves down by recounting good things. This versicle is the peak of that section, where the narrator comforts themself with the knowledge that Elohim works wonders.

Around the outside of the triangle is the name שדי (Shaddai). Within the triangle is אלוה (Eloah), which is a singular version of Elohim. I have been taught that when the name Eloah is used (in preference to Elohim or El), it is to emphasize the Eternity of G-d, whereas El connotes Strength, and Elohim leans into the essential Unity of all things. Given this, I understand this pentacle to be designed to communicate to any spirit (אל) that the bearing magician is operating under the auspices of the Eternal Spirit (אלוה) and thus "outranks" them.

I rarely have occasion to instill wrath and discord,[6] so I don't use this pentacle very much. When I do, it is usually for commanding hostile spirits, particularly those of the restless dead. When made for that purpose, I hold the kavvanah that it serve as a "badge of authority" that I operate under the sanction of Elohim, the Eternal Spirit. Occasionally, I combine this pentacle on my left hand with the Countenance of Shaddai on my right. I find this combination especially effective as a "badge" of spiritual authority and personal sovereignty.

♂ 4: The Cross of AGLA

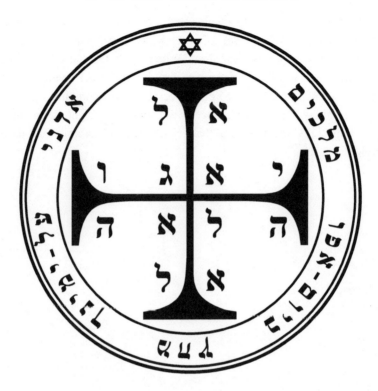

ABOUT THIS STRAIGHTFORWARD pentacle, Mathers says: "It is of great power and virtue in war, wherefore without doubt it will give you victory." The versicle is from Tehillim 110:5: "Adonai is at your right side; he will crush kings on the day of his wrath." This psalm is traditionally[7] understood to be written by King David about Abraham the Patriarch and primarily focuses on reminding the people Israel that G-d (here referenced by the Most Holy Name) will grant victory over enemies. Opinions vary as to whether the "you" in the verse is Father Abraham, the kingdom of Israel under the rule of David, or the entire people Israel throughout all time.

At the top and bottom is the name אל (El). Split across the right and left is the Most Holy Name. At the center of this pentacle is the Name of Power אגלא (AGLA). As we discussed in the previous chapter, this name is generally understood as an acronym for the phrase אתה גבור לעולם אדני (Atah Gibor Leolam Adonai), which means "You are mighty forever, Adonai." For example, the 16th century Polish Kabbalist Yeshayahu Levi Horovitz says about this name: "The letters אגלא are the Name of the attribute גבורה [*geborah;* power], Isaac's special characteristic. The Kabbalists have adopted this name from the words in our daily prayer."[8] אתה גבור לעולם א-דני.

Geborah (גבורה) and gibor (גבור) are both forms of the same root, גבר, GBR, which gives rise to a family of words and names related to bravery, physical strength, political power, and male virility. For example, the angel Gabriel (גבריאל) is the GBR of El. The name AGLA is quite common on protective amulets, both Jewish and Christian.

On one occasion, I was instructed by Saint George to make a steel pentacle with the Shield of Yeshua on one side and the Cross of AGLA on the other for a soldier shipping back out to war. I was instructed that they should wear it with the Shield of Yeshua inside to "heal the broken heart"[9] and the Cross of AGLA on the outside to protect them. Saint George called this a "Templar Shield" and said that it should be worn on a chain with a Saint George medal.

Saint George medals are very common Greek Orthodox amulets, often worn by soldiers. They depict Saint George on horseback using a lance to subdue a dragon. I did not know this at the time I was taught to make the Templar Shield, but while researching for this book, I learned that Saint George's iconography likely derives from older Greek magical gems which depict Solomon.[10]

Drawing by Jon Goodfellow after amulet in the British Museum.

The particular amulet pictured[11] was carved into black hematite[12] in the 4th century CE. One side depicts King Solomon, with his name ΣΟΛΟΜωΝ in Greek on the left and top, on horseback spearing a demoness, whom some say is Lilith. The back reads σφραγὶς θεοῦ ("seal of God").

♂ 5: Scorpion Power

ABOUT THIS PENTACLE, MATHERS SAYS: "Write this pentacle on virgin[13] parchment or paper. It is terrible unto demons, and at its sight they will obey you, for they cannot resist its presence." The versicle is from Tehillim 91:13. It says: "You will tread on cubs and vipers; you will trample lions and asps."[14] As I mentioned in the previous chapter, this psalm is common in Jewish protective amulets.

Around the inner perimeter of Mathers's pentacle is the word הול (*hul*) four times. I do not believe that to be a word. However, the very similar-looking word חיל (*khayil*) means "power," "valor," or "military might" and can also mean more specifically "army corps." This seems far more fitting for this pentacle, and so that is what I use when I make it. Another option is to read it as a variation of הלל, a root closely related to the Egyptian hieroglyph hilul, which we discussed earlier in this chapter.

In the center of the talisman is a scorpion. For the most part, in Jewish teaching, scorpions are considered aggressive omens of ill fortune. However, they are also sometimes used as protective symbols, a usage also common in many other Levantine cultures.

For example, on Turkish *kilim* rugs, this symbol (a stylized scorpion, with six legs, a head, and a tail) is called *akrep*[15] and is used for protection.[16] Described as a scorpion, or sometimes a dragon,[17] it is used to protect against scorpions and, more generally, against evil spirits. Because I find the scorpion very difficult to engrave, I often use this symbol instead of a scorpion when I make this pentacle, particularly when I intend it primarily for protection. When I do so, I hold the kavvanah that Akraviel (עקרביאל), the Scorpion El, awaken the pentacle to stand as my sentry.

♂ 6 Elohim of the Grave

THIS PENTACLE, SAYS MATHERS, ". . . hath so great virtue that, being armed therewith, thou shalt neither be injured nor wounded when thou fightest with him, and his own weapons shall turn against him." The versicle is from Tehillim 37:15, and says: "Their swords shall pierce their own hearts, and their bows shall be broken." The antecedent of "their" is in the previous verse: "the wicked . . . [who] bring down the lowly and needy [and] slaughter upright men." That is to say, this pentacle serves to turn the weapons of wicked oppressors back onto them. Mathers accompanies the versicle with a symbol, which I understand to represent a broken arrow. He draws it as an arrow with a box around it, but we have chosen a more modern way to represent a broken arrow.

The symbols around the spokes of the wheel are from a magical cipher called the Secret Alphabet of the Malachim popularized by Heinrich Cornelius Agrippa in his 16th century *Three Books of Occult Philosophy*. Using the table below, we can decrypt it. Counterclockwise from the top, it reads אלהים קבר

(Elohim Kavar). QBR (קבר) gives rise to a family of words related to burial, tombs, and graves. It is related to a larger family of words that include the root קב (QB), which related to downward or inward motion.[18]

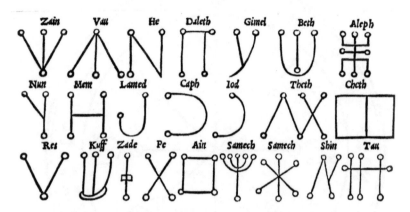

The Secret Alphabet of the Malachim. Cornelius Agrippa, 1651.

In the context of the pentacle, I understand Elohim QBR as "Elohim of the Grave" or "Elohim Undertaker," suggesting that the intent of the pentacle is not just to turn your enemies' weapons away from you, but to turn them against your enemies, putting them in their grave, just as Mathers says.

♂ 7 The Martial Octagram

MATHERS SAYS THAT THIS, his final martial pentacle, produces hail and tempest when "you invoke the names of the Demons written herein, and uncover it within the Circle." The versicle for this pentacle is from Tehillim 105: 32-33.

:נתן גשמיהם ברד אש להבות בארצם

.ויך גפנם ותאנתם וישבר עץ גבולם

He gave them hail for rain, and flaming fire in their land. He struck their vines and fig trees, broke down the trees of their boundaries.

Unfortunately, the names of those demons Mathers references are not entirely clear. In the center is the familiar name אל (El) along with the uncommon ייאי. This obscure name occurs in the 17th century kabbalistic text *Sha'ar ha-Kavvanot* (Gate of Intention).[19] The section in which the name

יא״י appears deals with kavvanot to be held during the bedtime prayers, in order to induce a soul-dismemberment dream (or perhaps trance experience) for the purposes of hastening one's escape from the cycle of *gilgulim* (reincarnation). This is a dense and difficult text that I do not recommend except to Kabbalah nerds.

The text[20] recommends the following mind experiment to form the name יא״י from the Most Holy Name:

1. Spell out each letter
   - yod (יד)
   - heh (הי)
   - vav (ואו)
   - heh (הי)

2. Eliminate all letters except yod and aleph: יד הי ואו הי.

3. Pray Tehillim 31:6, "Into your hand I entrust my spirit; you redeem me, HaShem El Emet."

4. While you pray, focus on this name (יא״י) in conjunction with the name El (אל).

The connection between the two names is this: Three yods can be combined into a lamed, thus connecting יא״י with אל. This is for two reasons: The character used for the letter yod (י) is also used for the number ten, and the character used for lamed (ל) is also used for thirty. However, it is also because the character ל is composed of three strokes, each of which is itself a yod.

The text continues, explaining that יא״י can also be produced from a similar expansion of Ehyeh (אהיה) as אלף הי יד הי. It relates this formulation to the Divine Mother, saying ". . . Imma [Mother], who is the secret of אהיה [Ehyeh] . . . consisting of three yods and an aleph which is the name יא״י. And from it are formed אל." We will discuss this enigmatic name further in the next chapter, in conjunction with the pentacle called Square of Saturn.

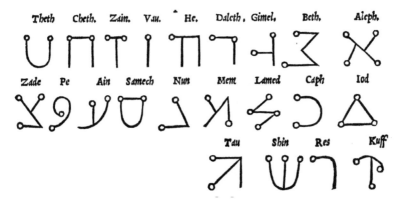

The cipher called *Scriptura Celestis*. Cornelius Agrippa, 1651.

Using another cipher of Agrippa, we can decrypt the symbols on the exterior of the octagram back into Hebrew, which gives the pentacle in our book. Because I am intensely opposed to the weaponization of weather in a destabilized climate, I have chosen not to translate this pentacle further. Proceed at your own risk.

4

The Pentacles of Jupiter

And the statement which comes fifth [i.e., the fifth commandment],
which is "honor" [your parents], is in relation to the sphere Jupiter
and points toward peace and justice and compassion, and the
payment of wages and resect which are owed.

—IBN EZRA, COMMENTARY ON EXODUS 20:14:1

Jupiter is the largest of the planets; it is more than twice as massive as all the other planets put together. In traditional astrology, one name for this planet is "Greater Beneficent." Jupiter rules expansion: it can help grow your bank account, your influence, and your empire. As the planet of expansion, Jupiter is a complex and sometimes fraught power in our culture. Unchecked expansion is fucking up our planet and our lives very badly right now.

Jupiter's English name, like that of most of the planets, derives from the name of the Roman god associated with it. Roman Iupiter is part of a family of gods whose names all arise from the Indo-European *Dyēu-pəter* ("Sky Father" or "God the Father"). For example, "Zeus Pater" is his Greek incarnation. Jupiter rules Patriarchy, as well as both leadership and fatherhood more broadly. For a long time, I didn't really get on with this power, but when I became a school administrator, I found myself in a position of power over people I barely knew. It was Jupiter to whom I turned for help leading wisely and well.

The planet Jupiter is a god of kings and a king of gods. He wields lightning with absolute authority. Jupiter's colors are the light bright blue of the sky and imperial purple. He is associated with eagles, bulls, and oak trees. To my mind, there are no strong number associations for Jupiter, but if pressed, I would say four, twelve, and one hundred. The scent I most strongly associate with Jupiter is cedar, and his traditional metal is tin.

The Hebrew name for Jupiter is צדק (*Tzedek*), which is difficult to translate, but I like "Righteous One." It is closely related to many other Semitic names for the god of the planet Jupiter, including the Phoenician Sydyk and the Ugaritic Ṣaduq. The root צדק gives rise to a huge family of difficult-to-translate words with meanings like "to give charity," "mercy," "compassion," "loving-kindness," "righteous," "saint," and "right action."

The angel of Jupiter is, unsurprisingly, Tzadkiel (צדקיאל). This is the angel that, they say, stayed Abraham's hand when he raised it to kill Isaac. He is said, by some, to be the leader of the Hasmalim, and by others to be the Angel of the Violet Flame. However, he is most renowned as the angel of *tzedakah*. Tzedakah (צדקה) is usually translated as "mercy" or "charity," but those are not good translations because of cultural differences in the way charity is understood. The Lubavitcher Rebbe explains: "'Charity' commonly means alms, gratuitous benefactions for the poor. The giver of charity is a benevolent person, giving when he need not. He does not owe the poor anything, but gives because of his generosity. 'Tzedakah' has a completely opposite meaning. Instead of connoting benevolence, it is the idea of justice—that it is only right and just that one gives tzedakah."[1] On this particular issue, I agree with him.

♃ 1: The Wheel of Jupiter

THIS PENTACLE, MATHERS SAYS, "serveth to invoke the Spirits of Jupiter, and especially those whose Names are written around the Pentacle, among whom Parasiel is the Lord and Master of Treasures, and teacheth how to become possessor of places wherein they are." Although I do not disagree with Mathers's assessment of this pentacle, I think it is better understood, in our modern world, as distributing gifts and treasure to the righteous as well as wiping away bad reports and unfavorable accounting. I most often make it for clients who are hoping to improve their credit score, particularly in combination with the Triangle of Shaddai, which we discussed in the Mars chapter.

Like all of the wheel pentacles, this one features an eight-pointed asterisk tipped with a variety of mystical characters and surrounded by four names of power. In this case, the names are (counterclockwise from the top):

- נתוניאל Netanial
- דוחיה Duachiah
- צדקיה Tzedekiah
- פרסיאל Parsiel or Parasiel

Compared to the other wheel pentacles, it is unusual that Tzedekiah appears at the bottom instead of the top. However, since I understand them to be, literally, wheels, I do not think these pentacles have a correct orientation; they are intended to spin.

Focusing in on the three remaining names helps us learn more about this pentacle and its uses. The name at the top, Netanial, appears to me to derive from the root נתנ (*natan*) which is both a word meaning "to give" or "gift," and also the proper name, Nathan. Solomon's teacher, the great prophet, bore this name. Notice that this name (נתוניאל) is spelled slightly differently from the more familiar נתנאל (Nathaniel), which is normally translated as "El Has Given." This name I would translate as "El Will Have Given." In the context of the pentacle, it seems clear that what El will have given is treasure and Jovial bounty.

On the right, is the name פרסיאל, Parasiel. The root פרס can mean "spread out" or "divide," but can also mean "reward," "treasure," or "prize." As in many ancient languages, these two meanings are closely related—such reward was generally communal, with each receiving their own cut. In the context of the pentacle, it seems clear that Parasiel is the angel who distributes treasures.

Finally, the name on the left, Duachiah, comes from the word דוח (*duach*) appended to the divine name Jah. In biblical Hebrew, the root דוח (DVKh) means "rinse away" and that may be the root in play here. However, דוח (D.V.Kh.) is also a rabbinic abbreviation for דין וחשבון (*din v'kheshbon*) a phrase that literally means "law and account" and figuratively means "legal obligation." For example, the Jerusalem Talmud makes use of this phrase while discussing the legal obligation of cities to provide free public access to doctors, bathhouses, courts of justice, and vegetable gardens.[2] Later, it uses the same phrase to say that each of us will, after our death, be held legally liable for every pleasure from which we abstained.[3] Personally, I often use a bit of rabbinic-style wordplay magic with both meanings to construct kavvanot for this name. I exhort Duachiah to fulfill his lawful obligation to uphold the rights of the underclass by rinsing away bad reports from financial power structures, such as credit reporting agencies.

As with most wheel pentacles, I most often use this one as a crank to build power for other pentacles. In particular, I often employ it on the reverse of the Hexagram of Ab Ehyeh or the Wheel of Fortune, both of which we discuss later in this chapter.

♃ 2: The Hexagram of Ab Ehyeh

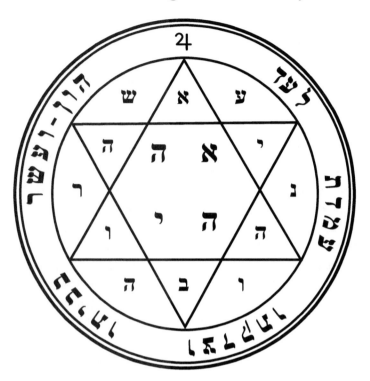

THIS PENTACLE, WHICH I CALL the Hexagram of Ab Ehyeh, is one of my favorites. About it, Mathers says: "This is proper for acquiring glory, honours, dignities of all kinds, together with great tranquility of mind; also to discover Treasures and chase away the Spirits who preside over them." He further instructs it should be "written on virgin paper[4] with the blood of a swallow and a screech owl."[5] In my personal practice, I use this pentacle almost exclusively for "acquiring glory, honours, and dignities of all kinds," particularly for acquiring patronage from rich and powerful benefactors, both human and otherwise. This pentacle is of particular value to people named Sarah (or Sara) for reasons which will soon be clear.

The versicle is from Tehillim 112:3 and reads: "Wealth and riches will be in their house, and their beneficence endures forever." In the context of the psalm, "them" does not refer to G-d, but rather "the person who is in awe of the Lord, who greatly desires His instruction." Talmud suggests that the verse also applies to "everybody who keeps a Torah scroll in his house."[6] Notice that the word וצדקתו, which I have translated here as "beneficence," is a form of צדקה (Tzedakah).

The hexagram is a very important symbol in modern Judaism, but it was less important in the days of Solomon. Today, it is used as the primary sign of Jewish identity, but that usage did not arise until the late 16th century. As we discussed previously, the hexagram is sometimes associated with the Seal of Solomon, but today it is more often called the Shield of David. As we discussed in the Venus chapter, hexagrams often represent the fertile union of complementary forces. For example, the upward pointing triangle is often associated with Great Father and the element of fire, whereas the downward pointing one can represent Great Mother and the element of water. Thus, the hexagram represents the essential harmony of creation.

Inside the center hexagon is the by-now-familiar name אהיה (Ehyeh), which means "I will be." In the top and bottom interior triangles, we have אב (Ab), which means "Father." In the horizontal interior triangles is יהוה, the Most Holy Name. On the outside of the hexagram, down the left side, is written שרה, which is the proper name Sarah and means chieftainess.[7] On the right side is written ענו (anu), which is an imperative form of ענה (ana) and means "listen!" or "respond!"

I choose to interpret this pentacle as calling on Ab, the Great Patron, in the name of the Holy One, and saying, "Listen to Sarah!" but I understand why, if your name is not Sarah, you might not want to read it that way. I encourage you to find your own meanings. One option is to start reading the outer letters with the ע in the top-right and continue counterclockwise, which yields עשר הון, which means "ten wealth." Under this reading, the pentacle can be intended to call on the power of Ab Ehyeh with the Most Holy Name to multiply one's wealth tenfold. I particularly like to use this pentacle in combination with the Seal of Sheba for charitable fundraising.

♃ 3: The Conjurer's Seal

ABOUT THIS, MATHERS SAYS: "This defendeth and protecteth those who invoke and cause the Spirits to come. When they appear, show unto them this pentacle, and immediately they will obey." Its versicle is from Tehillim 125:1. It says: "A song of ascents: Those who trust in HaShem are like Mount Zion[8] that cannot be moved, enduring forever." This psalm[9] is called a "song of ascents" because it was traditionally sung by pilgrims climbing to Jerusalem's acropolis.[10] This passage reminds the conjurer of their spiritual authority; like a mountain, the magician cannot be moved from their chosen path.

As we discussed in the Mercury chapter, with The Cross of Father El, the Sun cross ⊕ is generally also a sign of the Sacred Center of Holy Mountain. To use this pentacle to conjure, hold yourself at the Sacred Center, and know that your spiritual authority, rooted in trust of HaShem, is unmovable and eternal.

Mathers's version of this pentacle has the name Adonai in the top right and the Most Holy Name in the bottom left. However, many older manuscripts instead have צדק (Tzedek) at the top right and רוחיה (Ruachiah) below. The names Adonai (Lord) and Tzedek (Righteous/Jupiter) are closely related; they both frame G-d as an overseeing king. Whichever you choose to use, you should hold the kavvanah of G-d as a righteous king while writing those names. Similarly, the Most Holy Name and Ruachiah both call to mind G-d as an enlivening spirit that moment by moment breathes the Becoming into Being. Focus on that kavvanah, no matter which of those two names you use.

Ruach (רוח) arises from a very old Proto-West-Semitic root meaning "wind." It is generally translated as "soul," "spirit," or "breath" in a more literal sense. It is the enlivening essence that departs, never to return, at the moment of death. The word can also mean "cardinal direction."[11]

In the top right, the Most Holy Name is inside a seal, which Agrippa[12] assigns to Jupiter. The seal mimics the cross shape of the whole seal and suggests a pairing between the letters of the Most Holy Name and the four quadrants of the pentacle. In the bottom left is the seal Agrippa gave for the intelligence of Jupiter, Yofiel (יופיאל), whose name is sometimes spelled "Jophiel."[13] The root יפה (YFI) means "to be beautiful." Yofiel is a well-known angel about whom much lore exists.[14] Zohar says that they are "high minister and superior over the camps under the dominion of Michael . . . Yofiel, high minister, is in charge over all of them, for his name does not change."[15] Other sources teach that Yofiel is the chief ministering angel of Torah.[16] The 16th century kabbalistic text Pardes Rimonim (The Orchard of Pomegranates)[17] says: "A level above the four holy creatures, is Yofiel, the angel of Torah, with all the keys of wisdom in his hand."[18] Some say Yofiel is another name for Metatron,[19] others that the two are companions or lovers.

Legendarily, Yofiel is among the angels who buried Moses: "Michael and Gabriel spread forth the golden bed, fastened with chrysolites, gems, and beryls, adorned with hangings of purple silk, and satin, and white linens. Metatron, Jophiel, and Uriel, and Jephephya, the wise sages, laid him upon it, and by His Word He conducted him four miles, and buried him . . . but no man knoweth his sepulchre unto this day."[20]

♃ 4: Wealth Bringer

OF THIS PENTACLE, his fourth Jovial one, Mathers says, "It serves to acquire riches and honor, and to possess much wealth. Its Angel is Bariel. It should be engraved upon silver in the day and hour of Jupiter when he is in the sign of Cancer."

This is not one of my favorite pentacles, particularly because the astrological timing is currently inconvenient. At the time of publication, the next time Jupiter will be in Cancer is June 9, 2025–June 30, 2026. The next after that is May 23, 2037–June 12, 2038. (These dates are for the US Eastern time zone and may require light adjustment elsewhere.) Personally, I believe the geometry of this pentacle to be some sort of astrological diagram. I expect those with sufficient proficiency in astrological magic can adapt the diagram to other Jovially auspicious times.

The versicle here is the same as on the Hexagram of Ab Ehyeh, "Wealth and riches are in his house, and his beneficence lasts forever."[21] Beneath the box on the left is the name אדניאל, Adonai-El. I understand the symbol ⊞ to be a diagram of a building, with four pillars at its corners. The letter ב (*beth*) in the middle, in addition to opening Bariel's name, also means "house." I understand this to be an illustration of the house in the versicle, within which wealth and riches dwell.

The name Bariel (בריאל), whom Mathers mentions, appears on the right-hand side of the pentacle and in the box on the left. It means "The Wholesome El" or "The Nutritious El" and comes from the root ברא (BRA) which means "to fatten." Since this is a pentacle to increase wealth and, for the overwhelming majority of human history, wealth was measured in calories, this makes perfect sense. Some say Bariel is the same as Barachiel (ברכיאל) "The Blessing El," but I do not believe this to be true.

4 5: Jakob's Chariot

THIS, MATHERS'S FOURTH Jovial pentacle, is one of my very favorites. About it, Mathers says: "This hath great power. It serveth for assured visions. Jacob being armed with this Pentacle beheld the ladder which reached unto heaven." The story he references is told in Bereshit 28:11-15. In the story, Jakob lies down to sleep at a holy place and has a powerful dream, wherein he sees a ladder from Earth to Heaven, with angels going up and down it. If you do not already know this story, you should read it before continuing.

This is an important story in Jewish mysticism, and there are many ways to understand it. Ibn Ezra presents many of these in his commentary to verse 12:

> The nature of a ladder [*sulam*] is a symbol [*semel*], or it is an explana-
> tion of the Gematria valuation of "Sinai" (Genesis Rabbah 68:12-14).
> And Rabbi Shlomo HaSefardi said that "ladder" hints at the highest
> soul and "G-d's angels" hints at wise thoughts. Rabbi Joshua said that

the reason for the ladder is that his (Jacob's) prayer rose on it and his salvation from the heavens came down on it. These explanations do not explain it in light of the prophecy of Zecharia (1:8), Amos (7:1), and Jeremiah (1:11). The reason for the ladder here is a metaphor, for nothing is concealed from G-d. Worldly things hang onto the heavens as though there is a ladder between them, upon which the angels go up to report on things after they have been walking along the earth. Likewise, it is written that other angels descend to fulfill G-d's tasks, like a king with his servants.

Because Mathers associates this with Jakob's dream, it would be natural to assume that this pentacle is to be used for dream incubation, and it certainly can be, especially in combination with The Dreamer's Servant. However, its geometry inspires another usage. Recall the so-called Metatron's Cube from the Sun chapter, which we promised to discuss more? I believe the image on this pentacle to be an old-fashioned way to draw the same orthographic projection.

The versicle of this pentacle is Ezekiel 1:1: "And I [Ezekiel] was in the community of exiles[22] by the Chebar Canal,[23] the heavens opened and I saw visions of[24] Elohim."

This passage opens the prophet Ezekiel's account of his first divine vision, his calling to prophecy, which makes up the first chapter of his book. It begins with a storm rolling in from the north, morphs into a chariot drawn by angels, forms into a fractal cloud of wheels and eye and fire and confusion, and then resolves into the Presence of G-d at the end of the chapter.

Although I, like Ezekiel, have described this as a sequence, these things are all happening at once. Even if you are familiar with the story, I encourage you to go read it again now, before continuing the discussion here.

The 18th century Kabbalistic genius (some say, heretic) Moshe Chaim Luzzatto explains: "In some cases the particular components of the power in question unfolded in stages, one after the other, in a gradual developmental sequence. In other cases, the components of the power in question were separated from one another, with one being placed in one location and another in a different location far away from the first. Afterwards, the circuit of the spirit that circulates around all the different parts was instituted, and everything reaches the overall form."[25]

This passage is the mythic backbone of a very old[26] type of Kabbalah, the ecstatic trancework called מעשה מרכבה (Ma'aseh Merkavah) or the Work of the

Chariot. Ma'aseh Merkavah[27] is, at its most basic, a type of spirit-travel to the upper world. Another name for the practice is *Hekhalot* (היכלת), which means "palaces," or "sanctuaries." That name is a reference to the places one travels in the chariot.

Merkavah is almost certainly the oldest living form of Kabbalah; similar techniques of kabbalistic travel are well documented in Talmud, the Dead Sea Scrolls, and much of the apocrypha. The goal of Merkavah mysticism is to partially recreate Ezekiel's experience and ride the chariot (merkavah) into the heavens, there to explore the many palaces (hekhalot). Merkavah is a huge, complex, and sprawling topic outside the scope of this book,[28] but this pentacle can help you learn it. The pentacle can also be used with other types of trance-journey.

The twenty-five letters within the geometric diagram are difficult to understand. They are a rearrangement of the final five words of the versicle: "The heavens opened, and I saw visions of Elohim." The kavvanah I propose for the construction of this pentacle involves making a few minor transpositions from Mathers's version, as shown in the picture below. I will explain my reasoning for these changes below, but it may be difficult to follow if you are entirely unfamiliar with trance journey.

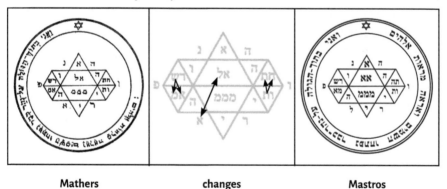

| Mathers | changes | Mastros |

Begin by noticing the ממם in the middle. It's clearly not a word; if it were, the final mem would look like ם. Instead, I understand it as a word-picture. The letter מ represents ocean waves. Remember when I instructed you in Going Below with the Lunar Lock & Key? Recall the "curtain of static" I mentioned? Remember how I said some people interpret it as a waterfall? That's what this is a picture of. Above that, we have a triangle of alephs. Aleph (א) is the first letter; it represents the sound of silence. Imagine saying "uh-oh." Aleph is the sound of your breath between the two syllables. Above the curtain of water is the sacred silence, the veil of Mystery. This is, indeed, the key to Merkavah.

Next, look at the interior triangles on the right and left of the ones we just discussed. Starting in the bottom right and reading counterclockwise, we have the Most Holy Name, יהוה.

Next, we turn our attention to the exterior letters. Starting in the top left and reading counterclockwise, we have נפל (NFL), a root word meaning fall, or descend. Starting at the top right and reading clockwise (including the י at the bottom) we get הורי, which I understand as a form of הורים, which means "parents" or "ancestors."

Finally, let's tackle the two-letter combinations in the triangles on the sides. For these, we connect them each with the א at the top, which gives:

- Top left: ארש (*arash*) which means "compact" or "wish."
- Top right: אתה (*atah*) which means "you."
- Bottom left: אמא (imma) which means "mother."
- Bottom right: אות (oht) which means "sign" or "seal."

Putting all that together, I derive a kavvanah something like: "Descend below to seal the covenant of your mother(s). Do so by holding the sacred silence at your center and sinking though the curtain of water." I find this completely in keeping with both Mathers's description of the purpose of the pentacle, as well as the versicle and geometry. I very often write this pentacle back-to-back with the Countenance of Shaddai, drawn with a Metatron's Cube rather than a face.

♃ 6: Simple Angelic Cross

THIS PENTACLE IS A simpler version of the Angelic Iron Cross of the Sun we previously discussed. Mathers says that it is for ". . . protection against all earthly dangers, by regarding it each day devotedly, and repeating the versicle which surrounded it. Thus, shalt thou never perish." I like to add this pentacle inside mezuzot. The versicle around the edge is from Tehillim 22:16-17: "They pierced my hands and feet; I can count all my bones."[29]

This psalm is often referred to by its first line: "My G-d, my G-d, why hast thou forsaken me?" Jews generally understand the "me" here to be King David (its legendary author); Christians associate it with Jesus. On this pentacle, given the context of the cross, I suspect Mathers intended it to relate to the crucifixion.

The angelic names on this pentacle are the same as those on the Angelic Iron Cross of the Sun—the chiefs of the four elemental orders. A summary of our discussion from that chapter appears in the table on page 200.

	Hebrew	English	Meaning	Choir	Mathers	Me
bottom	אריאל	Ariel	Lion of El	Erelim	Water	Air
top	שרף	Seraph	Venomous Serpent	Seraphim	Earth	Fire
left	כרוב	Cherub	Griffin? Blessing?	Keruvim	Fire	Earth
right	תרשיש	Tarshish	A place. A gem?	Tarshishim	Air	Water

♃ 7: The Wheel of Fortune

THIS IS MATHERS'S SEVENTH, and final, pentacle of Jupiter. He says it has great power against poverty if considered with devotion, repeating the versicle. Further, he says, it serves to discover Treasures and drive away Spirits that guard them. The circumferential versicle is from Tehillim 113:7: "He raises the poor from the dust, from the garbage heap he lifts up the needy." Many people keep a copy of this pentacle in their wallet. I often use it in social justice work, sometimes in conjunction with Elohim of the Grave.

Exercises

- Teach at least one Jupiter pentacle to your Book. I recommend Jakob's chariot.

- Make a pentacle for someone else, give it to them as a gift, and teach them to understand it. Explain why you chose it for them, and give them clear instructions on how to use it.

- Develop your own kavvanah for one of the pentacles you've learned. I recommend the Hexagram of Ab Ehyeh. Remember to ground your kavvanah in the text, geometry, and features of the pentacle. Ask Solomon to help inspire you.

♄

The Pentacles of Saturn

One of the most distinguished words in the Bible is the word kadosh, *holy; a word which more than any other is representative of the mystery and majesty of the divine. Now what was the first holy object in the history of the world? Was it a mountain? Was it an altar?*

It is, indeed, a unique occasion at which the distinguished word kadosh *is used for the first time: in the Book of Genesis at the end of the story of creation. How extremely significant is the fact that it is applied to time: "And God blessed the seventh day and made it holy." There is no reference in the record of creation to any object in space that would be endowed with the quality of holiness.*

—SHABBAT AS A SANCTUARY IN TIME, FROM
THE SABBATH: ITS MEANING FOR MODERN MAN BY RABBI ABRAHAM JOSHUA HESCHEL

Of the planets visible to the naked eye from earth, Saturn is the furthest away and the slowest in its movement across the field of the (apparently) fixed stars. It is thus the most liminal classical planet, standing as it does on the boundary of our sensible solar system and the vast invisible darkness of outer space. For this reason, Saturn is associated with boundaries, both literal and metaphoric. Saturn holds the line between the known and the unknown; between the understood and the maddening. Saturn is the eternal avant-garde, an auspice of death, but also of liberation.

Saturn's English name comes from the Latin, whose etymology is unclear, possibly from the root, "*serere*," meaning "to sow," although some ancient sources associate it with the Latin *satis,* which is the root of our English "saturate" and "satiate." In Greek, Saturn is called Kronos (Κρόνος), which I understand to derive from "sickle" or "claw" (Κείρω), but which is of uncertain origin. As this name implies, Saturn is associated with restriction. Because of our culture's unhealthy obsession with limitless growth, Saturn is often vilified in this role and called the Greater Malefic. Personally, I believe this to be in error. Saturn is malefic toward Jupiterian ends, but the enemy of the Great

Patriarch is often the ally of the People. When the slavedriver cracks his whip, it is Saturn who says, "Enough!"

Although the two names/spirits were sometimes understood as distinct, Kronos was often understood as interchangeable with Chronos (Χρόνος), Father Time, who rules the orderly progression of the seasons. This association between the agricultural and the temporal underlines Saturn's role as ruler of the calendar. Saturn directs the flow of the seasons, particularly as they relate to plow/grain farming.

In the ancient world, both Baal Haman (the chief god of the Carthage) and the god of Israel were equated with the planet Saturn. This association remained very tight until the European Renaissance and is still referenced in unsavory internet backwaters. As the enemies of the Roman empire, some of the only peoples to long withstand Roman conquest, our gods and cultures were vilified, and part of the "Western" distaste for Saturn is rooted in this. Not just Africans and Jews, but witches too, with our dreadful sabbats, are understood to be children of Saturn. This mythic tension between Rome/Christendom and peoples of Saturn makes many Saturnian spirits especially good magical allies for containing, restricting, and cutting down Patriarchy, white supremacy, antisemitism, Christian supremacy, and many (but not all) forms of fascism.

The Hebrew name for the planet Saturn is *Shabbatai* (שבתי), from the root שבת (shabbat), which means "resting" or "not working" or "being on strike." Presumably, the planet is so named because it moves so slowly.

When Solomon built the temple in Jerusalem, high on the acropolis of Mount Moriah, it was the Eternal Temple of the sabbath which he sought to embody. His design is described in detail in 1 Kings, chapter 6. I encourage you to use that passage, as well as the many, many reconstructed images and videos online, to construct a mental temple of your own, in which you can clearly imagine yourself, and to hold this kavvanah of abiding in the Eternal Temple while constructing the pentacles of this chapter.

Especially if you, like me, do not have a strong visual imagination, I encourage you to fill your inner temple with your other senses. We do not know what music played in the Temple, although we know there was both a choir and an orchestra. The internet will allow you to listen to modern reconstructions of music from ancient Israel, Egypt, and Mesopotamia, which I encourage you to listen to as inspiration for your imagining. We do, however, know exactly what the Temple smelled like, because Vayikra (Leviticus) 16:12-13 provides a recipe for the Holy Incense, *ketoret,* which was used. A translated recipe interpreted in modern measurements can be found in my *The Big Book of Magical Incense.*

♄ 1: The Square of Saturn

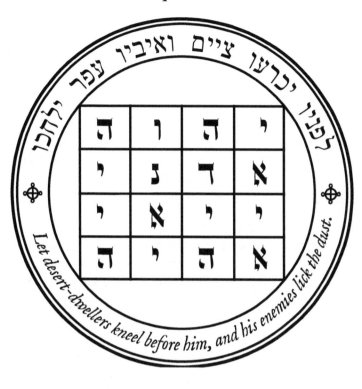

AS I MENTIONED EARLIER, Mathers, and most other texts of the pentacles, present the Saturn pentacles first, and then move their way down to the Moon. Thus, this is the first pentacle Mathers presents. He says that it is ". . . of great value and utility for striking terror into the Spirits. Wherefore, upon its being shown to them they submit, and kneeling upon the earth before it, they obey." The versicle is from Tehillim (Psalms) 72:9, the psalm that David sings over the infant Solomon: "Let desert-dwellers kneel before him, and his enemies lick the dust."

Inside the square, from top to bottom we have:

1. The Most Holy Name, יהוה

2. Adonai (Lord) אדני

3. The uncommon name ייא, which also appears on the Martial Octagram

4. Ehyeh (I Am) אהיה

This exact list of four names also occurs in *The Book of Contemplation,* a 13th century text from the Circle of Contemplation, whom we mentioned in Part Two. Mark Verman offers this translation:[1]

> [Continue] until you investigate, consider, seek out, reconcile, and establish the four Names dependent upon the yod. This constitutes the explanation of the four Names dependent upon the yod . . . like a coal connected to a flame, and the flame divides into four heads. . . . a gushing fountain and its waters speak out into 24 parts. Each part has four roots. Each of the roots has four branches. Each branch has four vocalizations . . . Similarly, [this applies to] these four Names of which we spoke. There are four of these Names. The first is אהיה; the second is יהוה; the third is אדני; the fourth is ייא.

> Know, understand, investigate, consider, comprehend, and juxtapose one thing against another and consider the analogies, until you fathom the explanation of these matters. For all wisdom and understanding, all comprehension, and through inquiry, knowledge, vocalization, reflection, speech, whispering, voice, action, guarding, and undertaking—all are found in this [16 letter] Name . . . Then you will understand the words of man, the speech of domesticated animals, the chirping of birds . . . [all of] which are accessible for the wise to know . . . you will attain complete clarity and tranquility, in order to consider the thought of the Supreme One who dwells in the Ether; there is no level higher than this.

♄ 2: SATOR Square

MATHERS TELLS US that "This pentacle is of great value against adversities and of especial use in repressing the pride of Spirits." The versicle is from Tehillim 72, the previously discussed psalm David wrote for newborn Solomon. In this, the eighth verse, we have "Let him rule from sea to sea, from the river to the ends of the earth."

Within, we have the famed SATOR square, an acrostic word square containing a five letter palindrome here. Mathers writes his with Hebrew characters. This magic square is of largely unknown origin. The oldest known examples of it are in Roman graffiti from late antiquity, including in the ruins of Pompei. It is most likely either Jewish or Christian in origin, although it may arise from the cult of Mithras. There is a long, fascinating, and complex history of translations of this square, which I encourage you to investigate. I especially recommend the excellent essay "And the Rotas Go 'Round" by Stieg Hedlund.[2]

♄ 3: The Wheel of Saturn

MATHERS'S THIRD PENTACLE of Saturn is the wheel, about which he says, "This should be made within the Magical Circle, and it is good for use at night when thou invokest the Spirits of the nature of Saturn." The names around the rim are, counterclockwise from the top, עמליאל (Emeliel), אנצחיה (Anetzach-iah), ארוכיה (Arokhiah), and אנחיאל (Anachiel). All four of these are relatively straightforward to interpret.

Emiliel's name appears to arise from the root עמל, which means "work" or "toil," although that translation loses some of the connotation. *Emil* (עמל) work is particularly the worst, most soul-crushing, body-breaking kind of work. It could also be translated as "hardship" or "travail." I generally hold a kavvanah of Emiliel as the "The Workers' El" when I make this pentacle.

Next is the name Anetzachiah. The root נצח (NZCh) means "to excel," "to be infinite," "to endure," or "to be victorious." The aleph at the beginning moves it to the first-person future tense, "I will prevail." Thus, Anetzachiah's name means "I will prevail in (as/by) Jah."

The name on the bottom is Arokhiah (ארוכיה), whose name means "The Long El," which in this context I understand as "El, the Long-Lasting." However, there is also a connection to be made here to the Arikh Anpin (אריך אנפין), the "Long Face" or "Macroprosopus," a complex kabbalistic concept outside the scope of this book. If you are familiar with it, I encourage you to create your own kavvanot making use of this connection.

Finally, we come to Anachiel (אנחיאל), whose name appears to mean Moaning (אנח) El (אל). It is difficult to understand why this name is here. However, the Greek translation of אנח is γοάω (goao), which similarly means "moaning," but is also the root of the word "goetia" which means "sorcery." I wonder if such a connotation isn't present here as well? Whether this etymology is genuine or not, I often hold such a kavvanah when writing this pentacle; Anachiel is an angel who groans out barbarous names for sorcery.

As with all the wheel pentacles, I primarily understand this one as a crank to churn up Saturnian power, and I most commonly use it on the backs of other Saturnian pentacles.

♄ 4: The Triangle of Doom

THIS BEAUTIFUL PENTACLE is Mathers's fourth pentacle of Saturn. About it, he says, "This pentacle serveth principally for executing all the experiments and operations of ruin, destruction, and death. When it is made in full perfection, it serveth also for those Spirits which bring news, when thou invokest them from the side of the South." My experience with it is almost entirely in operations of ruin and destruction, generally in a political context. I do not normally use it to conjure spirits who bring news, no matter what direction they come from, because I prefer other methods for that purpose.

The versicle is taken from Tehillim 109:18: "May he be clothed in curse like a garment, may it enter his body like water, his bones like oil." This is a powerful image for *malefica*, and it deeply informs my kavvanah for use of this pentacle.

Around the outside of the pentacle, starting on the right, is written: "Listen, Israel! HaShem is our god. HaShem in One." This prayer, commonly named after its first word, *Shema,* is taken from Devarim 6:4. It is unquestionably the most important prayer in modern Judaism; in some ways, it is our central "statement of belief." It is very common in amulets and phylacteries, including both mezuzot and tefillin. It can be understood in many ways, some of which I'll briefly discuss.

The famed medieval Ashkenaz commentator Rashi says: "The Lord who is now our God and not the God of the other peoples of the world, He will at some future time be the One."[3] His Sefardic contemporary Ibn Ezra instead suggests that "The Name [יהוה] is then further repeated, to say: God, who is our Lord, is one God—in other words, He is absolutely unique."[4] Talmud Berakhot offers a take that especially emphasizes the unity of the Jewish people: "You have made Me a single entity in the world . . . because of this, I will make you a single entity in the world, unique. . . ." The 14th century commentator Rabbeinu Bahya most closely reflects my own sentiments: "Had he only mentioned ה' אחד (G-d is One), there would have been a chance for the nations to understand the name Hashem as the way the Jews describe the god of the Gentiles in their language. This is why Moses had to add the word אלו-הינו (our God), to make plain that Hashem is the name of our G-d, the G-d of the Jewish people."

Because of these close connections between the Shema and not just Jewish religion, but also Jewish tribal identity, I believe the use of this prayer by non-Jews to be inappropriate. Instead, I recommend they use the seventh verse of Isaiah 45 for this pentacle, which provides a stronger basis for the coming conjuration. Arrange it like so around the triangle, in either Hebrew or your preferred translation:

Left	יוצר אור ובורא חשך	I form light and create darkness;
Bottom	עשה שלום ובורא רע	I make weal and create woe—
Right	אני יהוה עשה כל־אלה	I, the LORD, do all these things.

At the center of the pentacle is the letter י (yod). Yod is the smallest letter; it is the single calligraphic stroke from which all other letters are formed. In magical contexts, including this one, the yod can be understood as a divine singularity, a flame ascending toward the heavens. Its origin is a pictograph representing a hand; for this reason, there is a Jewish aphorism that "A yod is a Yid (Jew) is a yad (hand)," which suggests that we act as G-d's "hands" in the world.

The striking geometry of this pentacle suggests a ritual for its use. One version of such is below.

HOW TO USE THE TRIANGLE OF DOOM

1. Recall: Pentacles can be understood as diagrams of rituals.

2. Write a large pentacle (or use the one in your Book if it's big enough).

3. Make a poppet of your target and put it in the center of the pentacle, at the yod.

4. Infuse power into the center, until . . .

5. The hand of the yod grasps the target, holding them tight.

6. Energetically reinforce the circular boundary around the yod, trapping the target inside.

7. Assert spiritual authority with the Shema (Jews) or the seventh verse of Isaiah 45.

8. Awaken the words around the triangle (which should match what you used in the previous step), creating a one-way boundary that allows energy to enter the triangle, but not leave.

9. Awaken the versicle.

10. Pour energy into the versicle, and feel it tighten around your target, your curse clinging to them like a garment, soaking into them like water, seeping into their bones like viscous black oil.

11. When you cannot push more energy, detach yourself from the energy flow.

12. Seal the outer circumference of the pentacle.

13. Wrap the pentacle and poppet and put them in a plastic zipper bag.

14. Put the bag somewhere it will remain undisturbed.

15. Wash your hands with soap and salt, paying attention to fully detaching from the work.

16. Take a shower and make sure you're fully disconnected before you go to sleep.

♄ 5: The Cross of Eloah

THIS SHIELD-STYLE PENTACLE is the fifth Mathers presents under Saturn. He says that it "defendeth those who invoke spirits of Saturn during the night; and chaseth away the Spirits which guard treasures." I use this pentacle for spiritual protection and to ward off malicious magics. I often recommend it to people who have recently broken a curse, cut energetic cords, or are otherwise energetically vulnerable, as well as those who live or work in miasmic or curse-dense environments like prisons and mental hospitals. For these purposes, I like a steel pentacle on a string of hematite beads. It can also be used on/with a scrying mirror for communicating with unknown or suspect spirits.

The versicle is the middle part of Devarim 10:17 and says: "The El, The Great, The Mighty, and The Awesome." In the inner circle, starting in the top right and proceeding counterclockwise, is written the Most Holy Name, יהוה. In the corners of the square is written אלוה, or Eloah, a singular form of Elohim.

Around the outside square, counterclockwise from the top left, are four uncommon angel names: רכניאל (Rakhaniel), רואלהיפר (Rualhipar), נואפיאל (Noyefial), and ארהנה (Arhanah). The first name is difficult to decrypt. The root רכנ (RKN) gives rise to a family of words related to bending, such as "soften" or "cause to faint" or "bend down." Given that it is next to the El on a pentacle designed to protect, I think "The Softening of El" is an appropriate interpretation; this name calls El in his most tender face.

Rualhipar (רואלהיפר) is an extremely difficult name to understand. By stretching the imagination a bit, one can intend it to mean רואה אל פרי or "See the fruit of El." I understand this name to be related to finding treasure.

Noyefial appears to begin with the word נואף, which means "adulterer," arising from the root נאפ (NAF), which engenders a family of words related to licentiousness, adultery, and idolatry. However, it could possibly be related to the root נופ (NUF), which gives rise to a diverse family of words related to winnowing grain, sprinkling, lifting, and wielding tools, which seems more in keeping with a Saturnian pentacle.

The name on the top right, Arhanah (ארהנה), can be understood as a variation of the name of the legendary original owner of the land on which Solomon's Temple would later be built. The story is told in the second book of Samuel and again in the first book of Chronicles. G-d was angry with Israel, and specifically with King David. A plague descended on the land, but it was stopped by an angel at the threshing floor of a man whose name is given several variant spellings: ארונה (Araunah[5]), ארניה (Araniah[6]), ארנן (Ornon[7]), or האורנה (The Avranah[8]), where King David was. The etymology of the name is unclear. It may be related to אַרָן (aran), which means joyful.

Seeing the angel, the king finally acknowledged his own guilt and pled for the lives of his people. The Lord was softened, and the plague abated. G-d spoke through his prophet, Gad, telling David to buy the threshing floor and erect an altar there. We are told in 1 Chronicles 3:1 that "Solomon began to build the House of the LORD in Jerusalem on Mount Moriah, where [the LORD] had appeared to his father David, at the place which David had designated, at the threshing floor of Ornan the Jebusite." I believe ארהנה to be the very same angel of the Lord that stopped the plague, an angel of the threshing floor, a messenger of El as the Sower, the Satiating, the god of worker and harvest.

♄ 6: Wheel of Obsession

ABOUT THIS PENTACLE, Mathers says, "The person against whom thou shalt pronounce it shall be obsessed by Demons." The versicle is from Tehillim 109:6 and says: "Set Thou a wicked man over him; And let an adversary stand at his right hand." The Hebrew word translated as "an adversary" is שטן (satan), which some interpret as a proper name, rather than a title. The context of the verse is that David is crying out to G-d, saying that wicked people are being mean to him, and asking G-d to hurt them. I very rarely use this pentacle, partly because, like the other wheel pentacles, I do not fully understand the symbols on it, but mostly because I rarely want to obsess others with demons. In my experience, doing so makes an enemy less predictable, more dangerous, and more difficult to control.

♄ 7: The Earthshaker

THIS IS MATHERS'S FINAL pentacle of Saturn. About it, he says, "This pentacle is fit for exciting earthquakes, seeing that the power of each order of Angels herein invoked is sufficient to make the whole Universe tremble." The circumferential versicle is taken from Tehillim 18:8: "Then the earth rocked and quaked; the foundations of the mountains shook, rocked by His indignation." Contextually, the psalm was written by David while he fled Saul's persecution. In this particular verse, G-d is angry that people are messing with David.

Inside the innermost triangle, clockwise from the top, are the three names אלהים (Elohim), כרובים (Keruvim or Cherubim[9]), and בני אלהים (B'nai Elohim, or "Children of the Gods"). The phrase B'nai Elohim is first found in Bereshit 6: "When men began to increase on earth and daughters were born to them, the B'nai Elohim saw how beautiful the daughters of men were and took wives from among those that pleased them." Rashi says that the B'nai Elohim in this passage are "The sons of princes and rulers . . ." although he admits "Another explanation [that they are] . . . princely angels." His

Sefardic contemporary Ibn Ezra says instead that those meant are astrological magicians.

The middle triangle is written in the Passing the River cipher, which we discussed previously (see page 142). Counterclockwise from the top are the names of three choirs of angels: חשמלים (Hashmalim), שרפים (Seraphim), and מלחים (Malakim). The top name, Hashmalim, is usually understood as the plural of חשמל (*hashmal*), which appears in Ezekiel's vision of the chariot and is usually understood as a gemstone, often electrum (amber). However hashmal is also an acronym. The ח stands for חכמה (chokmah, which means "wisdom"), ש for שלום (shalom, peace), the מ stands for ממשלה (*memshala*, dominion), and the final ל stands for לבוש הדר (*lavash hadar*, garment of splendor). These four attributes of Solomon—wisdom, peace, dominion, and a "garment of splendor"—are also the gifts of the angels called Hashmalim.

The Seraphim (venomous serpents) were discussed in the Sun chapter. The final name, Malakim (also spelled Malachim), is both the generic name for all types of angels (and, occasionally, human messengers) as well as a specific choir of angels of middle rank. Malachim are generally understood to appear in human form.

Finally, around the outer triangle, counterclockwise from the top, are written the names of three more choirs of angels, חיות הקדש (Chayot H'Kadosh, Holy Creatures), אופנים (Ophanim, Wheels), and אראלים (Arelim, Heroes), the last two of which we discussed in the Sun.

The first name, Chayot H'Kadosh, is usually translated "Holy Living Beings" or "Holy Creatures." The root of the first word חיות is חיה, which means "to live" and is also the root of All-Mother Eve's Hebrew name, חוה (Chava). The second word, קדש (*kadosh*) is usually translated as "sacred," from a root meaning "set apart as special." The Chayot H'Kadosh are beings of Ezekiel's vision, angels that hold up the throne of the Most High. They are, in most Jewish reckonings, the highest choir of angels.

I have never used this pentacle to provoke an earthquake, nor do I recommend you do so. However, I do find this pentacle useful in works designed to incite Divine retribution for injustice, which I most often use in a political context, especially the sorts of Saturnian contexts about which I spoke at the beginning of the chapter.

Exercises

- Incubate a dream visitation to the Temple of Solomon with King Solomon.

- Teach at least one Saturnian pentacle to your Book.

- Develop your own kavvanah for at least one pentacle in your Book.

Now What?

If you've successfully completed all the exercises in this book, you should have a basic understanding of the forty-four Mathers pentacles, as well as a solid vocabulary of Hebrew Names of Power. You've developed a relationship with Solomon, the Magician King, as well as some beginner skills in dream incubation, trance journey, and spirit communication. You've written many awakened pentacles and magically deployed them using a variety of techniques and kavvanot. Perhaps most importantly, you have birthed a powerful magical familiar, your awakened and enchanted Magic Book of Pentacles.

As you continue to work with the pentacles, record what you learn in your Book. What do you wish you'd done differently? What intentions do you hold when using the pentacles? Where do you disagree with me? What secrets have you discovered? What new pentacles have you created? As it says in Skinner and Rankine's *The Veritable Key of Solomon*: "Even though I may give a significant number of designs for Talismans in this Book, you should not avoid working with them and stop making new and appropriate figures because of that. I am not offering these designs for that purpose, but to make it easier to create new ones."

As your Book begins to wear from use, start thinking about what your Master Book of Pentacles will be like. Consult with Solomon and your current Book. How will the pentacles be different from the ones in your first book? What other pentacles, incantations, or other magic you will include? How will you decorate it? Is it even a book at all?

Recommended Reading

- Visit the Solomon Extras section at my website, *MastrosZealot.com,* to see supplemental materials related to this text.

- If you'd like to learn more from me, visit *WitchLessons.com* to see all my books and courses, including the companion course to this book.

- If you'd like to learn more Solomonic magic, I recommend Stephen Skinner's seminal book *Techniques of Solomonic Magic.*

- If you'd like to learn more about the Hebrew amulet tradition, I recommend Gideon Bohak's fabulous book, *Ancient Jewish Magic.*

- If you'd like to learn more about the fascinating history of Solomonic magic, I very strongly recommend Joseph Peterson's extraordinary online archive of Solomonic grimoires and other traditional European occult texts at *EsotericArchives.com.* It is not only a fabulous resource for a Solomonic deep dive, but also a treasure trove of other materials.

The End

ברוך אתה, יהוה אלוהינו, מלך העולם, שהחינו וקימנו והגיענו לזמן הזה

Blessed are You, HaShem our god, King of the Forever,
who has kept us alive,
sustained us, and brought us to this day.

Notes

Introduction

1. Kohelet (Ecclesiastes) 12:10. My translation. Throughout this book, I will use the original Hebrew names for some books of the bible, rather than their Christian names. You can view a table of these names in the Supplemental Material at *MastrosZealot.com.*

2. Except where otherwise noted, all biblical translations are my own.

3. "Hermeneutes" is the anglicization of the Greek Ἑρμηνευτής, which literally means "Hermes-er" and is usually translated into English as "interpreter" or "translator," but sometimes as "mediator" or "go-between." You can learn more about it as a magical practice in the Introduction to my book, *Orphic Hymns Grimoire* (Hadean Press, 2022).

4. Mashal (Proverbs) 2:2.

5. Many Anglophone Jews use "G-d" as a proper name for our tribal god, the god of Israel (as Athena is the god of Athenians), distinct from the gods of all other peoples and religions. That is to say, "god" is a word for a type of spirit; "G-d" is a name for a particular god. The hyphen is partly because of a custom, older than the invention of writing, of not speaking the proper name of our god (יהוה) aloud. We discuss this in greater detail in Chapter 2.5, in the section titled The Most Holy Name.

6. In this book (and in most other contexts), the "G-d of Israel" means the god of the people Israel (aka Jews), that is to say, the god of the Hebrew bible. It does not refer to the modern nation-state of Israel.

7. The Babylonian Talmud is the core traditional collection of rabbinic Jewish teachings. Indeed, the word itself means "teachings." It was written by a collection of rabbis and sages in Jewish Babylonia from the 3rd to 6th centuries CE and claims to faithfully record much older oral teachings. You will read many passages of Talmud throughout this book and can read the entire thing, in multiple translations, online at Sefaria, a nonprofit organization offering free access to Jewish texts. I recommend the more modern William Davidson translation, although in this book I'll be using the 1921 A. Cohen translation. There is, additionally, an older Jerusalem Talmud, but when people say simply "Talmud," they usually mean the Babylonian Talmud.

8. We discuss this more in the chapter titled The Mathers Edition of the Key of Solomon, where we learn more about Moina and her husband.

9. Find it under Middle Eastern Music Generator at *mynoise.net/NoiseMachines/middle EasternMusicGenerator.php*

Chapter 1.1

1. This phrase, לדור ודור (l'dor v'dor) or "generation to/with generation," is an important facet of Jewish identity. It describes the central relationship between the Jewish people and our wisdom teachings. While many gentiles understand Judaism to be a religion passed "by the book," Jews generally understand it primarily as a tribal/cultural inheritance passed "from generation to generation" and as a collective struggle that extends across space and time, "generation with generation."

2. Torijano, P. *Solomon the Esoteric King: From King to Magus, Development of a Tradition.* Leiden, The Netherlands: Brill, 2012. Page 211.

Chapter 1.2

1. Despite the name, Wisdom Literature is comprised of both written and oral materials.

2. TaNaKh is an acronym for the parts of the Hebrew bible: Torah (The Five Books of Moses), Nevi'im (Prophets), and Ketuvim (Writings).

3. Additionally, there is an apocryphal text called the Psalms of Solomon, which is known only from late medieval Greek manuscripts. It was probably originally written in Hebrew around the 1st or 2nd century CE. There are eighteen psalms in the collection, the penultimate of which is very similar to 72, the babe-blessing which we discussed above.

4. Kings 3

5. Note that this is a permutation of our familiar שלמ (SLM).

6. Proverbs 22:17–24:22: "Bend Your Ears to the Sayings of the Wise," for example, closely parallels the late New Kingdom Egyptian "The Instruction of Amenemope."

7. See, for example, Boeck, B. "Proverbs 30:18 in the Light of Ancient Mesopotamian Cuneiform Texts." *Sefarad,* 2009. *digital.csic.es.*

8. Rashi on Song of Songs 1:1.

9. It is particularly effective, in my experience, as a working script for sex magic involving Ishtar (Venus) and Tammuz (Adonis) or Solomon and the Queen of Sheba, a pairing we discuss further in the chapter on the Venus pentacles.

10. "Reception of the Sabbath." This is the Jewish Friday night ritual.

11. "Sacred marriage," a type of devotional sex ritual.

12. Although most modern Jews do not consider this text canonical, it was accepted by the Hellenized Jews of its time.

13. Φρόνησις (*phronesis*). The most common Latin translation is *prudentia,* the root of the English word "prudence."

14. πνεῦμα σοφίας (*pneuma sofias*). This could also be translated as "breath of wisdom."

15. Wisdom 7:21.

Chapter 1.3

1. Whiston, W. *The Genuine Works of Flavius Josephus the Jewish Historian.* London: University of Cambridge, 1737. 8.2.5, *penelope.uchicago.edu.*

2. Remember this when we discuss the Lunar pentacle called "The Conjurer's Hook."

3. Psalm Scroll of Qumran Cave 11, psalm 3.

4. Today, we often hear "Lilith" as the proper name for the Queen of Demons, but in earlier Semitic literature, it is also the name for a whole category of demons.

5. Torijano, P. *Solomon the Esoteric King: From King to Magus, Development of a Tradition.* Leiden, The Netherlands: Brill, 2012.

6. PGM XCII 1–16.

7. Isbell, Charles D. *Corpus of the Aramaic Incantation Bowls.* Oregon: Wipf and Stock, 2009.

Chapter 1.4

1. Torijano, P. Solomon the Esoteric King: From King to Magus, Development of a Tradition. Leiden, The Netherlands: Brill, 2012. Page 72.

2. McCown, C. C. *The Testament of Solomon: Edited from Manuscripts at Mount Athos, Bologna, Holkham Hall, Jerusalem, London, Milan, Paris and Vienna.* Germany: J. C. Hinrichs, 1922. Pages 2–3.

3. Sparks, H. F. D. *The Apocryphal Old Testament.* Oxford: Oxford University Press, 1984. Pages 733–4.

4. The word means scrying in water, but that technique does not appear in the surviving text. When queried, Solomon told me it was because the spirits should be called in "mirrors" of still pools of clear living water, and their voices listened for in running water.

Chapter 1.5

1. At this time, much of the Iberian Peninsula was Muslim-controlled.

2. Others translate this title רוקח (*Rokeach*) as "Perfumer" or "Apothecary."

3. Today's Hasidim are the result of a different movement, which arose in 18th-century Podolia (modern Ukraine). One of the main political protectors and financial benefactors of that revival was Reb Temerl Bergson, the great-grandmother of Mina Bergson, whom most occultists know by her married name, Moina Mathers. We discuss this more in the chapter titled The Mathers Editions of the Key of Solomon.

4. Many believe Reb Eleazer to be the author of The Sacred Magic of Abramelin the Mage, although I am not entirely convinced. However, I do believe there is a literary relationship between Abramelin and Eleazer's legendary ancestor, Abu Aaron ben Samuel ha-Nasi of Babylonia.

5. The Jewish community in Muslim-controlled Iberia (modern Spain and Portugal).

6. Quoted in Verman, M. *The Books of Contemplation: Medieval Jewish Mystical Sources.* State University of New York Press, 2012. Page 29.

7. Or, more accurately, a whole family of closely related texts.

Chapter 1.6

1. This is possibly another name for the mythic Hermes Trismegistus.

2. You can see a scan of the complete manuscript (in Hebrew) here: מפתח שלמה L. Fuks, Catalogue of the manuscripts of the Biblioteca Rosenthaliana University Library (Leiden, The Netherlands, 1973), no. 242, *nli.org.il/en.*

3. This is a very common Sefardic name, which is one among many reasons I believe this text to originate in Seferad (Muslim-controlled Iberia), despite the antecedent copy being in London.

4. I'm working on a translation which will be available in the winter of 2024.

5. The Hebrew word here is אשפנים (ashpinim), which appears to be a plural of the Aramaic אשפין (ashpin), a type of magician referenced in Daniel 2:27, often translated as "conjurer" or "astrologer." However, ashpin is already plural, so it is unclear why it is doubly pluralized here.

Chapter 1.7

1. One of the defining characteristics of the Golden Dawn was that it was (then) the only Masonic/Rosicrucian order to admit women.

2. Some say that their marriage was celibate, but I see no evidence to support that claim except that Moina once described their love as "pure," which, to my ear, is just the sort of glib romantic nonsense twenty-five-year-old newlyweds say.

3. They were right. The young couple were supported almost entirely by the largess of Moina's rich friend Annie Horniman, who had attended the Slade School with her.

Chapter 2.1

1. I have a complex personal mythology wherein "Bat Sheba" (Daughter of Sheba) is a title, not a proper name, and that the Daughters of Sheba were an elite unit of spies in service to the Queen of Sheba.

2. Some say Ethiopia, others Yemen. Possibly "Sheba" was not a specific place at all, but a general word Hebrews used for several advanced cultures to their south.

3. His age at the time of David's death is unclear. Some say he was as young as fifteen, others that he was a young man in his mid-twenties.

4. More literally, the kings of Israel swear not to hoard horses, wealth, or wives.

5. Tehillim 127.

6. We learn to seek teaching dreams later in this chapter.

7. This could also be translated "my father, David," because "David" means "Beloved."

8. 1 Kings 3:6-9.

9. 1 Kings 3:11-13.

10. What I have translated as "with" is sometimes rendered as "about," which, in my opinion, obfuscates the meaning.

11. I Kings 5:9-13.

12. Search for "Kebra Negast" to learn more about this.

13. Is this the same as the demon princess mentioned in the Zohar? Or is she the same Na'amah that was sister to Tubal-Cain? Or someone else entirely? Accounts vary.

14. And quite a few other women on the side.

Chapter 2.2

1. The new Moon is the first night on which the Moon is visible following a dark Moon.

2. Two Sundays before Christmas.

3. Talmud Berakhot 57b.

Chapter 2.3

1. Nachman of Breslov, Sefer h'Middot, Dreams, Part II:1.

2. Berakhot 55a:15 (William Davidson Edition). *sefaria.org.*

3. Solomon's desirability and prowess as a lover are legendary. The central Jewish text on erotic love (the Song of Songs) is both about him and, they say, written by him. If it sounds appealing, I encourage you to invite him into erotic dreams as well.

4. Loosely based on PGM VII: 1009–1016.

5. Ibn Attar, C. *Or HaChaim on Genesis.* Translated by Eliyahu Munk. New York: KTAV Publishing House, 1998. *sefaria.org.*

Chapter 2.4

1. Kalisch, I. Sefer Yezirah. New York, 1877. *sefaria.org.*

2. That is, Jewish, but pretending otherwise.

3. That is, not Jewish, but pretending otherwise.

4. Phylactery, as a term in Anglophone magic, means an amulet whose power derives from words written on it. The word comes to English from a Greek word for a protective talisman. In a Jewish context, however, it typically refers to a specific kind of written protective talisman called tefillin. Because of this confusion, I will mostly avoid using the term in this book.

5. The masculine form is Ba'al Shem (בעל שם).

6. The most famous of these wonder workers was the early 18th-century Ashkenazi rabbi Israel ben Eliezer, usually called the Baal Shem Tov (Master of the Good Name) or the Holy Besht. (BeShT is an acronym for Baal Shem Tov.) He founded a (then) radical movement today called Hasidism (Pious Ones), which focuses on inculcation of a mystic state of consciousness called דבקות (*devukut*). Devekut, which literally means "clinging," is an ecstatic experience of union with the divine.

7. Aramaic is the only other surviving Northwestern Semitic language family.

8. I am not among them; my Hebrew is passable, but not fluent.

9. Christo-centrism and white supremacy deeply inform this research, so it's hard to really know.

10. Who may or may not have been enslaved; history isn't always clear.

11. That is to say, strictly phonographic writing systems. Many Asian languages do not use alphabets, but rather logograms, where characters represent ideas, rather than just sounds.

12. Note that the letter *mem* has two forms. Usually, it's written like this: מ, but when it occurs at the end of a word, it is written like this: ם. It makes an M sound.

13. When Torah says, "spare the rod and spoil the child," this is the word being used. It does not mean a rod with which to beat the child. It means a shepherd's staff, with which one offers support and guidance. Whenever you read a translation of holy or magical texts (including the ones in this book), you should be very alert to the biases and motivations of the translator.

14. Not all evolutionary anthropologists agree. The model I am describing here is called "ritual/speech coevolution theory." I encourage you to research it further.

Chapter 2.5

1. A mezuzah is an extremely common type of Hebrew house-blessing amulet. Mezuzot (plural) contain small scrolls with written blessings. They are traditionally placed at doorways.

2. Written in the 13th century CE by Yosef Giqatillah, a student of the famed Abraham Abulafia, Shaarei Orah is a dictionary and Kabbalistic analysis of 300 Names of Power. It is also an important source for the Kabbalistic underpinnings of the Smith-Rider-Waite tarot. (See *Tarot and the Gates of Light* by Mark Horn for more on this.)

3. Shaarei Orah, Introduction 4. Tanakh: The Holy Scriptures. Sefaria community translation, *sefaria.org.*

4. See the section called "The True Tree of Knowledge is the Fruit of PRDS" in the Supplementary Materials on my website.

5. PRDS is actually a Hebrew acronym: פרדס. It stands for Peshat (straight), Remez (hinted), Derash (inquiry), Sod (mystery). I have chosen looser English translations in order to preserve the acronym.

6. I had trouble choosing a word for this that began with an R. When I teach this material out loud, I sometimes use arcane and say it like a pirate: *ahr*-cane.

7. In Judaism, the number seven's sacredness is largely inherited from its ancestral Mesopotamian astrotheology. Whenever you see a group of seven sacred things, spend a moment considering whether what you're looking at is related to the seven classical planets. It isn't always a strong connection, but it's rarely completely unrelated.

8. You can learn more about how to respect names as animate beings in the section entitled "How to Dispose of This Book" in the Supplemental Materials at my website.

9. Talmud Sotah 14a:6.

10. "Directed intention," "meditative frame of mind," or "mystic intention." The plural is kavvanot. The root כבנ means "to be present." We discuss this much more extensively in the chapter with the Mercury pentacles.

11. The Zohar, translated and annotated by Rahmiel-Hayyim Drizin. The author is putting a hyphen in the middle of E-l for the same reason I put one in G-d—out of an abundance of caution to not accidentally profane a holy name.

12. The most important work of modern Hasidic philosophy. You can read the Tanya online at Sefaria.

13. Tanya, Part IV, *Iggeret HaKodesh* 7.

14. Ibn Ezra, commentary on Bereshit 1.1, Sefaria community translation, *sefaria.org*. License: COO.

15. A 12th-century CE Judeo-Arabic text that describes the story of how an (apocryphal) 8th-century CE king of the pagan Khazar (Turkic) people gathered to himself great thinkers and teachers of all faiths and had them teach him, so he could determine which faith was the true one. Spoiler: he chose Judaism. This book was not intended as a history lesson; it is generally understood to be a thinly veiled metaphor for multi-faith politics in Al Andalusian (Muslim-controlled Iberian) society.

16. I am endlessly delighted by the fact that, in the United States, this is also a colloquial phrase for "naughty word."

17. Note that, when writing Hebrew in English letters, Y, I, and J generally all code for the same letter י (yod).

18. Jerusalem Talmud Sanhedrin 10:1. The "Jerusalem Talmud" is an earlier and smaller collection than the Babylonian Talmud, which is what people usually mean when they just say "Talmud."

19. Tanya, Part II; *Sha'ar HaYichud VehaEmunah* 4:2.

20. Out of an abundance of caution, in order to not accidentally take the Most Holy Name in vain (that is to say, without acknowledging its special holiness and funneling that power into the world), the author has interjected a blessing immediately after his use of this name.

21. *Shaarei Orah, Introduction 4. Tanakh: The Holy Scriptures*. Philadelphia: Jewish Publication Society, 1985. *sefaria.org*.

22. But that's just me and my issues. If it works for you, work it!

23. *Sha'ar HaEmunah VeYesod HaChasidut* 20:2.

24. One Jewish folktale says that the bush had been on fire for years, and every day Moses walked past it but never noticed because his attention was caught up in his head and not on the world around him. Finally, he clears his mind, looks around, and sees the obvious miracle has been there all along.

25. Asherah is a very old pan-Semitic mother goddess, the consort of El. Her name basically means "goddess." Like my name, Sara, it derives from the Semitic root SRR, which means "rule over." She is often understood as the Queen of Heaven. Asherah is a goddess of the grove, often associated with prophecy. Some understand her to be the same as the goddess of the oracle of Dodona, whose Greek name is Dione (which also just means "goddess").

26. The " in the middle of this name is another technique to prevent profanation of a holy name by casually invoking it.

27. *Shaarei Orah, Introduction 5, Tanakh: The Holy Scriptures.* Sefaria community translation, *sefaria.org.*

28. *Kuzari* of Yehuda HaLevi, 4:3. *sefaria.org.*

29. For example, the Hebrew name for what English-speakers call the "Israeli Defense Forces" is אבצ הנגהה לארשיל (Tsva ha-Hagana le-Yisra'el or "Army of Defense for Israel").

30. For example, in Talmud Shevuot 35b:5, Rabbi Yosei expresses this opinion.

31. Her prayer was answered; her son becomes Samuel, the prophet.

32. For example, Ibn Ezra reads it thus in his commentary on Isaiah 6:3.

33. In fact, as in the title of Sefer H'Otot (The Book of Seals), it is the Hebrew word used to describe the pentacles on which this book focuses.

34. It's also possible that the name was imported from a non-Semitic language.

35. That is, "we hold the following kavvanah."

36. Remember that our English "Sh" sound is a single letter, ש (shin), in Hebrew.

37. Ezekiel 1:24.

38. Technically, every letter is, by its very nature, a Name of Power, and all Names are Names of Power constructed letter by letter.

39. This list is not intended to be exhaustive.

Chapter 2.6

1. My imagination of this cloak owes a lot to Doctor Strange's Cloak of Levitation.

2. In Judaism, and especially in the Hebrew amulet tradition, it is not permitted to throw out books or other writings that contain holy Names. Instead, such materials are ritually placed into special "book coffins" called *genizoht* (the singular is "genizah"). These book coffins are often buried with the bodies of sages, but others are stored indefinitely in attics, basements, or closets. There is more information about genizoht, including complete instructions for making your own, in the Solomon Extras section online at *MastrosZealot.com*.

3. It's always best to speak your own words, directly from your heart. Remember that you're speaking in Solomon's voice, not just your own. If you've invoked him properly, your hearts should be aligned, and you should speak from that shared heart.

4. As we discuss in the section called Five Holy Names, you should choose a divine name that is close to your heart. In this book, I pretty consistently use "Elohim," a genderqueer plural Hebrew godname which literally means "gods."

5. In Devarim (Deuteronomy) 22:12.

6. See supplemental instructions for beginners concerning planetary hours in the Solomon Extras section online at *MastrosZealot.com*.

7. You can find a "diabetic lancet," which is perfect for this purpose, in any pharmacy.

8. If, like me, you are not neat handed, I recommend practicing on scrap paper first.

Chapter 2.7

1. This is not a fully technical statement of the Fundamental Theorem of Arithmetic. If you're interested, I encourage you to learn more about this topic.

2. For obvious reasons, two is the only even prime.

3. If you'd like to understand why, Google "compass straightedge pentagram construction golden ratio."

4. If you'd like to understand more deeply why that's true, I strongly encourage you to read *Philosophy of Mathematics: Selected Readings* edited by Paul Benacerraf.

5. This is just a more nuanced way to say "sense of touch" and includes sensations like "muscle ache" or "hunger," which are not explicitly in the skin.

6. The Asklepion of Kos was where Hippocrates, the so-called "father of medicine," trained, and he later ran his medical school in association with that temple. I have a special affinity for Kos, which is the home of my paternal ancestors.

7. Efrat Bocher and Oded Lipschits, "The yršlm Stamp Impressions on Jar Handles: Distribution, Chronology, Iconography and Function." *Tel Aviv* 40 (2013), pp. 99–116.

8. Two wounds on Jesus's hands, two on his feet, and one on his chest.

9. Annunciation, Visitation, Nativity, Presentation of Jesus to the Temple, and Jesus's Debate in the Temple.

10. Friendship, generosity, chastity, courtesy, and piety.

11. The Greek word αἰθήρ (aither) means something like "upper atmosphere" or "the air of outer space."

12. Shabbat 55a.

13. Even though, to most English speakers, El and Elyon sound related, in Hebrew, they are spelled differently and come from different intermediary roots. However, it is entirely possible that the Proto-Semitic EL is related to the Proto-Afroasiatic ELH. This supposition seems well-supported because many gods named El are, in fact, gods of the high places.

14. The sacred founding ancestors of the Jewish people. Sarah, Rebekkah, Leah, Rachael, Jakob, Isaac, and Abraham.

15. "God of your Father," sometimes translated "God the Father."

16. For example, in the 7th-century BCE Arslan Tash amulet incantation.

17. A Semitic Queen of Heaven and Great Mother of All. She is often portrayed, in myth both ancient and modern, as a lover of El. She is among the many gods Solomon worshipped; her idol remained in the Temple until the time of Josiah (mid 600s BCE).

18. Joshua 3:10.

19. You'll want to rewrite this based on the names you've chosen.

20. Until you're draining yourself. But that's hard to do with this kind of magic.

21. Although the exact meaning of the biblical "selah" הלס is not fully clear, I (and most scholars) understand it to be a "stage direction" meaning something like "stop and listen" or "pause for music." Most often, it appears as I used it in the invocation, to end a psalm or other prayer.

22. Not like a pet, which is a very rude way to treat a god(s).

23. Many, but by no means all, of my students, especially but not exclusively those who are attracted to men, have reported sexual dreams starring Solomon after this work. He is famed as a great lover; if you're into it, enjoy! If you're not, don't worry about it. It's just the magic working itself through your unconscious.

Part Three: Planetary Pentacles

1. This breakdown is articulated by Agrippa at the very beginning of the Three Books of Occult Philosophy. There are, of course, many other ways to categorize things.

2. That is not to say that they must be exactly as written in this, or any other, book, including the most antique of grimoire manuscripts. Rather, they need to be correct, and the only way to know they are correct is to understand what they are, and why they are on that particular amulet. You can add to or change the names on a pentacle, but only if you know what you're doing.

Moon

1. Of course, using a word like "prince" conjures up a whole complex sociopolitical structure very different from that of the time and place the name arose. "Chieftain" or "leader" is probably more accurate.

2. It's important to understand that these sorts of attributions are by no means fixed, because they are deeply informed by the magician referencing them. Magical associations are not scientific equivalences; they are poetic metaphors.

3. It actually describes doors with five interlocking recessed frames. See: Mumcuoglu, M., and Y. Garfinkel. "The Puzzling Doorways of Solomon's Temple." Biblical Archaeology Society Online Archive. *baslibrary.org.*

4. Although רבש is generally translated as "has broken" it could also mean "has separated," which, in the context of a door, is just the normal opening mechanism.

5. You may have noticed that, over the course of this book, I use the words angel, spirit, and daimon more or less interchangeably. I rotate between them intentionally to get you used to the idea that spirit "categories" are very subjective and flexible. For the most part, the "types" of spirits are not "species" but more like job descriptions that tell you about the relationship between the speaker and the spirit in question. The descriptor "angel," for example, means "messenger."

6. In the same way that "cee" is the name of the English letter C.

7. Technically, at this point, you're not exactly in the Underworld, but in a sort of intersubjective lobby to the Underworld.

8. "Adorcism" is the process of conjuration to intentional possession. The word is the opposite of "exorcism."

9. 1 Samuel 28:7.

10. Like the English "huff," the word is onomatopoetic; it describes the sound of a snort.

11. The Hebrew could also be read as "discoursed *about* trees."

12. A 16th-century French Catholic magician and cryptographer.

13. Shem H'Mephorash means "Name Which Has Been Explained" and is sometimes another noa-name for the Most Holy Name. It is sometimes (strangely, to my mind) referred to as the "Hidden Name" or "Secret Name" instead. In later Kabbalah, this same name refers to the so-called "Name of 72 Letters" cryptographically derived from She-mot 14:19–21. Splitting the name into three-letter sections and El-ifying them produces seventy-two angelic names.

14. Late April.

15. Sometimes called "Worry."

16. A kind of fancy geometry related to boundary cases of infinite things.

17. סוד (sod=secret, the S in PRDS). Learn more in the Solomon Extras section online at *MastrosZealot.com*.

18. Not to be confused with the more well-known עזראל (Azrael), a psychopomp daimon.

19. The tenth.

20. Whose Proto-Semitic roots are ABD-AL, Abad-El, meaning "slave of Allah."

21. I encourage you to read the Grimm's fairy tale *Frau Holle* about a little girl who falls down a well and visits with a witch-queen whose name means "Mrs. Hell." *Frau Holle* is closely related to a very ancient Germanic chthonic goddess of winter, witchcraft, and weaving.

22. Greyhounds are a very old breed. The oldest confirmed greyhound skeleton found is about 4000 years old and from modern Syria.

Mercury

1. Google, the search engine, is named after this number. It is a very big number, on the order of the number of grains of sand on Earth times the number of elementary particles in the universe. For comparison, as of 2019, the amount of bits stored (collectively) by Google, Amazon, Microsoft, and Facebook is about 1/10 the number of the grains of sand on Earth.

2. The male form is sofer (ספר).

3. Albright, W. F. "A Teacher to a Man of Shechem about 1400 B. C." Bulletin of the American Schools of Oriental Research, no. 86, 1942, pp. 28–31. *doi.org*. Accessed Aug. 25, 2022.

4. Bauer, B. T., and L. Holstein, "The Power of the Scribe," *Craftmanship*, Spring 2017. *craftsmanship.net*.

5. Eruvin 13a.

6. I am a proponent of the PRDS method, which you can learn in the Solomon Extras section online at *MastrosZealot.com.*

7. I believe (as do many rabbis) that the prohibition against carrying on Shabbat (like most sabbath rules) is, at its root, a communal-labor protection law to ensure that people cannot be forced to work on their divinely mandated day off.

8. Sola, D. A., and M. J. Raphall. *Mishnah Shabbat,* 1845. *sefaria.org.*

9. The Hebrew word for "chariot" is מרכבה (merkavah), which is also the name of a type of Kabbalah focused on trance journey. We discuss this further in the Jupiter chapter.

10. These same words appear as the second half of verse seven.

11. The word I have translated "abundance," הכבוד (*h'kavod*), comes from a root that means "to be heavy" and could be translated as any of abundance, wealth, bounty, gravitas, honor, or glory. "Glory" is the most common.

12. Chayyot (חיות) are a type of angel, whose name is usually translated as "living creature," although I prefer "non-human sentient being." The singular is חיה, from the root חי (chai), which means "living." We discuss that divine name of power in the Great Seal chapter.

13. Zohar, Bereshit 17:191–192. Sefaria community translation. *sefaria.org.*

14. For examples, see: Bosworth, David. *House of Weeping: The Motif of Tears in Akkadian and Hebrew Prayer.* Atlanta: SBL Press, 2019.

15. For examples, see: Grambo, Ronald. "Ritual Crying in Folk Tradition." Anthropos 66, no. 5/6 (1971): 938–45. *jstor.org.*

16. Please recall that, in this book, my goal is to explain and contextualize Mathers's pentacles, not to reconstruct the historical sources on which he based them, which often provide many more uses.

17. It derives from a root that means "to hammer thin."

18. There is no known linguistic link between the names Giael and Gaia. And yet, as we have discussed, all names are spells woven with the breath. Names that sound the same share a certain quality of shape, and so do the spirits they name.

19. In particular, this is the unique regular dodecagram, {12,5}.

20. To learn more, search for "superior highly composite numbers."

21. For example, many experts believe some early Germanic counting systems were base twelve. That's why eleven and twelve have their own words, instead of being "one-teen" and "two-teen."

22. To learn more, search for "Mesopotamian duodecimal numbers."

23. The name ארבעתאל means Four-of-El. I understand it to be "four" in the context of a crossroad or compass rose.

24. It could also be read ". . . was everything."

25. In fact, stability over time is the primary virtue of written (versus spoken) language.

26. Although the text we know today is likely from the 11th to 13th centuries CE, it is compiled from much older traditions.

27. In a Jewish context, of course, all angels are in service to heaven, but the fallen are less directly so.

28. This was my original interpretation, but application of All-Knowing Dodecagram yielded further insight.

29. Sefer Chokmah (the Book of Wisdom) 8:2.

Venus

1. In English, our day is named after the Norse goddess Freya, whom the Romans equated with their Venus.

2. Such amulets are extremely common in other collections of Hebrew amulets.

3. MS 214 of the Bavarian State Library in Munich, folios 154a–158b. A complete translation of the conjuration is available in The Love Factor in a Hebrew-Arabic Conjuration by Raphael Patai.

4. Kolatch, Alfred J., *The New Name Dictionary: Modern English and Hebrew Names.* New York: Jonathan David Co., Inc., 1994.

5. Personally, I call them first in this order, but then I repeat them in a variety of permutations glossalaically, bouncing between them as the spirit moves me.

6. The daylit hours of Venus on a Friday.

7. It is also the first word, and thus the Jewish name, of the book Christians call Deuteronomy.

8. Bereshit Rabbah 68:4.

9. The Red Sea, which G-d parted for Moses.

10. The river in question is the Euphrates.

The Sun

1. In the northern hemisphere. In the south, all this needs to be reversed.

2. In older systems, which are sometimes used in astrology, 0' is in the south, and the angle of a sunrise shadow is measured. This makes east +90' and west -90'.

3. Or sometimes a demon queen.

4. Some people will try to tell you that Amun's name is the root of the Hebrew אמן (amen). That is not true. The word אמן (amen) means "truly." It is closely related to the name El Emet, the El of Truth.

5. That is, without indents or bumps sticking out. More technically, a shape is convex if and only if a line segment connecting two points on its surface lies entirely inside the shape.

6. A polyhedron is "regular" if all its faces are the same size and shape.

7. A polyhedron (plural = polyhedra) is a three-dimensional shape whose faces are each polygons. That is to say, whose edges are straight line segments.

8. The reason there are only five is as follows: At every vertex, three faces must meet, so their interior angles must sum to less than 360 degrees. If the sum of their angles was exactly 360 degrees, then the "vertex" would fold flat. If there were more than 360 degrees, then the vertex would "pop" inside the shape. Since the faces all need to be the same, and must all be regular, they must have interior angles of less than 120 degrees. The only such regular polygons are triangles, squares, and pentagons.

9. Octahedron=Mercury, Icosahedron=Venus, Dodecahedron=Mars, Tetrahedron=Jupiter, Cube=Saturn.

10. A discovery Kepler credited to direct angelic inspiration.

11. In Greek, as in English, there is a close relationship with the specific word for a "ratio" and a broader word about "rational" thinking. Ratio:rational = αναλογία (analogia): λόγος (logos).

12. You can also achieve this same trance state by contemplation of a pentagram, which was the preferred method for Pythagoreans, but it's a little harder.

13. If you need some hints, search the internet for "proof that $\sqrt{2}$ is irrational." Do not trust a chatbot to answer technical math questions. They are routinely wrong on the details.

14. No, it does not. The universe is much, much, much weirder than human brains can fathom.

15. Given this, it's kind of weird that we have only nine jurists on the American Supreme Court.

16. Pesachim 119a:3.

17. Other people translate this as "In the beginning . . ."

18. For example, in Isaiah 29:1, 2, and 7.

19. Daniel 10:5 (JPS), *sefaria.org.*

Mars

1. In fact, it is the iron in hemoglobin that gives human blood its red color.

2. Whereas orcharding, beekeeping, and permaculture are Venus's domain.

3. In Mathers's illustration, this name is in the top left.

4. In English, the only words that change form in the accusative are pronouns. "Them" is the accusative version of "they," for example. In English, the accusative is sometimes also called the objective case.

5. The earliest known uses of this spelling are by Christian Renaissance occultists. I believe it was first used by Johan Reuchlin in his 1494 Liber De Verbo Mirifico.

6. Personally, I generally prefer Mercurial or Venereal methods to Martial ones. That is to say, I'm the sort of person who would usually rather talk or manipulate my way through a conflict rather than all-out fight. Everyone has different strengths.

7. For example, Rashi explicitly says this in his commentary to the first verse of this psalm.

8. Rabbi Isaiah HaLevi Horovitz. Shenei Luchot HaBerit. *sefaria.org.*

9. Which I understood to mean something like battle PTSD.

10. Torijano, P. *Solomon the Esoteric King: From King to Magus, Development of a Tradition.* Leiden, The Netherlands: Brill, 2012.

11. Drawing by Jon Goodfellow based on item in the collection of the British Museum, reference number: EA 56204. *britishmuseum.org.*

12. Hematite (Fe_2O_3) is crystalized iron oxide, the same material that makes Mars red. It is an excellent materia for martial talismans of all types, although it is difficult to carve with the precision required for Solomonic pentacles.

13. "Virgin" means it should never have had writing on it before, even if it's been erased. Most modern paper is virgin.

14. The Hebrew word here, תנין, can also mean "sea-serpent," "crocodile," or just "enemy."

15. This is very similar to the Hebrew word for scorpion, עקרב (*akrav*).

16. "Scorpion—Akrep," *rugstoreonline.co.uk.*

17. I don't know for sure, but I suspect it is called "dragon" mostly in areas where scorpions are not common.

18. *abarim-publications.com.*

19. This text was written by Shmuel Vital, the son of Hayim Vital. It explains and clarifies his father's famous work *Etz Chayim* (Tree of Life) and recounts the teachings of Hayim Vital's teacher, the famed kabbalist Isaac Luria.

20. Ish-Shalom, Zvi. *Sleep, Death, and Rebirth: Mystical Practices of Lurianic Kabbalah.* Boston: Academic Studies Press, 2021.

Jupiter

1. "Teshuva, Tefillah, Tzedakah: The Ten Days of Repentance." Chabad. *chabad.org.*

2. Jerusalem Talmud Kiddushin 4:12:2-3.

3. Jerusalem Talmud, Kiddushin 66b.

4. That is, paper on which nothing has previously been written.

5. He means *strix aluco,* who is modernly called a "tawny owl," not what we moderns call screech owls, which are found only in the Americas.

6. Jerusalem Talmud Bikkurim 3:6:4.

7. Many people translate it as "princess," but I believe that misrepresents the nature of ancient Hebrew political structures.

8. That is, Jerusalem's Temple Mount.

9. Like its neighbors; psalms 120–134.

10. Others say that it was also sung at the dedication of Solomon's Temple.

11. Because the "four winds" are so closely associated with the cardinal directions.

12. Recall that many manuscripts of the Key predate Agrippa's work. It is more likely that Agrippa learned the seal from the Key than vice-versa, although I believe they both share common ancestry.

13. Christian sources usually anglicize this as "Jophiel."

14. For example, Ma'aseh Merkavah (a mystic text we will discuss further below) provides an extended conjuration of Yofiel, which begins on page 235 of the Swartz translation.

15. Zohar, Vayikra 12.

16. See, for example: Balak 234 and Beha'alot'cha 102.

17. A primary text in Kabbalistic ethics, published in 1548 by Moshe Cordovero.

18. Pardes Rimonim, Gate of Sanctuaries: 1. As quoted in *Shemirat HaLashon, Book I, The Gate of Discerning* 14:7 by Rabbi Shraga Silverstein. *sefaria.org.*

19. For example: Lesses' *Ritual Practices to Gain Power: Angels, Incantations, and Revelation in Early Jewish Mysticism,* p. 357; Orlov's *From Apocalypticism to Merkabah Mysticism,* p. 352.

20. The Targum of Jonathan ben Uzziel, translation by J. W. Etheridge, London, 1862. *sefaria.org.*

21. Tehillim 112:3.

22. By the end of the Jewish Babylonian War (601–586 BCE), the Kingdom of Judah had fallen to Babylonian conquest, the Temple was destroyed, and many Jews were taken as enslaved prisoners of war back to Babylon. This community of exiles is commonly called the "Babylonian Captivity." The book of Ezekiel is set in this community, and there is good evidence that the book probably was originally written there, with some changes being made later.

23. Probably in/near ancient Nippur, about 200 km north of modern Baghdad. In ancient days, this was the seat of the god Enlil, a storm god who was chief of the Sumerian pantheon. Many equate him with Jupiter.

24. Or "from."

25. Kalach Pitchei Chokhmah 34:11.

26. The authorship of the earliest surviving complete Merkavah texts is unclear, although they are traditionally attributed to the inner circle of Rabbi Akiva's 1st-century CE school. We discussed Rabbi Akiva and his school in the Moon chapter, along with a story about his trance journey practices.

27. In addition to being a name for the practice, this is also the name of a specific text.

28. If you'd like to learn more about Merkavah, I recommend the book *Shamanic Trance in Modern Kabbalah* by Dr. Jonathan Garb, the Gershom Scholem chair in Kabbalah at Hebrew University. If you already have a strong background in Kabbalah and are willing to slog through same difficult prose, I recommend *Mystical Prayer in Ancient Judaism: An Analysis of Ma'aseh Merkavah* by Michael Swartz, which includes an English translation of Ma'aseh Merkavah.

29. I.e., "I am emaciated."

Saturn

1. Verman, *The Books of Contemplation,* p 52–53.

2. Hedlund, Stieg. "And the Rotas Go 'Round." *Deru Kugi,* February 2017. *derukugiblog.com.*

3. Rashi, Rosenbaum, Rashi, M., and and A. M. Silbermann. Pentateuch with Targum Onkelos, Haphtaroth and Rashi's Commentary: Genesis, Exodus, Leviticus, Numbers, Deuteronomy. New York: Hebrew Publishing Company, 1972.

4. *The Commentary of Abraham, Ibn Ezra on the Pentateuch,* trans. By Jay F. Shachter, Hoboken, NJ: Ktav Pubishing House 1986–2003.

5. 2 Samuel except . . .

6. 2 Samuel 24:18.

7. 1 Chronicles 21:15.

8. 2 Samuel 24:16.

9. This name is discussed in the Sun chapter.

Bibliography

Abarim Publications. "Abarim Publications' Biblical Dictionary: The Old Testament Hebrew word: קָב." *Abarim Publications' Biblical Dictionary.*
abarim-publications.com.

Abrams, D. *Sexual Symbolism and Merkavah Speculation in Medieval Germany: A Study of the Sod h-Egoz Texts.* Tübingen, Germany: Mohr
Siebeck, 1997.

Abusch, I. T. *Essays on Babylonian and Biblical Literature and Religion.*
Leiden, The Netherlands: Brill, 2020.

Almirantis, Yannis. (2005). "The Paradox of the Planetary Metals." *Journal of
Scientific Exploration,* 19. 31-42. *researchgate.net.*

Andrew, James. *Hebrew Dictionary and Grammar: Without Points, Together
with a Complete List of Such Chaldee Words as Occur in the Old
Testament, and a Brief Sketch of Chaldee Grammar . . . To Which Is
Added, a New . . . Account of Scripture Chronology . . . with Several
Useful Tables of Chronology, and of Ancient Weights and Measures.*
London: Messrs. Ogle, Duncan, and Co., 1823.

Avigad, N. "Three Ornamented Hebrew Seals." *Israel Exploration Journal,*
vol. 4, no. 3/4, 1954. *jstor.org.* Accessed Aug. 3, 2022.

Avioz, Michael. "King Solomon in Josephus' Writings." *Writing and Rewriting History in Ancient Israel and Near Eastern Cultures,* edited by
Isaac Kalimi, 1st ed., Harrassowitz Verlag, 2020. *doi.org.*

Bailey, R. (2017). "Greek Manuscripts of the Testament of Solomon in the
Biblioteca Apostolica Vaticana." In *The Embroidered Bible.* Leiden,
The Netherlands: Brill. *doi.org.*

Bauer, B. T., and L. Holstein. "The Power of the Scribe." *Craftmanship,* 2017.
craftsmanship.net.

Boeck, Barbara. "Proverbs 30:18-19 in the Light of Ancient Mesopotamian
Cuneiform Texts." *Sefarad,* vol. 69:2, 2009. *doi.org.*

Bohak, Gideon. "Some "Mass Produced" Scorpion-Amulets from the Cairo
Genizah." In *A Wandering Galilean: Essays in Honour of Seán
Freyne.* Leiden, The Netherlands: Brill, 2009.

Bonner, Campbell. "Amulets Chiefly in the British Museum." *ascsa.edu.gr.*

Bonner, Campbell. "The Technique of Exorcism." *The Harvard Theological Review,* vol. 36, no. 1. Cambridge, UK: Cambridge University Press, 1943. *jstor.org.*

Bose, Mishtooni. "From Exegesis to Appropriation: The Medieval Solomon." *Medium Ævum,* vol. 65, no. 2, Society for the Study of Medieval Languages and Literature, 1996. *doi.org.*

Bosworth, David A. *House of Weeping: The Motif of Tears in Akkadian and Hebrew Prayers.* Atlanta: SBL Press, 2019.

Brauner, Reuven. "Shimush Pesukim." *halakhah.com.*

Brauner, Reuven. "Shimush Tehillim." *halakhah.com.*

Brauner, Reuven. *Shoroshim: The Ultimate and Unique English Thesaurus of Hebrew Verb Roots.* Ra'anana, Israel: R. Brauner, 2014.

Briggs, K. M. "Some Seventeenth-Century Books of Magic," *Folklore,* 64:4, 445-462. United Kingdom: Taylor & Francis, Ltd., 1953. *doi.org.*

Butler, Elizabeth M. *Ritual Magic.* Cambridge, UK: Cambridge University Press, 1979.

Clines, David J. A. *The Dictionary of Classical Hebrew.* Sheffield, UK: Sheffield Academic Press, 1993.

Conybeare, F. C. *The Testament of Solomon.* Piscataway, NJ: Gorgias Press, 2007.

Dafni, Amots, et al. "Ritual Plants of Muslim Graveyards in Northern Israel." *Journal of Ethnobiology and Ethnomedicine,* vol. 2, no. 38. 2006. *doi.org.*

Dan, J. *Jewish Mysticism: The Middle Ages.* Maryland: Jason Aronson, 1998.

Dasen, Véronique. "Magic and Medicine: Gems and the Power of Seals." In Entwistle, C. and N. Adams. *'Gems of Heaven': Recent Research on Engraved Gemstones in Late Antiquity c. AD 200-600.* London: British Museum, 2011.

Davidson, G. *A Dictionary of Angels.* United Kingdom: Free Press, 1994.

Duling, D. C. "Solomon, Exorcism, and the Son of David." *Harvard Theological Review,* 68(3–4), 235–252, 1975. *doi.org.*

Fanger, Claire. *Invoking Angels: Theurgic Ideas and Practices, Thirteenth to Sixteenth Centuries.* University Park, PA: Pennsylvania State University Press, 2012.

Farrell, Nick. *Making Talismans: Living Entities of Power.* Woodbury, MN: Llewellyn Publications, 2001.

Feldman, Louis. *Jewish Life and Thought among Greeks and Romans: Primary Readings.* Minneapolis, MN: Fortress Press, 1996.

Feldman, Louis H. "Josephus' Portrait of Solomon." *Hebrew Union College Annual,* vol. 66, 1995. *jstor.org.*

Fine, Lawrence. *Essential Papers on Kabbalah.* New York: New York University Press, 1995.

Fodor, Alexander. "A Group of Iraqi Arm Amulets (Popular Islam in Mesopotamia)." *Quaderni di Studi Arabi,* Vol. 5/6, Istituto per l'Oriente C. A. Nallino, 1987. *jstor.org*

Fuks, L. Sefer h'Otot in *Catalogue of the Manuscripts of the Bibliotheca Rosenthaliana,* University Library of Amsterdam, no. 242. Leiden, The Netherlands, 1973.

Garb, J. *Shamanic Trance in Modern Kabbalah.* Chicago: University of Chicago Press, 2011.

Gikatilla, J. b. A. *Gates of Light: Sha'are Orah.* Lanham, MD: AltaMira Press, 1998.

Goodenough, E. R. "Review of Studies in Magical Amulets, Chiefly Graeco-Egyptian, by C. Bonner." *The American Journal of Philology,* 72(3), 308–316, 1951. *doi.org.*

Greer, M. K. *Women of the Golden Dawn: Rebels and Priestesses: Maud Gonne, Moina Bergson Mathers, Annie Horniman, Florence Farr.* Rochester, VT: Park Street Press, 1996.

Guggenheimer, Heinrich W. *The Jerusalem Talmud.* Berlin: De Gruyter, 1999–2015.

HaLevi, Yehuda. *Sefer haKuzari.* Project Ben-Yehuda. *benyehuda.org.*

Hamburger, Anit. "A Greco-Samaritan Amulet From Caesarea." *Israel Exploration Journal,* vol. 9, no. 1, Israel Exploration Society, 1959. *jstor.org.*

Harari, Y. *Jewish Magic Before the Rise of Kabbalah.* Detroit, Michigan: Wayne State University Press, 2017.

Harden, D. (1953). "Studies in Magical Amulets, Chiefly Graeco-Egyptian." By C. Bonner. Pp. xxiv +334, with 25 pll. Ann Arbor, MI: University of Michigan Press, 1950. *The Journal of Hellenic Studies,* 73. *doi.org*

Heather, P. J. "The Seven Planets." *Folklore,* vol. 54, no. 3, 1943. *jstor.org.* Accessed Nov. 4, 2022.

Hedlund, Stieg. "And the Rotas Go 'Round." *Deru Kugi,* February 2017. *derukugiblog.com.*

Isaac, Ephraim. "The Princeton Collection of Ethiopic Manuscripts." *The Princeton University Library Chronicle,* vol. 42, no. 1, 1980. *doi.org.*

Ish-Shalom, Zvi. *Sleep, Death, and Rebirth: Mystical Practices of Lurianic Kabbalah.* Boston: Academic Studies Press, 2021.

Jackson, H. M. "Notes on the Testament of Solomon." *Journal for the Study of Judaism in the Persian, Hellenistic, and Roman Period,* vol. 19, no. 1, 1988. *jstor.org.*

James, M. R. *The Lost Apocrypha of the Old Testament: Their Titles and Fragments.* United Kingdom: Society for Promoting Christian Knowledge, 1920.

Johnston, Sarah Iles. "The Testament of Solomon from Late Antiquity to the Renaissance." J. Bremmer and J. Veenstra, eds., *The Metamorphosis of Magic from Late Antiquity to the Early Modern Period.* 2002.

Kalimi, Isaac. *Writing and Rewriting the Story of Solomon in Ancient Israel.* Cambridge, UK: Cambridge University Press, 2018.

Kalisch, Isidor. *Sefer Yetzirah.* New York, 1877. *sefaria.org.*

Kaplan, Aryeh. *Meditation and Kabbalah.* Newburyport, MA: Weiser Books, 1985.

Kaplan, Aryeh. *Sefer Yetzirah.* Newburyport, MA: Weiser Books, 1997.

Keiter, Sheila Tuller. *The Jewish Understanding of the Scriptural Solomon Narrative: Examining Biblical, Classical Rabbinic, and Major Medieval Responses.* A dissertation submitted in partial satisfaction of the requirements for the degree of Doctor of Philosophy in Near Eastern Languages and Cultures, 2018.

Keyser, Paul T. "Alchemy in the Ancient World: From Science to Magic." *Illinois Classical Studies,* vol. 15, no. 2, 1990. *jstor.org.* Accessed October 21, 2022.

Klein, E. *A Comprehensive Etymological Dictionary of the Hebrew Language for Readers of English.* Edited by B. Sarel. Israel: Carta, 1987.

Klutz, Todd. *Rewriting the Testament of Solomon: Tradition, Conflict and Identity in a Late Antique Pseudepigraphon.* London: T&T Clark International, 2005.

Kolatch, Alfred J., *The New Name Dictionary: Modern English and Hebrew Names.* New York: Jonathan David Co., Inc., 1994.

Krappe, Alexander Haggerty. "Solomon and Ashmodai." *The American Journal of Philology,* vol. 54, no. 3, 1933. *doi.org.*

Lassner, J. *Demonizing the Queen of Sheba: Boundaries of Gender and Culture in Postbiblical Judaism and Medieval Islam.* Chicago: University of Chicago Press, 1993.

Leiner, Gershon Henoch of Radzin. *The Introduction to the Beit Yaakov.* Translated and annotated by Betzalel Edwards. *sefaria.org.*

Lesses, R. M. *Ritual Practices to Gain Power: Angels, Incantations, and Revelation in Early Jewish Mysticism*. Harrisburg, PA: Trinity Press International, 1988.

Levy, B. B. *Planets, Potions, and Parchments: Scientifica Hebraica from the Dead Sea Scrolls to the Eighteenth Century*. Montreal: McGill-Queen's University Press, 1990.

Levy, Yaakov. *The Oxford English-Hebrew Dictionary*. Oxford, UK: Oxford University Press, 1998.

Libourel, Paul-Antoine, Baptiste Barrillot, Sébastien Arthaud, Bertrand Massot, Anne-Laure Morel, Olivier Beuf, Anthony Herrel, Pierre-Hervé Luppi. "Partial Homologies between Sleep States in Lizards, Mammals, and Birds Suggest a Complex Evolution of Sleep States in Amniotes." *PLOS Biology,* October 11, 2018. *doi.org.*

Mathers, S. L. M. *The Golden Dawn Legacy of MacGregor Mathers*. Washington: Holmes Publishing Group LLC, 1998.

Mathers, S. L. M. *The Key of Solomon the King: Clavicula Salomonis.* Newburyport, MA: Weiser Books, 2016.

Mathers, S. L. M. *The* Key of Solomon *the King: Clavicula Salomonis*. Revised by J. H. Peterson, "The Key of Solomon." *esotericarchives.com.*

Mathiesen, Robert. "The Key of Solomon: Towards a Typology of the Manuscripts." *Societas Magica Newsletter,* 17.1, 2007: 3–9.

Matt, Daniel C. *Zohar: The Book of Enlightenment*. New Jersey: Paulist Press, 1983.

McBryde, J. M. "The Sator-Acrostic." *Modern Language Notes,* vol. 22, no. 8, 1907. *doi.org.* Accessed July 28, 2022.

McCown, Chester C. *The Testament of Solomon*. Leipzig, Germany: J. C. Hinrichs, 1922.

Meyer, M. W., and P. A. Mirecki. *Magic and Ritual in the Ancient World*. Leiden , The Netherlands: Brill, 2002.

Miller, M. T. *The Name of God in Jewish Thought: A Philosophical Analysis of Mystical Traditions from Apocalyptic to Kabbalah*. United Kingdom: Taylor & Francis, 2015.

Ó Maoilearca, J. *Vestiges of a Philosophy: Matter, the Meta-Spiritual, and the Forgotten Bergson.* New York: Oxford University Press, 2022.

O'Donald, Megan. "The ROTAS 'Wheel': Form and Content in a Pompeian Graffito." *Zeitschrift für Papyrologie und Epigraphik,* vol. 205, 2018. *jstor.org.* Accessed July 28, 2022.

Orlov, A. A. *From Apocalypticism to Merkabah Mysticism: Studies in the Slavonic Pseudepigrapha*. Leiden, The Netherlands: Brill, 2007.

Parpola, Simo. "The Assyrian Tree of Life: Tracing the Origins of Jewish Monotheism and Greek Philosophy." *Journal of Near Eastern Studies*, vol. 52, no. 3, 1993. *jstor.org*

Patai, Raphael. "The Love Factor in a Hebrew-Arabic Conjuration." *The Jewish Quarterly Review*, vol. 70, no. 4, 1980. *doi.org*.

Peterson, Joseph. *The Sworn Book of Honorius*. Lake Worth, FL: Ibis Press, 2016.

Peterson, Joseph. "The Veritable Clavicles of Solomon: Translated from Hebrew into the Latin Language by Rabbi Abognazar." *Esoteric Archives*. *esotericarchives.com*.

Pingree, David. "Indian Planetary Images and the Tradition of Astral Magic." *Journal of the Warburg and Courtauld Institutes*, vol. 52, 1989. *doi.org*. Accessed Oct. 21, 2022.

Rashi, *Commentary on Song of Songs 1:1*. Sefaria community translation. *sefaria.org*

Rashi, M. Rosenbaum, and A.M. Silbermann. *Pentateuch with Targum Onkelos, Haphtaroth and Rashi's Commentary: Genesis, Exodus, Leviticus, Numbers, Deuteronomy*. New York: Hebrew Publishing Company, 1972.

Rayner, J. D. *Jewish Religious Law: A Progressive Perspective*. Oxford, UK: Berghahn Books, 1998.

Rodkinson, M. L. and I. M. Wise. *New Edition of the Babylonian Talmud: Tract Sabbath (1896)*. Charlestown, SC: Nabu Press, 2012.

Rohrbacher-Sticker, Claudia. "From Sense to Nonsense, From Incantation Prayer to Magical Spell." *Jewish Studies Quarterly*, vol. 3, no. 1, 1996. *jstor.org*.

Rohrbacher-Sticker, Claudia. "A Hebrew Manuscript of Clavicula Salomonis, Part II." *The British Library Journal*, vol. 21, no. 1, 1995. *jstor.org*.

Rohrbacher-Sticker, Claudia. "Mafteah Shelomoh: A New Acquisition of the British Library." *Jewish Studies Quarterly*, vol. 1, no. 3, 1993. *jstor.org*.

Roth, Norman. "Jewish Seals," in Norman Roth, ed., *Medieval Jewish Civilization: An Encyclopedia*. New York and London: Routledge, 2003.

Runyon, C. *The Book of Solomon's Magick*. Silverado, CA: Church of the Hermetic Science Incorporated, 1996.

Schäfer, P. *The Origins of Jewish Mysticism*. Princeton, NJ: Princeton University Press, 2011.

Schäfer, P., and H. G. Kippenberg. *Envisioning Magic: A Princeton Seminar and Symposium*. Leiden, The Netherlands: Brill, 1997.

Schaff, P. *A Religious Encyclopaedia: Or Dictionary of Biblical, Historical, Doctrinal, and Practical Theology: Based on the Real-Encyklopädie of Herzog, Plitt, and Hauck*. New York: Funk & Wagnalls, 1889.

Schrire, T. *Hebrew Amulets: Their Decipherment and Interpretation*. United Kingdom: Routledge & Kegan Paul, 1966.

Schwartz, H. *Reimagining the Bible: The Storytelling of the Rabbis*. Oxford, UK: Oxford University Press, 1998.

Sefaria community translation. *Jerusalem Talmud Sanhedrin. sefaria.org.*

Seidenberg, D. "Kiddush Levanah: Sanctification of the Moon." *Open Siddur. opensiddur.org.*

Shah, I. *Secret Lore of Magic*. London: ISF Publishing, 2016.

Shemesh, A.O. 2018, "'And God Gave Solomon Wisdom': Proficiency in Ornithomancy. *HTS Teologiese Studies/Theological Studies"* 74(1), a4904. *doi.org.*

Skemer, Don C. *Binding Words: Textual Amulets in the Middle Ages: Magic in History*. University Park, PA: Pennsylvania State University Press, 2006.

Skemer, Don C. "Cover Note." *The Princeton University Library Chronicle*, vol. 74, no. 1, 2012.

Skemer, Don C. "Magic Writ: Textual Amulets Worn on the Body for Protection." In *Schriftträger-Textträger: Zur materialen Präsenz des Geschriebenen in frühen Gesellschaften*, edited by Annette Kehnel and Diamantis Panagiotopoulos. Berlin: De Gruyter, 2015. *doi.org*

Skinner, Stephen. "Magical Techniques and Implements Present in Graeco-Egyptian Magical Papyri, Byzantine Greek Solomonic Manuscripts and European Grimoires: Transmission, Continuity and Commonality." Submitted in total fulfilment of the requirements of the degree of Doctor of Philosophy (Classics). University of Newcastle, 2013.

Skinner, Stephen, and David Rankine. *The Veritable Key of Solomon*. Woodbury, MN: Llewellyn, 2008.

Skoss, Solomon L. "An Ethiopic Book of Magic." *The Jewish Quarterly Review*, vol. 23, no. 4, 1933. *doi.org.*

Soucek, Priscilla P. "Solomon's Throne/Solomon's Bath, UK: Model or Metaphor?" *Ars Orientalis*, vol. 23, 1993. *jstor.org.*

Sparks, H. F. D. *The Apocryphal Old Testament*. Oxford, UK: Oxford University Press, 1984.

Sparks, H. F. D. "The Testament of Solomon." In *The Apocryphal Old Testament*. Oxford, UK: Clarendon Press, 1984. Oxford Biblical Studies Online. Accessed March 27, 2022.

Stieglitz, Robert R. "The Hebrew Names of the Seven Planets." *Journal of Near Eastern Studies,* vol. 40, no. 2, 1981. *jstor.org.* Accessed Apr. 4, 2022.

Strong, James. *Strong's Hebrew Dictionary of the Bible.* New York: Beta Nu Publishing, 2012.

Swart, J. G. *The Book of Sacred Names.* South Africa: Sangreal Sodality Press, 2012.

Swart, J. G. *The Book of Seals & Amulets.* South Africa: Sangreal Sodality Press, 2017.

Swartz, M. D. *Mystical Prayer in Ancient Judaism: An Analysis of Ma'aseh Merkavah.* Tübingen, Germany: J. C. B. Mohr, 1992.

Swartz, M. D. "Scribal Magic and Its Rhetoric: Formal Patterns in Medieval Hebrew and Aramaic Incantation Texts from the Cairo Genizah." *The Harvard Theological Review,* vol. 83, no. 2, 1990. *jstor.org.* Accessed Aug. 25, 2022.

Swartz, M. D., Schiffmann, L., Swartz, M. *Hebrew and Aramaic incantation texts from the Cairo Genizah: selected texts from Taylor-Schechter Box K1.* Sheffield, UK: JSOT Press, 1992.

Torijano, P., *Solomon the Esoteric King: From King to Magus, Development of a Tradition.* Leiden, The Netherlands: Brill, 2012.

Tully, C. J., and S. Crooks. "Dropping Ecstasy? Minoan Cult and the Tropes of Shamanism." *Time and Mind: The Journal of Archaeology, Consciousness and Culture,* 8.2: 129–158, 2015.

Van der Toorn, K., B. Becking, and Pieter W. van der Horst. *Dictionary of Deities and Demons in the Bible (DDD).* Second edition. Cambridge, UK: William B. Eerdmans Publishing Company, 1999.

Verheyden, Joseph. *The Figure of Solomon in Jewish, Christian and Islamic Tradition: King, Sage and Architect.* Leiden, The Netherlands: Brill, 2012.

Verman, Mark. *The Books of Contemplation: Medieval Jewish Mystical Sources.* New York: State University of New York Press, 2012.

Verman, Mark. "Classifying the 'Hug Ha-Iyyun.'" *Proceedings of the World Congress of Jewish Studies*, vol. ʾ, 1989. *jstor.org.* Accessed Oct. 28, 2022.

Verman, Mark. "The Development of Yihudim in Spanish Kabbalah." *Jerusalem Studies in Jewish Thought,* vol. ה, 1989, *jstor.org.* Accessed July 24, 2022.

Waite, A. E. *The Book of Black Magic and of Pacts: Including the Rites and Mysteries of Goetic Theurgy, Sorcery, and Infernal Necromancy.* Chicago: De Laurence, Scott & Co., 1910.

Wall Kimmerer, Robin. *Braiding Sweetgrass.* Minneapolis, MN: Milkweed Editions, 2015.

Weitzman, S. *Solomon: The Lure of Wisdom.* New Haven, CT: Yale University Press, 2011.

Wellcome Collection. "Pseudo-Solomon." *wellcomecollection.org.*

Whiston, W. *The Genuine Works of Flavius Josephus the Jewish Historian.* *penelope.uchicago.edu*

Yamauchi, Edwin M. *Mandaic Incantation Texts.* New Jersey: Gorgias Press, 2005. *doi.org.*

Zalman, Schneur. *Shaar Hayichud Vehaemunah.* New York: Kehot Publication Society. *chabad.org.*

About the Author

Sara L. Mastros has been called "the single most important living teacher in witchcraft today." Recognized by her peers as a brilliant and original thinker, an engaging and inspiring teacher, a compelling and clever writer, and a generally decent human being, Sara spends a lot of time dreaming, thinking, enchanting, writing, and teaching about witchcraft, magic, and myth. She's especially interested in magical communication, translation, and cryptography. But her true passion is raising up an army of inspired, educated, empowered witches prepared to weave weird new ways of being in a world that desperately needs us. Rise up.

Visit Sara at *WitchLessons.com*.

To Our Readers

Weiser Books, an imprint of Red Wheel/Weiser, publishes books across the entire spectrum of occult, esoteric, speculative, and New Age subjects. Our mission is to publish quality books that will make a difference in people's lives without advocating any one particular path or field of study. We value the integrity, originality, and depth of knowledge of our authors.

Our readers are our most important resource, and we appreciate your input, suggestions, and ideas about what you would like to see published.

Visit our website at *www.redwheelweiser.com*, where you can learn about our upcoming books and free downloads, and also find links to sign up for our newsletter and exclusive offers.

You can also contact us at *info@rwwbooks.com* or at

Red Wheel/Weiser, LLC
65 Parker Street, Suite 7
Newburyport, MA 01950